LEGACY OF MY FATHER

LEGACY OF MY FATHER

By
Waverley Traylor

iUniverse, Inc.
Bloomington

Legacy of My Father

Copyright © 2012 by Waverley Traylor.

All rights reserved. No part of this book may be used or reproduced by any means, graphic, electronic, or mechanical, including photocopying, recording, taping or by any information storage retrieval system without the written permission of the publisher except in the case of brief quotations embodied in critical articles and reviews.

iUniverse books may be ordered through booksellers or by contacting:

iUniverse
1663 Liberty Drive
Bloomington, IN 47403
www.iuniverse.com
1-800-Authors (1-800-288-4677)

Because of the dynamic nature of the Internet, any web addresses or links contained in this book may have changed since publication and may no longer be valid. The views expressed in this work are solely those of the author and do not necessarily reflect the views of the publisher, and the publisher hereby disclaims any responsibility for them.

Any people depicted in stock imagery provided by Thinkstock are models, and such images are being used for illustrative purposes only.
Certain stock imagery © Thinkstock.

ISBN: 978-1-4697-9640-6 (sc)
ISBN: 978-1-4697-9639-0 (hc)
ISBN: 978-1-4697-9638-3 (ebk)

Library of Congress Control Number: 2012904497

Printed in the United States of America

iUniverse rev. date: 03/08/2012

TABLE OF CONTENTS

Acknowledgments ix
Dedication xi
Introduction xiii

Part I- The Man 1

Chapter 1- Father & Son 3
Chapter 2- The Beginning 7
Chapter 3- Growing Up 25
Chapter 4- Love and Marriage 47

Part II- The Marine 65

Chapter 5-   Pride of the Corps 67
Chapter 6-   Off to War 93
Chapter 7-   Onward to Glory 105
Chapter 8-   Duty in Hell 121
Chapter 9-   Cheating Death 139
Chapter 10- Recovery 147

Part III- The Survivor 157

Chapter 11- Rebuilding a Life 159
Chapter 12- Building a Family 171
Chapter 13- Jekyll & Hyde 187
Chapter 14- Rough Times 203

Chapter 15- The Agony 219
Chapter 16- Sunset 229
Chapter 17- The Legacy 251
Chapter 18- Epitaph 259

Epilogue 263
Glossary 265
About the Author 279

List of Illustrations

Figure 1	Waverley Sr. with partner on their pie delivery truck.	9
Figure 2	Junior with dog Zorro and playmate Randi	10
Figure 3	Junior and Grandpa George at the granite sculptures' shop.	12
Figure 4	Junior on the running board of his uncle's Model T.	14
Figure 5	Junior swinging on the exercise bar in the park.	15
Figure 6	Junior and friend William on Junior's racing wagon.	27
Figure 7	Uncle Edward's 1936 Dodge with Waverley Jr. claiming first riding rights.	38
Figure 8	Junior dressed out on the practice field at Petersburg High School.	42
Figure 9	The lovebirds could always be found together while visiting the Unruh's cottage.	54
Figure 10	The Newlyweds on Honeymoon Rock at Richmond's Maymont Park.	57
Figure 11	Waverley's Uncle Edward and Aunt Margaret attend Waverley's Marine Corps Graduation.	77
Figure 12	Waverley Jr. home on leave from Boot Camp.	79
Figure 13	Waverley Jr. with ammunition handler during Machine Gun qualifications on the range at Camp Lejeune.	81
Figure 14	Limited resistance on the Green Beach was quickly dispatched.	111

Figure 15	Fox Company cleaning up after the firefight on Okinawa's Motobu Peninsula.	119
Figure 16	Waverley's Machine Gun Squad displays the captured Japanese Battle Flag.	133
Figure 17	Waverley Jr. proudly presents his new son to the world.	165
Figure 18	The children playing with their new friends from across the road.	174
Figure 19	Waverley Sr. sporting his infamous Brown Fedora.	178
Figure 20	Waverley Jr. on the piers in Key West when visiting his Navy son.	224
Figure 21	Peg and Wave just minutes after vowing to Love, Honor, and Respect.	226
Figure 22	Baby Christine met her grandparents for the first time.	227
Figure 23	Waverley Jr. taking "Missy" for a ride.	230
Figure 24	Cindy's father was determined he would walk his daughter down the aisle.	244

Acknowledgments

During the time it has taken to research this book, I had, on occasion, become obsessed with the work and therefore wish to thank my wonderful, understanding, and beautiful wife (Margaret) for her support, assistance, proofing, and encouragement in making the completion of this book a reality. I also wish to thank my good friends Verna Brainard and Liz Yeaw whose time and input proved to be a valuable asset.

I also wish to thank the friends and family for their indulgence in providing the information so vital in the assembly of the facts which made this story possible: William Stewart, Forrest Traylor, Kathy Holzer, Nancy Traylor, Lorene Stewart, Margaret Traylor, Susan Traylor, Marie Crawford, Margaret Roark, and Dr. Gail Furman.

Stories from the following friends, family and acquaintances had been relayed to me before their passing, but in remembering, filled the vacant periods of my father's life: Waverley Traylor Sr., Frances Traylor, Waverley Traylor Jr., Marie Venner, Fred Landrum Jr., Clarence Venner, Leon Boisseau, Hettie Landrum, James Ellis, Calvin Minton, Edward Traylor, Katherine Northington, Lloyd Goulder, Bertha Thomas, Jesse Traylor, and Doris Twilley. May ye all rest in peaceful slumber.

Dedicated to the veterans that have served honorably in all of our wars and who have returned home suffering the consequences, not of giving their lives, but of sacrificing their living; you are not alone.

"No person was ever honored for what he received. Honor has been the reward for what he gave."

Calvin Coolidge

INTRODUCTION

As I was growing up, my father played a very important part in my life, however, I was totally unaware of this fact at the time. I knew a little about his life and what made him tick, or so I thought. There was a definitive purpose when I began to write this book but as with life itself, time breeds change.

As I began my research, I learned a little more each day of Dad's life. It seems that for every question I answered, five more questions surfaced. I talked with his childhood friends, I read every book I could find on the battles of World War II in which my father fought, I visited family and comrades across the country and sorted through thousands of photographs, newspaper articles, letters, and cards. I listened to, and recorded, a multitude of stories from his birth until his death.

After nearly a year of concentrated research, I believe the pieces finally fit together as to who my father really was. This was nothing, of course, to what I thought I knew just a short time ago. I have been intrigued, shocked, and totally amazed at finding out how his life has paralleled my own so closely.

This story contains my attempt to compile his life journey, uncovering the uncanny parallels with my own. I tried to reconstruct how he had been raised with all of his wants and aspirations and how, in only a few short months, his life was changed so drastically and permanently.

I have used this venue to examine his life from his birth following World War I to his death that came too early in his years. All he did in life, that I had never quite understood, has now become clear to me and he has emerged as a most wonderful caring man with a severe problem, caused by war, and never properly treated to relieve his constant pain and agony. A man I never understood while I was growing up, but now can comprehend his every action. I realize now that my real ambition in life was to be just like him, not as a professional, but as a person.

The book presents three distinct periods in his life. The first describes the boy to the man and how he grew up in pre- and post depression America. The second period delineates his participation in World War II and the events that rocked his world. Finally, how the severe impact of the war destroyed his life and changed the man he once was so drastically.

Every available source was examined to extract the details of his life including photographs, letters, history books, films, and newspapers. In the process I learned the post war fate of thousands of Marines who deserved a better life but were restricted by the shortsightedness of 1940's technology as described herein. Thousands of Veterans have lived through and suffered in like ways over the years and it is about time that the Veterans became aware that they were not alone in their anguish.

Any resemblance between the characters in this book and real persons, either living or deceased, is purely intentional. The names of several of these characters has been changed to protect the innocent from further embarrassment.

Know Your Waverleys

This story covers the life through three generations of Traylors, all with identical names. To attempt to alleviate any confusion, the names are covered here along with all of the alias' used. This is the key for unraveling the Waverleys of Traylor:

Waverley Lahmeyer Traylor Sr.—A.K.A. Waverley Sr., Old Man Traylor, Wave

Waverley Lahmeyer Traylor Jr.—A.K.A. Junior, Waverley, Waverley Jr., Wave, Big Waverley, Dad

Waverley Lahmeyer Traylor 3rd—A.K.A. Waverley 3rd, Waverley III, Little Waverley, Young Waverley, Brother, Butch, Wave

Part I
The Man

"Don't let anyone look down on you because you are young, but set an example for the believers in speech, in life, in love, in faith and in purity."

Timothy 4:12

Chapter 1
Father & Son

A man, from birth, is a product of several molding factors. Among these are the genes passed on to him through his biological parents, the experiences he encounters throughout his lifetime, and the lessons learned by direct interaction with his father.

The father is the most influential character in the development of a male child, whether it is the way his father lived or the way his father dreamed. The son is molded into his father's image and takes on the characteristics of the parent physically, mentally, and socially. My father was no different, and his father before him, but it was only after I became a grandfather that I saw the parallels and discovered the lessons that I had somehow learned along the way.

I grew up with what I would consider the normal childhood of an average country boy. But as with most sons, life was confusing and contradictory. This was especially true having two sisters and me being stuck in the middle. I loved my older sister very much in spite of, or maybe because of, the fights we had each day. I loved my younger sister very much in spite of, or maybe because of, the fact that we never had a cross word between us. Family, you gotta love 'em.

Dad, on the other hand, was himself a packet of contradictions, a loving parent who I never heard speak the word "Love." He was a humorous man with a strange sense of the funny. His most frequent uttering was his claim of psychic powers in that he could predict the winner of a football game before the game was played: "the team with the most points." Funny, but it got old; yet we all laughed on every occasion. It made us all feel good. But in an instant the tide might turn, as if some imperceptible switch had been activated transforming him into a force to be feared. Although no one in the family was ever physically harmed, his outburst would scare the quills off a porcupines' back and I am certain that it had a lot to do with the condition of my hair today, wherever it is.

At the time a lot of this uncertainty was laid off on the "Traylor Temper." An uncontrollable rage which would explode at the most inopportune time or place. This family malady can be traced back for generations through the family tree. From Frederick Traylor and his service in the Revolutionary War, to Waverley Junior in World War II, and every generation in the wars in between. This really brings into question the validity of a congenital disorder and lends itself to more of a history of battle stress passed down and supplemented by each generation.

My father was born and raised during the roaring 20's when life was good and sustenance plentiful. His house was huge by standards of the time and he always had what every child his age desired: a bike, a wagon, and a best friend. As he moved toward his teen years "The Great Depression" had struck with a paralyzing blow to everyone. The basic items of sustenance were no longer readily available and daily life became a chore unto itself. It was no help that his new baby brother was born the year of the crash and life within the family was surrounded by an atmosphere of stress.

He served in the Marine Corps during World War II, but I seldom ever heard him speak of this time in his life. I had learned from my mother that he had been wounded and the one document that I had access to, the book of the 6th Marine Division History, bore this out. He was listed as one of many who received the Order of the Purple Heart, an award first authorized by General George Washington and given now to the soldiers wounded in combat by enemy fire.

I had asked once to see the award but he confessed that he had never received the actual medal. He spent an inordinate amount of time making calls and writing letters in his attempt to obtain it. This medal would have given him extra bonus points as he applied for several jobs in government service. He never made much progress in his quest, but continued to desire the physical award up to the day he died.

He had expressed to me on several occasions the importance of his pursuit, so following his passing, I took over his quest and was determined that I would see his medal one day. It took 25 years to accomplish this feat and what I discovered along the journey was both amazing and shocking. I believe that, for the first time, I actually learned about my father and discovered why and how he lived his life. I really knew him for the first time and finally understood the events and attitudes that had for so long haunted me.

The man who went to war, never returned "home." He died on that horrific day in a foxhole on the other side of the world. The man who came home in his place was completely unrecognizable to family and friends but did his utmost to live a good and clean life, successfully raising three children, despite their becoming teenagers, and surviving the ordeal.

CHAPTER 2
The Beginning

Waverley Lahmeyer Traylor Jr. was born on his grandfather Ethan Allen's farm in Chesterfield County, Virginia, to Waverley Sr. and Jesse Traylor, on the 4th of August in the year 1921. The war to end all wars had recently ended and the soldiers returning from France were being discharged back into civilian life. Prior to the war, Waverley Sr. had been a veterinary assistant working for Doc Fisher on South Sycamore Street in Petersburg. His mother had been a student at the Southern Girls College in the same city. His parents had married the year before his birth having been together throughout the war years. Waverley Sr. was a handsome man standing six foot with a slender build, that was tightly bound in his uniform when he returned home from the fighting in France. His exceptionally slim hands bore long fingers that made his hands look like those of an artist. The early onset of Arthritis was apparent in his knuckles which gave the appearance of those hands being near skeletal. His face was triangular with a slender chin balanced out by his larger than average ears. Jesse was a beautiful girl, brown hair, blue eyed, tall at five foot eight inches, slender, and shapely. They made the perfect post war couple when they stood before the minister. When Waverley Jr. was born the New York Yankees were about to win the American League pennant and Warren G. Harding had just entered the White House, beginning the recovery to prosperity. A larger than normal number of babies were born during this period in celebration of the massive homecomings and belief that the economy would soon be taking a turn for the better.

The son of a Pie Truck driver, Junior, as he was known to his family, entered this world sporting a sparse head of hair and cheeks that appeared chocked full of dumpling cakes. As a baby he lived, impoverished, his first year in the post Wilson era. The economy was improving and the future was looking brighter for the new family. The rail strike was hanging over the health of the nation and generating great concern among local businesses. Farmers were enjoying the ability to sell their harvest for a decent price and prosperity was returning to both urban and rural inhabitants. Junior and his family would often visit the farm where he was born. He loved seeing his grandma and grandpa but he particularly enjoyed seeing his Aunt Marie. She was a beautiful young girl having recently celebrated her 20th birthday. She always fascinated Junior with her dark auburn hair and arms that had just enough strength to hold Junior and play *let the baby fly* with him. This always made him giggle and sometimes even laugh out loud. She always gave him her full attention and constantly doted over him. A lot of time was spent visiting the farm in the warmer months but the cold of winter kept the family in the city. As he began to take steps and explore the world of walking, his mother would dress him warmly against the winter cold to take him out in the yard to play. During the spring and autumn he could often be found in the back yard, cuddled in the old bentwood rocker with his mother, while she read the newspaper aloud to him for instance, about the schooner that had sunk just off of the coast of Virginia. It was not so much that he understood what she read, but rather that he just loved to listen to his mother reading to him.

Waverley Sr. with partner on their pie delivery truck.

As he grew and passed through his toddling phase, his family situation continued to improve and by the age of three, he had his very best friend living with him. She was a mix of multiple terrier ancestry weighing in at nearly ten pounds. Her coat was a pure white, save for her two large black spots that covered each ear and eye. She carried herself proudly on her short stocky legs, which brought her up to waist height on the two-year-old, Now, the early twenties sported a craze in the United States formed around a popular serialized book entitled "The Curse of Capistrano" by Johnston McCulley. The story was set around the time of the Mexican-American War in the Pueblo de Los Angeles when Don Diego de la Vega returns from serving in the Spanish army to find a corrupt regime exploiting and torturing the people.

Living the fantasy that all young boys of that time dreamt, the big black spots around his puppy's eyes naturally encouraged him to name her Zorro. Not a typical girlie name for a dog, but Zorro it was. After all, who was going to tell a stubborn three-year-old any different. His favorite pastimes were playing in the back yard with Zorro, rolling around the back porch on his new horsey with wheels, or visiting his favorite aunt in the country.

His closest human playmate was a young neighbor girl who liked to visit and play with Junior and Zorro in the back yard. Randi lived next door and came over often to play with Junior and roll down the hill behind his house in what was once an actual wooden wagon; a vehicle with wheels so wobbly that it took skill to balance in the wagon body without falling out. Of course it didn't help their ability to steer since there was no handle on the cart, the victim of a previous crash in the canyon out back.

Junior with dog Zorro and playmate Randi.

Zorro, they soon discovered, had become pregnant and that summer delivered six beautiful black and white puppies to the family. Junior and Randi loved chasing the puppies through the grass-challenged yard and the game was to see who could hide the best in the dust, dirt, and/or mud which would cover their entire bodies. It was often a tie and laying on the ground would render them invisible to Junior's mother when she would appear on the upper level porch to call them in for the evening. Before being allowed into the house though, the children always had to stop by the rain barrel to endure buckets of water emptied over their heads to dispose of a majority of the muck. During the hot summer, this was an enjoyable treat but when the ice had to be broken to dip the barrel, it wasn't quite as much fun.

The family received word of the passing of Waverley's Uncle Charlie. He was only 29 years of age and had been a patient at the Spring Grove Hospital in Maryland. Three years had passed since he began treatment for wounds suffered in France during World War I. Services were held at the home of Grandpa George on High Street. His mortal remains were interred at Blandford Cemetery with full military honors. Never before had so many people tried to pack themselves into the High Street home and they overflowed to the second floor. Junior had never met his Uncle Charlie so he really didn't miss him. He just wanted to go home and play with the puppies.

Eventually homes were found for all of the puppies and Junior spent a lot of time with his Grandpa George explaining to him how much he missed the furry little critters. They would sit out back on the steps and talk for hours. Grandpa would regale Junior with amazing tales of adventure and fantasy, or they might spend hours together at the park playing on the swings or feeding the pigeons. Junior had two favorite places to visit. He enjoyed spending time with his Grandpa at his friends' granite sculpture shop or with his mother when she would visit the family farm in the county. The road to the farm was genuine dirt paved with a layer of red clay mud. But there was so much room to run and play. On their ventures to the country they would often pass a cyclist on the road. This was a sport catching on in Petersburg.

Junior and Grandpa George at the granite sculptures' shop.

As a matter of fact, a group of boys bicycling from Petersburg to Atlantic City had recently been received at the White House by none other than Mister President Calvin Coolidge. This was quite a news event for all the citizens of Petersburg. Events such as this had always been considered big news but on this day they were bumped from the headlines by a real wiz-bang of a story out of the great state of Tennessee. It seemed that a battle was raging to the west when a biology teacher had been accused of teaching Evolution, against the law. The State of Tennessee versus John Thomas Scopes brought to the courtroom the likes of Clarence Darrow who could always outclass the classiest. It was really getting to be quite a ruckus.

Back in Virginia, the Traylor home was playing out a ruckus of its own. Junior's home was not the most pleasant of atmospheres. Junior's dad continued to suffer from his war experience in France. Maybe it was the stress of battle and maybe there was a little "survivor's guilt" thrown in on the side. He was, however, prone to mood changes and outbursts of rage directed at no one in particular and brought on by no apparent stimulus. These episodes were often attributed to the horrid Traylor temper which had been passed down through the men for many generations. The home lay in turmoil for only a short time and fortunately had humored up by the time the holidays had rolled around.

Christmas that year brought Junior a big surprise. He received a new riding horse, not with wheels, but with springs that allowed him to get the feel of a real bucking bronco. He nearly rode the springs off of that poor horse by the time warmer weather had arrived. How fortunate he was to have a father who could repair anything. Junior helped his dad with the repair chores whenever he could and began learning the contractor's trade from the young age of four.

As spring waned that year, another big surprise was in store for Junior. His most favorite uncle came down from Philadelphia for a visit. He always enjoyed time with his Uncle Ed, a physical contradiction of his brothers. Waverley Sr. and his brother Charles had always been tall and slender. Edward, while not fat, was of average height and just a bit on the stocky side. His brothers often teased him that the doctor spanked the wrong end when he was born. How well Uncle Ed fit the Traylor physical profile was irrelevant to Junior because his uncle always appeared to enjoy playing with young Waverley. His first indication that his uncle had arrived was when he spotted the shiny new Ford Model T four door parked outside. Its highly polished exterior shone like a beacon sitting on the street in front of the house. It had arrived with Uncle Ed, who was proud to take the family for a ride.

Junior became smitten with this sparkling black vehicle and at the age of four and a half entered into his "love affair with cars" phase which lasted well into his teens.

Junior on the running board of his uncle's Model T.

They drove around for an hour and discovered how much the city was growing. Across the river, the subdivision that had developed not all that long ago, had become a town. Junior and his mother were spending a lot of time across the growing city visiting the park where he spent hours on end playing on the swing and the exercise bar. He loved to swing on that bar but found it was more fun to swing on than to fall off. He often would take a tumble, but his mother was glad that he was never injured, or so she thought. He would also dress in his finest outfit with the bright red bow tie and accompany his mother to church each and every Sunday. They would walk a mile to the church on Sunday morning for church school and stay for the copious sermon lavished upon them each week. The walk became more enjoyable as the temperatures cooled and time ticked closer to the winter solstice.

Junior swinging on the exercise bar in the park.

Preparing for Christmas that year found Junior being really good for the time leading up to his annual letter to Santa Claus. The wagon he and Randi played in had gone way past its last leg and was presently decomposing at the bottom of the ravine. The tricycle he loved was in far greater need of repair than was available on this Earth. His mind drifted into daydreams about the new toys he wanted as his mother wrote down all he dictated. He kept the letter short and to the point as he bragged about how much he had helped his mother. The typical list of toys was headed by an automobile pedal car (thanks Uncle Ed), a wagon, and some games. He did not, however, overlook the more practical gifts such as a pair of galoshes and new gloves. After all, making a snowman can make your hands turn really,

really, red. His letter was addressed to Santa Claus at the North Pole. Junior believed so hard in the big man that he had no doubt the letter would find its way into his hands. He recovered the letter from where his mother had placed it and personally walked it down to the post box.

The Post Office began delivering North Pole letters to the local Progress Index newspaper, even those with drawn on stamps. The editors at the paper took a liking to Juniors letter that year and decided to print it as a seasonal special.

"Dear Santa Claus:

I am a little boy 5 years old, and try to be good and do the things my mother ask me to. Please bring me an automobile scooter, wagon, and some games. A pair of rubbers and a pair of gloves. Also bring me some fireworks, nuts, candles, and oranges.

Don't forget all the other little boys and girls. Your little boy, Waverley Traylor Jr, 226 High Street. I forgot to tell you to bring me a pistol and caps."

The Progress Index
December 2, 1926

In spite of his many attempts, on the playground equipment, to not continue to grow older, Junior reached the age of public school. He was to advance his education in a much different environment and learn of concepts, places, and hidden mysteries of the world in which he lived. The economy was improving and many rare commodities, once considered luxuries, became more commonplace. The food set upon the table was better and much more plentiful. Clothes were now frequently new, at least for Junior, who was growing like the proverbial beanstalk that Jack once climbed. Many of the older clothes were packed away and his play clothes reverted to cleaning rags for his mother or shop rags for his dad.

As he sailed through the school year, Junior began having a difficult time with an unexplainable numbness in his legs while he slept. They often would tingle and seemed to have a mind of their own. After a number of trips to the doctor, and a thorough evaluation, the medical experts decided that his trouble originated in the spine. They believed that pressure was being applied to his spinal cord by a slight case of scoliosis which mis-positioned his lower vertebra. He was treated by an orthopedist and fitted with a back brace which stabilized the vertebra with the intent of permanently relieving the pressure on his nerve column. The amazing resolution to this ailment lay in that back brace. That stupid little uncomfortable brace actually worked and within three years, he was declared cured and never had to endure such a thing again. Since Restless Leg Syndrome (RLS) was unknown to medicine in the 1920's, the cure had been primarily in his mind. The driving factor lay in the annoyance of having to wear that uncomfortable, stupid, brace.

His years in grammar school were, for the most part, uneventful. Oh, it was true that he was getting himself into trouble every couple of ~~months weeks~~ days. But what boy his age wasn't always pushing the envelope. But pushing the envelope with his dad was dangerous, knowing that there never had to be a good reason why his dad would explode. He was always able to find a retreat, out of the house, by playing on High Street hill and when restricted (the punishment for crimes unnamed) he found solace sitting out back with Zorro.

The end of the year, as the holiday approached, found Junior again passing his wishes to the big guy up north. His letter to Santa found its way again in the newspaper editor's office and his desire to have a new wagon and a raincoat were made public, much to the surprise of his mother. After all, she had hidden his letter pretty good and couldn't figure how it made it into the post box.

"Dear Santa Claus:

I am a little boy six years old, and I like school fine. I would like for you to bring me a raincoat, rain hat, a pair of gloves and rubbers, a wagon with sides on it, and a flashlight. Also bring me some fireworks, nuts, apples, and candy. Don't forget all the little boys and girls. I will try to be a good boy.

Bye, bye—Waverley Traylor Jr"

The Progress Index
Dec 1, 1927

That year he didn't exactly receive what he wanted but he was lavished with gifts that well made up for Santa's forgetfulness. His favorite was an Indian outfit that came with a double barrel pop gun. He also received a new winter coat, and a brand new scooter. He really enjoyed himself and thought of himself as a very lucky kid. Even at this age he showed a propensity for compassion and generosity. He had also just begun to discover how his concern for others was enhancing his own life.

As Waverley continued to grow and advanced through the elementary grades, his family continued living in the same three story duplex home that his Great Grandpa Addison built prior to the Great Southern Rebellion. His family lived in one side and Grandpa George lived in the other. His possessions while growing up contained many of the items of a middle class youth. Owning a rare two wheeler made him a popular youngster and living in a row house directly across the street was his bestiest friend in the world, William.

The boys became inseparable and could be found everywhere together. They would walk to school together but spend the day in separate classes. After school they could always be found getting into some kind of mischief. Weekends though, were when real trouble would raise its ugly head.

If the day was nice, the boys could nearly always be found in the nearby park playing on the swings, the exercise bar, or just riding their bikes and showing off. Being at the advanced age of seven brought about new adventures in their behavior in the form of showing off when the young girls were watching. Their many antics were often well received by the fairer sex observers, but again, things did not always go as planned, especially when they followed the exclamation "Watch This!"

William's mother Annie was a good friend with Mrs. Traylor. They often would sit on the front stoop and discuss the day's affairs, what to cook for dinner, or what the boys were doing at that time to cause trouble. Annie always had her thumb on the boys behavior. William's father was a city jailer and the threat of telling him what trouble they caused was a sure fire way to defuse the situation.

By this age, Junior was very much aware that the stork did not leave babies in the cabbage patch. His mother had become pregnant and the whole family looked forward to the new arrival. There was not much debate over the gender of the upcoming family addition. Junior did his praying for a little brother. After all, how much fun could a little sister be?

Often his mother did not feel well, "a woman's thing" his father would tell him. He now was spending a lot more time next door chatting with his Grandpa George. This kept him out of the house and away from the little arguments that permeated the living quarters. He and his grandpa would sometimes spend hours sitting on the back steps discussing everything from his dad as a young boy to how to keep the monsters, lurking beneath his bed at night, from sneaking up on him while he was asleep. One of the most significant contributions that Grandpa George made to young Waverley's education was teaching him how to efficiently climb a tree. That meant how to get up the tree without injuring yourself. Coming down, though, meant that you were on your own. There was no graceful way to de-tree a seven-year-old boy.

Christmas that year brought Junior a real treat. He received a shiny new wagon with high sides. The wheels were edged with rubber making them run smooth and quiet. He was so thrilled with this gift that he insisted on sending Santa Claus a thank you letter. Again without his mother's knowledge the letter was mailed and ended up on the newspaper editor's desk. His mother found out and sent a letter to the newspaper to try and halt its publication. Her request fell on deaf ears as the incident appeared in print.

> "Now the third letter is an amusing one, for two reasons: First the writing: 'Dear Santa Claus—I want to thank you for the wrecking truck, scooter, games, and wagon you painted so pretty for me. Daddy put one of his license tags on the back of my wagon. It is number 34502 circus wagon. You forgot all about my rubbers. If you have any left, send me some number seven. ABC chart, bird bang game, blocks, filling station, horns, harp, books and games, nuts, candies, and apples. I will be a good boy and be sure to see me next year.'
>
> I do not give the little boy's name, for today we received this letter from his mother: 'Just to amuse my son the other night, I wrote a letter to Santa Claus, thanking him for the presents. To please him I just mentioned everything he said and not letting me know, he dropped it in the mail box. So if you received same, just destroy it.' Out of respect for her wishes I didn't give the name, but it's a rather amusing incident. She overlooked the fact that her little boy is a firm believer in Santa Claus. The letter was addressed to the North Pole."

The Progress Index
8 January, 1929

Junior became industrious that year and enjoyed himself immensely in his own back yard. There he constructed a tent which served as a garage for his new wagon, determined not to let that shiny finish fade. He tried to get his two wheeler into a pup tent he erected but pre-calculations on the size were just a bit off. Lesson learned. His pedal car fit inside the garage tent really well but alas, Junior no longer fit more than one leg inside that pedal powered vehicle.

He also enjoyed spending time with his father and would accompany him on his weekend visits to the area battlefields. Being an accomplished relic hunter, the senior Traylor would collect minie balls, sabers, muskets, and pistols. Junior became quite an archeologist and relic hunter with his very own collection of mini-balls and arrow heads. He had a bountiful collection made from granite but his prized arrow heads were those made from quartz crystal. These were good times with his dad when his obvious sense of humor would creep through and he would joke about digging into the past. But care had to be taken to ensure that nothing was said to detonate that ticking time bomb concealed in his father's head. To prevent this from occurring, he tried his best to concentrate on his own collecting, hoping that this common interest would help his relationship with his dad. His private collection was kept in an old cigar box in his top dresser drawer, but was taken out most nights so that he could fondle the artifacts and daydream of the battles fought and the hunting parties taking down game for their camp. He was very proud of his collection and loved sharing his tiny portable museum. He often would place the cigar box in his beloved wagon and pay a visit to any neighbor who would take the time to stop and talk. Mostly he would end up at William's house where they would play with the souvenirs of his battlefield adventures and make up stories of times long ago.

Then there were the days when Junior would show up on William's doorstep without the cigar box but always with one of his objects of transportation in tow. His wagon was the best of his playthings when he and William were out together. They found great pleasure in pushing or pulling each other around the sidewalks or both would pile in for a quick plummet down High Street hill. Although he loved that wagon very much, it held a place in his heart just below that of his two-wheeler. This mode of enjoyment was perfect for when he played alone or visiting his friends further up the street. Now that bike could be a real menace at times. The frame rode real low, missing the ground by only a few inches, and sat on front and rear wheels that were barely 12 inches in diameter. When the bike was new, those wheels were honestly round, but after many jumps, hills, ditches, etc, several of the spokes had loosened and the wheel became more like a barrel hoop that had been driven too many times with a stick. Both the seat and the handle bars sat high up above the frame so when peddled, his feet, in those heavy boots he wore, would skim the ground oh so gently. When ridden in the dry dirt, a trail of smoke would trail out behind like an out-of-tune motorcycle. Oh wow, how spiffy was that. But when he rode it through the mud, well, it just fell over a lot. It was more than playing in the streets that caused Junior's parents to worry. Day to day life was always a challenge and growing up during the roaring twenties wasn't easy for a adolescent. He loved that two wheeler as much as he loved his wagon, even though it was such an odd looking contraption. He and William would sometimes take the bike up to the park where they had plenty of room to ride without getting into too much trouble.

Worrying about her son was just one of the daily chores of his mother. She had begun showing with child for the new year. She confessed to Junior that she wanted a daughter but he didn't relish the possibility of having to deal with a sister; a brother was still set in his mind. Then early in May the pains started and Junior was sent up the street to get her designated midwife while Poppa Traylor stayed busy practicing going berserk. Jumping on his bike and with wheels spinning and hair flickering in the wind, Junior flew up High Street hill and disappeared. Shortly Mrs. Bishop appeared, chugging up in front of the house in her family Model T. Although being a rather robust woman, she had no difficulty rapidly ascending the 11 steps to the front door.

Just then, a lone figure rose over the crest of the hill and rapidly grew bigger as he descended toward home. Apparently moving a slight bit faster than he was used to, Junior was beginning to have a little difficulty trying to stop. He really had no reason to be concerned because his brakes were supplemented by the rear end of Mrs. Bishop's Model T. This caused the bike to rapidly stop and Junior to fly over the rear of the car, ending up head down in the back seat. It was fortunate for him that she had left the top down on her automobile. He paid no notice of the condition of his bike and, touching only every third step, raced into the house.

Hours went by with no word coming from within the Traylor house. Suddenly, Junior came bursting out of the front door and, not touching any of the steps, well maybe just one, hit the sidewalk and shot across the street. Exploding in the front door of his friend William's home, he shouted "It's here! It's here! I have a brother! I have a brother!" William, it seems, was excited too and wanted to see the new baby. The pair adjourned to the Traylor house but as they approached the front steps Junior noticed a twisted piece of metal laying on the street directly behind Mrs. Bishop's car. May 6th, 1929, became a real day to remember for Junior. He was given a new baby brother and his beautiful bike had gone and gotten itself broken. For the next month Junior could be found in his backyard workshop, hammer in hand, attempting to straighten his front wheel into something that resembled a circle. He was successful in his venture but from that point on, his bike felt as though it was being ridden across railroad ties as he choo-chooed down the street.

CHAPTER 3
Growing Up

Times had been good but darkness loomed in the wings. Stocks on the financial market began a major decline in 1929. While not having any direct impact on the Traylor family, indirectly it proved their reliance on a healthy financial system. October 29th, 1929, Black Tuesday, the day America's financial system cascaded into chaotic ruin and drove the economy in a downward spiral. Times had become difficult once again. The family began relying on whatever work Waverley Sr. could muster, but then again everyone suffered. No one wanted their house painted, or wallpaper hung, or gutters repaired. No one wanted to buy the flowers they grew because these beautiful blooms were not fit for eating. He was fortunate that a lot of people couldn't afford the gasoline for their cars and began using bicycles. His bicycle repair business took a small shot of adrenalin which helped them survive. There was rent coming in from properties owned by the family, that is whenever it could be collected. But taxes had to be paid and later, several of the properties had to be sold to pay back taxes.

Life became difficult and, with a new baby to care for, stress enveloped every waking moment. "Old Man Traylor," to which he was affectionately known to his friends, was seemingly handling this stressful time well, but Junior's Mother, with the baby to care for, would occasionally lose control and scream for a little peace and quiet. There were no other factors surrounding that situation, which was occurring through most households of the era, but it made a lasting impression on the young man's delicate psyche. He would recall this impression later in his life and it would prove to be a monumental mistake on his part. The stress of the time never seemed to dissipate as events were constantly being stacked one upon another.

In February, Waverley's Grandpa George passed away at home, which was adjacent to Junior's home, in the Traylor family duplex. The funeral service, unlike his Uncle Charlie's, was held at a local funeral home in Petersburg and the body of this well loved man was laid to rest in Blandford Cemetery. Grandpa George's passing brought Waverley Sr.'s brother back into town. Junior, although depressed on the loss of his grandfather, was always glad to see his uncle. He swore, though, that it was not because of the swell presents that his Uncle Edward always brought him.

Waverley's Uncle Edward, having served in France with his father, brought Waverley a leather aviator's helmet. Since William was always like a member of the family, Uncle Edward would never forget to also bring along one for him. The helmets looked good on the boys with their matching leather jackets with fur collars. Wearing them with aviator goggles perched above their eyes, however, apparently gave them the illusion of indestructibility. Boys being the way boys are, they never buckled the helmets which allowed the straps to dangle loose like long pigtails extending below their cheeks. They wore these aviator duds everywhere they went, except for church. After all, the church was there to show off your fanciest of clothes. Even in spite of the times, everyone kept one set of good going-to-church clothes for this occasion.

Whether in church or playing on the street, Junior and William were known far and wide, at least on High Street. They were always together, wearing their aviator duds, and pulling their beautiful shiny wagons. These wagons were the envy of the neighborhood, big shiny red rectangular buckets that were a foot off of the ground and a good 5 inches deep. The guidance system locked firmly to the head of the vehicle and connected to the movable front axle where two shiny red solid metal ten inch wheels were attached. These wheels, and the two wheels in the rear, sported a thick rubber edging. It was believed by the young wagon racers that this made their rides smoother and therefore faster. In truth though, the rubber was probably there to make the wagons run quieter and therefore not drive the mothers so crazy by having to listen to them all day long.

Riding their speedier-than-the-wind wagons down High Street hill was a common pastime for the boys. Showing any regard for the traffic crossing below never occurred to them. Then came the morning when, as they raced neck and neck, their helmet straps flying out behind their heads, an automobile crossed just as the boys reached the base of the hill. Waverley swerved to the right and flew directly into the front door of Mr. Minton's grocery store. William cut sharply to the left, crossed the street behind the passing car and landed with an abrupt halt by braking, using the gas pump at the ESSO station as his braking medium. The boys were not immediately injured from the accident but that condition was not long lived, after their fathers were made aware of their afternoon's adventure. That was about the time that Junior wished he had been injured.

Junior and friend William on Junior's racing wagon.

It was not only the wagon which provided a source for trouble. His repaired-daily bike was also a great catalyst for misfortune, usually with a capital "M." He would often pose in the back yard with his bike because this was the spot where you could always find him working on his two wheeled monstrosity. Whenever anyone found Junior sporting his aviator helmet and brown aviators jacket, you could be assured that some kind of ordeal was coming his way. He would be preparing to race down High Street hill, or do something honestly just as foolish. But what else is there for an eight-year-old boy to do except find and challenge danger. These incidents were referred to as their game of pain. The game always started with the immortal words, "Hey, watch this," or "I dare ya." It was then they knew that pain would be coming very, very, soon.

Although Junior's baby brother, Allen, was not yet ready for the thrill rides down High Street, Junior would allow Allen to play in his wagon. He would often pull him up and down the street listening to his vocalizations of joy. There were few children in the neighborhood to play with his brother, so Junior became his best friend and playmate. They could often be found together or with William, the three of them would play silly games. Junior even taught Allen how to pull him around on a hand truck whenever they paid a visit to their father's shop on Bank Street.

Junior's father was working as a handyman, had sporadic work as a cabinet maker, and was growing flowers on a plot of land in the country purchased from Jesse's father. This was a small plot of only 22 acres once being a part of the Pamplin farm, which ironically had been purchased from the Traylor clan shortly after the American Revolution. It was quite amazing that these two long established families would intertwine more than 100 years later when Waverley Sr. and Jesse tied the matrimonial knot. Junior would try and help his dad on any of his jobs. He had been learning the handyman trade for several years and was presently learning agriculture while helping to establish the flower farm in the country. He was able, after school, to help his dad in the shop downtown, work on bicycles, and fill tobacco pouches for the Brown and Williamson Tobacco Company.

Tobacco was a big industry in Petersburg. Most of the country farms raised this commodity and the large tobacco companies had their warehouses in town. The cigarette tobacco would be made and sold in cloth bags for people to roll their own. The Traylor's had a home industry in which the whole family participated. The bags were picked up at a little shop on Taft Street and were turned in to the print shop to be embossed with the Brown & Williamson label. The family made their own frames out of a bent coat hanger which they would screw down to a piece of board. Using a needle, strings would be threaded through the sewn opening to produce the drawstrings for the pouches. They then would measure out the tobacco and fill the tiny bags. This was truly a family business and the way that food was put on the table most days. Spending so much time working with his father and family left Junior not spending any time with William. As a matter of fact, his entire social life was suffering and he barely had any time for his studies.

By the age of 11, Junior was becoming really socially conscious. He could often be found, weather permitting, sporting his knickers that allowed showing off his favorite striped socks, which he would pair with his white shirt and tie. Unlike his father, though, he never buttoned the top button nor pulled his tie up tight. This gave him that casual "man about town" look so vital to an up and coming teenager. His social carousing had taken a real blow that summer. His friend William became ill, suffering from Rheumatic Fever. It kept his buddy confined for a good bit of the time and Waverley found entertaining himself a very boring and difficult task.

Autumn came and Junior attempted a breakout of his social shell. He landed a role in the school play produced in memory of Edgar Allen Poe. A giant in the American Romantic Movement, Poe was an American author, poet, editor and literary critic. Junior played the role of a young Poe and pleased the audience with his convincing performance. This had the opposite effect than was intended for the poor lad. His portrayal of a secluded and introverted young Poe set in motion Junior's move toward social isolation that plagued him throughout high school and the remainder of his life. Without intention, he had become socially invisible. His only escape at this point was the work he performed to help in his father's latest money making scheme.

Junior's father was never one to allow the prospect of a good money making idea go untried. Attached to the rear of the house were the remains of slave quarters made up of a single room, two stories high. He used this building to raise Canaries, having built a multitude of cages for nesting and a large aviary. The canary business didn't last very long and he was soon turning the first floor into a workshop for his minor repairs and tool storage for his contracting business. The second floor was now used as storage. He would often buy wallpaper in bulk for pennies a roll and store the rolls on the second floor. When he needed wallpaper for a job, he would cut and trim the selected paper, and make up the wallpaper paste in his workshop, the night before the job began.

Each year, in the late winter, Waverley Sr. would shift gears and begin preparations for the spring flower harvest. This meant that work on the farm would pick up, which in turn meant several fun days for Junior. His father had taught him how to drive the tractor in order to plow and cut the fields. The tractor was a bright red International Harvester with large steel wheels that could grip dirt, mud, or asphalt, but would tear up the surface in doing so. A seat had been added by "Old Man Traylor" so that plowing chores could be done with a little comfort, very little. Junior also loved the trips to the farm because once they left the paved roads in the city and landed on the country dirt roads, he was allowed to drive his daddy's pickup truck. He really, really loved driving. What he didn't necessarily love was clearing the grasses from the flower fields. The broom straw had to be cleared in order to allow the flowers to thrive and bloom fully. This chore was accomplished by hand using a freshly sharpened sickle. A real backbreaker of a clearing operation but one that was ooh so important.

That same year, Waverley Sr. placed an order for a wide variety of new flower bulbs that would expand his operation and, with luck, equally expand his income. These new bulbs would not come until late summer because fall was the planting season for these beauties. Clearing the fields this year included plowing an additional acre in preparation for the fall planting. When the work was finished for the weekend, Junior and his dad returned to the city but remained too tired to do anything other than relax and listen to the radio. Sometimes, when everyone wasn't so tired, the family liked to go out to the movies and maybe even get to watch a talkie. Otherwise, the family would sit around the Magnavox and listen to the likes of "The Adventures of Gracie," "Amos 'n' Andy," or the "Fireside Chats" of President Roosevelt.

Winter melted into spring and the harvest days were upon them. April showers brought the flowers, and in the Traylor household, this meant work for everyone. The daffodils blooming on the farm were ready for picking and Junior, along with his Dad, would spend afternoons picking these flowers and trucking them into town. The back room over the workshop at 228 High Street was set up to handle the production with tray after tray filled with water in which the harvested flowers could soak. Mrs. Traylor would then take over sorting the mass of flowers into saleable bouquets. Junior was naturally conscripted to assist his mother in wrapping her beautiful bunches as he had been for the picking process. Nothing much could top working in that back room with the scent of such varied genus of daffodils, jonquils, and narcissus. The aroma in that room was created by a potpourri of fresh, sweet fragrances emanating from each bright luscious blossom.

Come the weekend, Junior, William, and several neighborhood boys were given the task of venturing into downtown with a basket filled with springtime joy and selling the flowers on the street. They would march out of the house with full baskets and return empty but with a full pocket of change. The money would be counted and the basket refilled in time to make another downtown run. This was a fair deal for all the young men. Junior managed to make just a little more than the other boys. After all, he did participate in all aspects of the business. This business was a saving grace during the bad economic times but remained lucrative as the country recovered.

When the flower season subsided, it indicated that summer break was just around the corner, but this break was only from school. Even for those who enjoyed learning, summer break was a welcome relief, especially this summer. Junior's Aunt Marie had been promising him a trip to the Big Apple. The long awaited journey finally began as his mother drove her sister and Junior to the train station at the upper end of High Street. They waited at the station and moved out onto the platform as time drew near for the train's arrival. Junior was the first to spot the engine. He could see the large plume of white smoke bellowing high above the tree tops to the south. Within a young man's instant, the gigantic locomotive appeared, approaching the station. As it neared the platform, the huge wheels on the engine began slowing down as a loud pulse of steam was emitted from the forward pistons. The squeal of the brakes sang in perfect harmony with the train's whistle announcing its arrival in Petersburg. The pair of New York bound adventurers boarded the coach when the conductor signaled and found their seats. Obviously Junior wanted the seat by the window so that he could better see the country as they sped through on their way north. Junior waved to his mother from the window as the train began pulling away from the station. His mother waved back and threw him a kiss. The train then disappeared around the bend.

The year 1933 marked his first train trip and Junior was giddy with anticipation. To ride along in the passenger coach looking out onto the world was a thrill like he had never known before. Towns would come and go as the whistle blew when passing each crossing. To see the cars waiting for the train to pass was as exciting as the smoke from the engine pouring back across the cars. It chugged up the track at a speed which the young boy from Petersburg had never before traveled. Waverley (he felt that he was too grown up to be called Junior any more) was so entranced that he nearly forgot about the sandwich his mother had packed for him. When the train pulled into Washington DC's Union Station. he pulled out his jacket, that he had been sitting on for the whole trip, dug into his pocket, and found what felt like a well wrapped flapjack. This was very unfortunate since he now realized how hungry he had become.

 Here in Washington they were to change trains because they were going to ride the new electric train into New York. They had a two hour wait so into the terminal they ventured. Upon entering the main lobby, Waverley was overtaken by its shear vastness. This was enough to render any young man speechless. The great arched ceiling rose nine stories above the floor giving him the feeling of being an ant running across a kitchen floor. Around the great room were gigantic, 40 foot high, arched windows providing sunlight enough to match the out of doors itself. Aunt Marie bought them a snack from an onsite vendor and they found comfortable seats up on the mezzanine from which they could enjoy their snack and watch the people below rush about. Time passes oh so slowly but as sure as his aunt promised, the moment finally arrived to prepare for boarding the train for the next leg of their adventure. They checked the time and found their way to the track 23 concourse.

 Their train was already in the station as they approached along the platform. There was still plenty of time before departure so Aunt Marie gave in to Waverley and they walked down the concourse to see the shiny new electric engine. The power end of the train was so much different than the locomotives that Waverley was used to seeing back home. There were no big wheels along each side, no smokestack, and no huge steel boilers. It so much reminded him of a character he had read about in a book titled "The Story of Doctor Doolittle." the character "pushmi-pullyu" resembled a llama with a head on each end. Much like that loveable character, the engine of this train looked like two that had been cut in half and glued together in the middle. On each end was an identical headlamp, an engineer's compartment, and a fold up device that would reach into the air and grab electricity from the heavy wires strung from the tall poles towering above the tracks. Wow!

They watched their luggage being loaded into the baggage car and heard the conductor call "All Aboard!" Waverley and his aunt stepped lively to where the conductor stood and stepping on the little stool he had placed in front of the door, entered the coach car. They found a pair of seats together with Waverley, of course, taking the seat by the window. As the train began to pull out of the station he noticed the sounds that weren't there. There was no whistle, no clanking of the bell, and no sound of steam escaping from the big drive pistons. It was truly eerie; the sounds that were conspicuously not there.

The ride from Washington to New York was so much different than the trip through Virginia. The train was very quiet which made it difficult to sleep. There was no *train lullaby* to caress you into a gentle sleep. In Virginia they passed through a lot of farm country which presented the wide open spaces of rural living. Now they were passing through urban country filled with tall buildings, factories, and the bustle of industry. They glided through Baltimore, Wilmington, Philadelphia, Trenton, and Newark before finally arriving in New York. It was as if each city touched the other with not very much breathing room between. It was well into the evening when they arrived at Grand Central Station.

They left the train using the same small stool that had been used to board in Washington. Walking along the long platform, they entered the main station. Waverley had only once seen anything so magnificent and that had been earlier in the day. The ceiling in the station was taller than his house and it was lit up as well as a bright sunny day. He struggled along behind his Aunt Marie, rather groggy and half asleep, as they stepped out on 42nd Street to hail a cab. The city streets were so bright that it was difficult to imagine that the sun had not yet risen. The bright illumination extended along the street in both directions appearing to form a mere point of light. A taxi cab pulled over in front of the weary travelers and they climbed in, which was another first for young Waverley. It whisked them through the night traffic, stopping at a fancy looking building. He appeared to sleepwalk all the way through the lobby and to their room at the Waldorf-Astoria. Later he remembered nothing after getting into the cab.

Their trip was an overwhelming event for an innocent twelve-year-old from the south. They visited the fairly new Empire State Building, which could be seen from nearly any place within the city. From the very top they walked out onto the deck and witnessed, first hand, the vastness of this city called New York. He had asked his aunt to point out the Big Apple, but felt embarrassed when he realized his naive mistake. Way away he spotted the Stature of Liberty which was going to be the next stop on their agenda. Aunt Marie and Waverley caught a cab to the south side docks and boarded a ferry bound for the Statue of Liberty park. The ride across the bay was fun because the breeze blowing across the ferry relieved the heat of the bright summer sun. Arrival at the park was interesting since the water had become a little rough as they tried to leave the boat. Aunt Marie had lost her balance and stumbled but was fortunately caught by her young nephew and saved from an embarrassing fall. The climb to the head of Lady Liberty was exhausting for his aunt but Waverley took the ascent like a trooper. The view from the crown was breathtaking, particularly being able to look back on the Empire State Building where they had just been. The entire lower side of Manhattan was visible with the ships, ferries, and small boats resembling toys in the bath tub. The wind had really picked up and the ride back to the mainland was a bit rougher than the trip out had been. The tiny ferry was tossed about in the choppy bay and the railings were packed with people who were obviously too excited to stay in their seats. Nearing the end of the transit across, Waverley too felt the necessity to lay upon the rail and make his contribution to the gods of the sea.

On Saturday night they met a young man who was obviously not a stranger to Aunt Marie. They dined at an upscale restaurant where young Waverley had the opportunity to practice the table manners his mother had been driving into him for years. After dinner they traveled by taxi to the NBC Studio where they had the good fortune to sit in the audience of the Shell Show, a musical variety show starring Al Jolson. During the week the pair were joined on several occasions by this same young man. One evening, they were treated to a stage play at the Times Square Theatre. The production of "Forsaking All Others" was having a very successful run. Young Waverley enjoyed his introduction to sophistication and the arts, in all of its forms. Just that afternoon they had spent several hours at the Metropolitan Museum of Art on 5th Avenue. On one of their exciting shopping adventures, the pair stopped at S.J. Shrubsole Jewelry on 57th Street just off of Park Avenue. Aunt Marie bought Waverley a shiny gold cross to wear and be protected forever. This was a fine present and Waverley promised to wear it always. His week on the town passed all too rapidly and it seemed to be over before it had even begun; it was time to go home.

Returning to Petersburg after such an exciting trip was not easy. Home had become a lonely place to live. Other than William, Waverley had very few friends. He would often spend hours alone in Central Park along Petersburg's Sycamore Street. Even when he traveled to have a good time, there was always an air of sadness about him. On a trip to Ocean View Amusement Park, he played the social game and rode the rides but the picture he had taken at the photo booth showed lines in his face resulting from an honest loneliness. He felt a true longing for his family and wanted so much to return home.

While twelve-year-old Waverley had spent the summer gallivanting around the east coast, his father had taken to headquartering himself in his workshop on Bank Street, just down from the A&P. The garage entrance was down the alleyway behind the George Williams Tire store, the entrance to which would become mucky when it rained. The price of having this area blacktopped was too high and Mr. Traylor was never known to spend a penny that wasn't absolutely necessary. Being the resourceful man that he was, he devised a method of mixing used motor oil with sand and voila, instant blacktop. Also that year the muleskinners came into town and rented the back lot from "Old Man Traylor." They installed a corral gate across the lot entrance and brought in their mules. They set up shop and were buying and selling mules from that location. This made another of the several rental incomes coming into the family, but yet another possibility had surfaced. Waverley Sr. had stored his old pie truck and several other old trucks in the garage, but had recently decided that instead of using the garage, he would rent it out. The pie truck he moved out to the farm and the others he sold. He then rented the workshop to a taxi cab company where they maintained their service garage and operated their fleet of taxis.

It was fortunate that "Old Man Traylor" had moved his shop to the old slave quarters behind his house. It would have been difficult trudging through the snow when colder weather arrived. The winter of that particular year was bitter and cold. The temperatures dropped well below freezing and remained below 20 degrees for over two weeks. Snow had been falling for more than two days and at least 15 inches covered the ground. That was when it happened. The water line buried in the back yard broke and the water forced its way to the surface. It looked rather amusing, like a big ice stalagmite growing in the yard. Waverley, his brother Allen, and their father dressed out warmly in their multi layered attire and began the daunting task of excavating the pipeline for repair. The boys cleared away the snow and made several attempts at digging the hole, but their shovels barely made a dent in the ice and frozen ground. Now the boy's dad, being the ingenious problem solver that he was, sent Junior, with their gas can, down the street to the ESSO station for a can of regular. Normally this would be a quick trip, but with so much snow covering the roads, and Waverley dragging out his sleigh for the journey, it was inherently going to take some time. Allen and his dad retreated into the house for a nice warm cup of cider to warm them while they waited.

After an abundant number of "tocks" on the grandfather clock, Waverley did finally return, struggling inch by inch with the full can of gasoline perched precariously on his sleigh. The gas was poured lightly on the snow cleared area and set ablaze. When the flames subsided, the boys would dig, clearing away an inch of thawed ground. This process was repeated for the rest of the afternoon until the pipe was ultimately uncovered. Their father made the repair as the boys watched and though it was unintentional, the boys had completed a valuable lesson in plumbing skills.

Uncle Edward's 1936 Dodge with Waverley Jr. claiming first riding rights.

The summer was approaching and Junior was hoping to get another trip to New York. His Aunt Marie was headed for the Big Apple but for a different purpose this year. The young man she had been seeing for a while had proposed to her. She was returning to New York this summer to get married. It looked like a fun trip with his favorite aunt was off for this year. He had to hang around home that summer but he used his time wisely and learned all he could about his Uncle Edward's new 1936 Dodge. At least he had his uncle to talk with when he came for a visit. He got rather excited when his uncle asked him to return to Atlanta with him for a summer visit. After all, what could have been any better.

They left on Saturday morning and drove straight through. Waverley couldn't believe how wonderful it was to watch the world passing by as they made their way down Route One toward Atlanta. Leaving the city, he found them passing through farm country. The wide open fields had fence lines separating the road from the cattle grazing within. Although the cows were actually far into the field, they could be identified by their distinctive odor which permeated the air and flowed gently throughout the car. He could feel the small town atmosphere as they approached the tiny town of South Hill. The streets were alive with shoppers shuffling in and out of the small shops. They motored through South Hill and back into the country. Waverley became mesmerized by the tree lined fields, filled with horses, cattle, and goats. As the day lazily passed into afternoon, Waverley became a little drowsy as he watched the telephone poles flash by in a hypnotic rhythm. He finally drifted off to sleep, also aided by the low hum of the tires on the pavement. When he awakened, they were passing through Raleigh with the tall buildings hovering overhead and the sound of the city filling the air with the rumble of people on the move. This so much reminded him of his recent New York adventure. They drove completely through the city and into the surrounding countryside. He particularly enjoyed watching for the series of signs along the roadway that entertained the drivers, breaking up an otherwise boring drive. "*At crossroads—Don't just trust to Luck—That other car—may be a Truck.—Burma Shave.*"

Late into the night, they arrived in the little Atlanta suburb of Decatur. Here he spent a couple of great weeks with his Uncle Ed and Aunt Margaret. Hailing from New Orleans, Aunt Margaret was a beautiful woman from an old southern aristocratic family. She always had an air of casual sophistication about her. On the first day of his visit her five foot seven inch frame wore a sued jacket with matching beret and a pair of beachcombers. This was a unique fashion statement but on her, it just seemed right. But she did look good, she always did. She took Waverley shopping to the city to put a little pizzazz in his wardrobe. On other afternoons she would take him to the pool. He did love to swim and also enjoyed watching his aunt gracefully take laps in the pool. He returned home to Petersburg in time to help his father around the shop while summer still dominated the weather.

Now Waverley Sr. had always been quite a collector of Civil War relics. He spent many afternoons on the Petersburg Battlefields searching for evidence of the battles fought there. On many occasions he didn't have to venture too far. While planting several rose bushes in the front yard, he dug up two cannonballs. Remembering the story that several union shells had pierced the house during the skirmish, it would not have been so out of place for the balls of steel to be found where they lay.

This gave Junior some really exciting stories when he returned to school. He began his High School studies and was thrilled with the "Snipe hunts" when several of the upperclassmen were kind enough to allow them to tag along. They taught him all of the finer points of hunting the dreaded snipe, although he was never able to trap one in his bag. Some of his new classes were more exciting than others which made him conflicted when it came to his love of learning. His interest was more attuned to the hands-on classes where he could learn by listening and doing. The classes relying on huge amounts of reading and memorization were more difficult to grasp. This resulted in his studies being sluggish when it came to history, english, and language arts. His grades in these classes expressed his extended boredom. He was a wiz, however, at math and science. His other favorite subjects were Mechanical Drawing, Woodworking, and Physics. In drawing he was allowed to express his imagination and display his natural engineering abilities. He was constantly drawing, whether it was a new style cabinet or a house that he one day would build. The skills he learned in woodworking classes served him well as he worked with his father in the afternoons as a cabinet maker. And whatever else could be said about studying physics, it was fun. This played on his natural abilities and fed his need of knowledge and understanding. This interest naturally led to his ability to solve any problem, understand how just about everything worked, and his skill to repair anything.

Waverley and his brother loved to venture out with their dad on Sunday afternoon artifact hunts. On one occasion, after relic hunting in Williamsburg, they were returning home on the Colonial Parkway in their father's pickup truck touting Waverley Seniors advertisement on the door, "*Interior* & *Exterior Decorator, Phone 3738-J*." Waverley and his father were in the seat and brother Allen was riding in the back. They were pulled over by a Colonial Parkway policeman and told that they ". . . couldn't have this truck on the Colonial Parkway. The parkway was for personal cars only." The boy's watched their father as he turned very indignant and explained to the officer, in not so uncertain terms, that ". . . this WAS his personal car." This was obviously one of the times that their dad vented his frustrations, which on occasion, was embarrassing to the boys.

Waverley had chosen an alternate method for venting, which involved physical exercise. Almost all of the boys at Petersburg High School played sports of one kind or the other. Maybe not for the school team, but with the same players in a sandlot after school or on weekends. He did play on the football team for one year but quickly learned that the regimented football in school just wasn't his bailiwick. He preferred the kind of game where he could use his imagination and change the play when needed. Most afternoons he was busy working with his father. When he could sneak away, he enjoyed a good game of whatever ball was being passed around the vacant lot. Whether it be softball, football, or baseball, Junior was always in the midst of the game. It was by far a most wonderful method of obtaining injury without being yelled at, or at least until he returned home. He was timid and not a very good mixer in other social environments. He seldom attended dances or parties and dreaded meeting new people in that type of environment. But, when the gang was on the field, he could get right in and mix it up with the best of them.

Junior dressed out on the practice field
at Petersburg High School.

It wasn't long into High School before a little "growing up" became a big change in his life. His focus was slowly turning from sports and academia to a much more interesting subject such as GIRLS; well, girls and cars. His passion for adventure filled his mind with daydreams of places both near and far. Of course he realized that girls and cars could be as dangerous as climbing tall mountains or rafting heavy white water in the west. With them it was much more likely that he might slip and fall. At least girls and cars were both good subjects for conversing with his best buddy.

Although he and William had no classes together the boys remained inseparable. Shortly after Junior's mother had received her driver's license, she wanted to treat the boys to an afternoon at the Southside Fair in Petersburg. She didn't have enough money to pay for all of their admittances, but Jesse Traylor was a very resourceful woman. She placed the boys, Waverley, William, and Allen, in the trunk of the car and drove into the fair grounds. When she got into the parking lot, she couldn't get the trunk open. The boys were locked in the trunk and a police officer came up to offer her help. She said "no—I don't need any help." There she was, trying to unlock the trunk and get rid of the police officer since she had snuck the boys into the fair. The trunk remained stubborn, refusing to lift. Jesse, at wits end, sat down on the running board as if to give up. The police officer left and shortly thereafter the trunk lid slowly opened on its own. It seemed that the trunk was unlatched while the policeman was standing there but Junior had held onto the trunk lid to prevent an embarrassing situation. The boys literally fell to the ground as they emerged from the vehicle. After getting their butts up off of the ground and dusting off their pants, with the help of mother, they all were finally able to enjoy a day at the fair. Yeah Mom!

The boys had remained the best of friends even though their interest were growing further apart. William loved bookkeeping and Waverley found his interest in science. His ambition was to seek a career as a Chemist or a Chemical Engineer. Between classes the boys would meet and look at girls. At lunch they would always arrange to sit with and talk to girls. This became their real common interest and the driving force that allowed them to get out of bed in the mornings. They always remained casual friends with the girls they knew, but a romantic interest just never seemed to develop. As younger boys, the engineers, as they were often called, would repeatedly do stupid things to get the girls' attention. Now they were growing up and had more mature thoughts on their minds. They would do stupid stuff to impress them and maybe, if they were lucky, they could hurt themselves and play for sympathy angle.

Although Waverley spent time with, and played with, his brother, Allen felt a deep resentment and a lot of jealousy for the one person whom he admired. This kept him conflicted between the love and the hate that he felt for Waverley. Allen never had any new clothes or toys. His possessions always seemed to be the hand-me-downs from his brother. Waverley spent a lot of time visiting his Uncle Edward in Georgia and his Aunt Marie in the country, but these were during the good years of the twenties. Allen never received the same considerations but it was difficult explaining to a pre-teen how the economy had turned so bad. Times were different and the boys grew up in entirely different eras, but he knew only his life and could never imagine what life was like a decade earlier.

Waverley continued to horse around with his brother at home and with his classmates in school. This was his meager attempt at becoming Mr. Popular. Although his grades weren't that good in social studies and languages, his excellence in math and science had him labeled as "The Brain" by his fellow inmates. This went over well in school and most of the student body knew his name. His social life, however, still registered low on the popularity-o-meter as he never seemed to get invites to parties or arrange for a Saturday night date. His entire array of social activity was surrounded by his participation in church activities. This gave him his close association with Christian principals. Through peer pressure, he had tried a cigarette or two, but his slender body didn't want anything to do with that nasty habit. He didn't attempt that trick again since the smoke left his lungs gasping for fresh air. He was raised in a home always filled with the smoke from his father but he swore that the suffocating smog would never again be purposely inhaled into his body. Alcohol was a completely unpleasant taste, he preferred a cold cola, and he pledged never again to let drink pass his lips. It was unfortunate that his future presented circumstances that caused a renege on these promises. He also was never known to curse. He had heard enough of the crude language in his own home and knew that he did not want to sound like his dad. He pledged to live a Christian life style and was devoted to his faith. Of course the church was his favorite place because this is where he had met Martha, the love of his life.

Martha was a beautiful girl and if ever there was a complete opposite from Waverley, this was the one. It is absolutely amazing how strongly that opposites attract, a principle of physics known all too well by Waverley. He was a gifted scientist and mathematician who liked to work on cars and motorcycles. She was a gifted artist as a painter, a musician, a singer, and a poet. This was evident even in high school when she composed a verse of Day Dreams.

"Day Dreams
By Martha Ellis

While all the world is passing by,
I sit content with my thought.
I dream of a gay and cheery land
That my heart alone has wrought
From out of the pages of history,
When knights for maidens fought.

My dream world is a world of romance;
Full of laughter, joy and fun,
And our minds will be free from toil and care,
And we rest when day is done.
Brave and gallant knights are there
Whose battles are bravely won.

Alas, I never will see that world,
A world that will please just me,
For each mortal would have a different thought
Of what the world should be,
But in my heart I'll treasure still
That beautiful memory."

The Petersburg High School Missile
Martha Ellis—Class of 1937

    These were the pleasures of Waverley's true love. These were the reasons for which he fell so deeply in love. He would love to hear her sing, he would love to hear her play the piano, and he could sit for hours in the park being read the poetry that she had written, just for his ears. Before all else happened, this was the true assemblage of love.

Chapter 4
Love and Marriage

They had been attending the same church for as long as Junior could remember. She came across the river from her parents' home in the county and he lived not far down the street from their church. The two of them knew each other and would often speak, but they ran in different circles and were separated by age. Martha was two years older than Waverley. This doesn't seem like an insurmountable difference when grown up but as a teenager, they were worlds apart. Their history had not much in common either. They grew up across the river from one another which naturally kept them apart. Martha was a beautiful girl and had her girlfriends keeping her company wherever she ventured. The church was the only escape she had from her friends and this is where she became the most vulnerable. The kids at the church would often travel together on adventures around the state, from weekend picnics at her pastors cottage on the Potomac river to a day trip to enjoy the beach and amusement park at Ocean View in Norfolk. The girls often spent the afternoon there at the Cavalier Beach Club on the oceanfront dancing and listening to big band music. This was really their favorite pastime.

Waverley did, however, run with a closer group of friends. His buddy William and his own baby brother Allen were all that he had. He had grown up as a ghost, invisible to all but a very select few. He had been keeping his eye on Martha as they both grew and often dreamed about going out with her. Their friends didn't mingle outside of the church but were always doing church related projects together and traveled together on church outings. On occasions, a group from the church would help out at the Veterinary Hospital taking care of the sick animals. This was where he picked up his love of animals and his ability to care for the sick and injured. After all, he had a dog. On the other hand, Martha loved her kittens. This, at least, gave them something in common.

Martha had graduated from Petersburg High School in 1937 and, although he was in the class of 1939, the difference in their ages didn't seem to hinder his desires. Waverley continued to keep a casual association with her. Although he wanted so much more in a relationship, he was too shy and nervous to expose any other intentions. To attempt to further impress her, he became more involved in functions and social activities of the church. Waverley also took the additional plunge and became baptized at the Easter services. He began attending night services when he knew she would be there and became closer to the popular minister, the Reverend Jack Unruh. As members of the Methodist Youth Fellowship, they attended the first summer retreat for teens held at the Unruh's summer cottage.

He became closer to Martha on this summer retreat and sparked what would continue back home as a mutual friendship. She had become attracted to his six foot frame since he towered over her height-challenged body. What she couldn't resist, though, were his bright Hazel eyes and how they sparkled each time he looked at her. He worked extremely hard when he returned to school in the fall. At least he worked hard at trying to summon up the courage to ask her out. Before Christmas, William maneuvered Waverley into a corner by telling Martha that there was something Waverley needed to ask her. The die was cast, resulting in Waverley setting up his first date ever.

"Friday Jan 13, 1939 First date with Martha."

Diary Entry
3 January 1939

Waverley borrowed his daddy's car for that evening and drove out to the county in Colonial Heights to pick up his companion for the evening. This is where he met James and Hettie Ellis for the first time. Oh, they had seen each other on occasion at church, but had never really had an opportunity to speak, much less have a conversation. As if fate had planned the evening, he arrived a bit early and of course she was not prepared for his arrival. This gave her parents the opportunity to have a nice chat with Waverley, and grill him they did. It was a wonder that he didn't leave on the date before Martha entered the room. She did though, and just in the nick of time.

They headed out for dinner and then off to the movies to watch "The Adventures of Robin Hood." They both enjoyed the evening. This shared occasion was a pivotal point in bringing them closer together as friends. There had also been a big change in Waverley after that night. Everyone at church could immediately bear witness to the fact that he was now wearing his ties cinched up tight to that closed top button. All knew that his life had changed and his close acquaintances would bet their weekly offering that they knew why.

The following summer, Martha attended the Methodist Youth Training Camp at Camp Bethel in the Blue Ridge mountains. Although he had only dated her once that year, he experienced empty longing for the first time. It became difficult to concentrate on his work and nearly impossible to sleep at night. At the end of each day, it became impossible to imagine another full day without her. Finally it was time for her return home and the entire gang at church was looking forward to her arrival, but none more so than Waverley.

It always seems that when the stew is in the pot and simmering, it becomes time for the pot to spring a leak. The Sunday morning following her return, Martha announced that her entire family was heading to New York to visit the World's Fair. Besides missing her most severely, Waverley also had just a wee smidgen of jealously. After all, his family was not able to afford trips such as this and definitely not as often. He was also envious of the fact that she had already graduated and he still remained tied down by school. Oh how glad he would be when he no longer had to worry about school and could be free to travel. By the following week, Martha had returned to her home in Chesterfield County and her precious little kittens.

In a desperate attempt not to be left alone again, Waverley arranged for a second date in the fall. By this time the two had become an item for gossip around the young adults at church and he had gotten used to seeing her through the window at school as she went to work each day. Of course the school was not directly on her way to work. A slight detour was required, about a quarter of a mile out of the way. He could also see her in the afternoons as she walked to the bus stop and passed by the library where he kept a part time job. He worked there after school to earn money to afford a wife. The pay wasn't much but it was honest work and it helped him gain the respect of those who worked around him.

Come October twentieth they were off on their afternoon date. They spent the entire day at Richmond's Maymont Park and sealed the deal in their decision to date steady. From this point on they were an item at the theatre or the corner drug store. This was when he discovered Martha's deep dark secret. It seemed that one of her sisters was married to a gentleman who was working his way up in the movie business. Her brother-in-law had become the manager of the Century Theater in Petersburg and if he knew that Martha was coming, would arrange for her free admittance and seats in the balcony. They went out with each other weekly or sometimes would just sit at home and talk or listen to Jack Benny on the radio. They would sit on the settee holding each other's hand and laughing together until they thought their sides would split. The Christmas holiday went by while the couple spent a lot of time at each other's home. Friday night was always a standing date at one another's house. They loved to listen to the Friday night fights. Of course there always seemed to be something on the radio. This made a wonderful excuse for sitting together and holding hands.

Early January became a special time as they attended an afternoon play in Richmond and stopped for an elegant dinner. They sat across the table and stared into each other's eyes which brought a mutual smile to their faces. They held hands and stared for what seemed an eternity until the waiter brought their check. They made a slow drive back to Martha' house and she retired from the parlor leaving Waverley alone with daddy. They made small talk for a bit while he conjured up enough courage to ask him for his daughter's hand in marriage. This brought a whole new serious tone to the conversation and daddy explained how much his daughter meant to him and how he would be very unhappy if she were to become discontented. He then explained how making him unhappy would surely lead to Waverley becoming miserable. Daddy then smiled and welcomed Waverley to the family. This was a family with three older sisters and two strappingly fit older brothers. What a glorious feeling it was to be accepted by such a wonderful family. He headed home after his whirlwind day and wrote just a few short words in his diary describing his life changing evening.

"Friday Jan 12, 1940 Boy oh Boy."

Diary Entry
12 January 1940

He had flown into the clouds and had not come down all weekend. His lack of sleep and absence of food had left him feeling a bit down on Sunday and unable to attend church. The week following when he saw Martha again, he asked her for a date the next week following services. On that day they found themselves again walking the pathways in Maymont Park and he was finally able to work "Will You Marry Me?" into the conversation. With a smile on her face and a gleam in her eye she said "Yes." It was really amazing how one word could really make you feel so dim-witted. It seemed that every word out of his mouth from that point on just couldn't coherently connect to any other uttering. They held on to each other and quietly walked the perimeter of the park, and then they walked it again. That evening he told his parents about his day but they were unsure as to how to accept the news, since he was still in High School. He naturally had to make a significant entry in his diary. Under these conditions, who could blame him for not knowing what year it was.

> "Sunday Jan 28, 1939. I was made the happiest man in this world and boy what a night. Am I glad we didn't go to church although I was made happy. I also had a thought in my mind settle that I have prayed over so much. God really answered my prayers in my love affair."
>
> Diary Entry
Sunday Jan 28, 1940

The Ellis family left on an extended vacation to the sunny and warm atmosphere of Florida's Gulf coast. They had planned on being gone for a couple of weeks and this left Waverley in a slow simmering stew at home.

> "Mr. & Mrs. J. T. Ellis, Miss Jennie Little, Miss Martha Ellis, and James Ellis all of Jackson Avenue left Friday for a vacation trip to points of interest in Florida."
>
> The Progress Index
10 February 1940

Even missing her as much as he did, he still had school to contend with. He also was working part time with his father in construction and cabinet making and part time at the library. Although these commitments kept him very busy, he still had difficulty with his ability to concentrate on anything except his sweetheart. His Industrial history was off to a very slow start. This was not what he wanted to do with his life and he was hoping for a change after graduation. After three days without his beloved Martha, he found himself inclined to sit down and draft an <u>I miss you</u> letter.

"My Dearest Darling Precious Martha:

Well I finally got down to writing after such a day as I have had today, or for that matter after such days that I have experienced these last three days with you away. Boy, have I missed you, like nobody's business. I missed you going to work and also returning as it has gotten to be a habit seeing you in the window every day. It seems as if you had gotten to be a piece of the setting.

Mother says she doesn't know what is going to become of me, for you have only been gone for three days and she claims that there is so much of a change in me. I haven't eaten hardly anything & everything I've tried to do has been wrong."

Letter to Martha
11 February 1940

In his life, Waverley had now identified his first regret. Having to repeat his classes in language arts had caused a year long delay in his graduation from school. He was missing so much by having to be in school each day, and having to delay the wedding is what hurt the most. Martha returned from her birthday vacation and immediately picked up on her relationship. In the spring, she made it a point to attend Waverley's graduation ceremony. Following graduation, the two of them went out for the evening to celebrate with dinner and a free movie.

July couldn't have come soon enough for Martha and Waverley to travel north with the church's young adult class to visit the Unruhs at their summer cottage. The lovebirds could always be found together. Anyone looking for petite Martha could always find her by spotting Waverley the tall. He was nearly always wearing his blue baseball cap with the gold trim. This really made him stand out wherever they went, whether it was enjoying watermelon on the lawn or rowing the small wooden boat on the river. Cookouts were the event of the day with a prayer session each evening. This was the way of Martha and Waverley. They both led a very Christian life.

The lovebirds could always be found together while visiting the Unruh's cottage.

Doris Twilley was Martha's best friend and through her, had become friends with Waverley. She lived in Portsmouth, which prevented all but weekend visits. Martha and Waverley would sometimes drive down to visit her and spend the day at her home on the Elizabeth River. As much time as they spent visiting each other, Waverley and Martha never double dated with Doris and her boyfriend. As a matter of fact, William and his girlfriend Lorene never managed to set up a double date with the couple either.

For Waverley's 19th birthday, Martha made her attempt at baking him a birthday cake. Martha was an excellent cook, as were all of the girls in her family, but she wasn't the baker that her sister Kitty was. The cake Martha baked was of outstanding quality, but her decorating skill left much to be desired. "Happy Birthday Wave" was written across the cake indicating just a slight case of nervous tension. The cake, on the other hand, was delicious, according to Waverley, and he particularly enjoyed his third piece. They settled in for a duo birthday party, sitting by the fire, and listening to the radio. That evening the President presented one of his ever popular "Fireside Chats."

Franklin Roosevelt announced that evening that conscription of soldiers was now an urgent matter. All young men from 18 to 35 were directed to register at the nearest Post Office for possible service in the Armed Forces. At only three days past his birthday, Waverley registered for the Armed Services call. Within the week, he was called on the application he had submitted for work at the DuPont Plant in Richmond. Although he had applied for a position in the research facility, he was offered an entry position in the textile factory. He went to work there as a textile operator in a position of Beamer III. His responsibility was to operate the Beaming & Winding machine, stopping and starting as necessary, winding the thread onto the large spools for transfer to the gigantic looms at another facility. In order to commute to this new job, Waverley had purchased a 1936 Dodge 4dr sedan with "suicide" rear doors. This "Black Beauty" was his pride and joy, giving him the independence to drive to work and to visit his girl friend without having to conform with the local bus schedule or his daddy's good graces. This had been the car that his Uncle Edward had first brought to town and had fueled his love affair with the internal combustion vehicle.

As summer passed, plans for the wedding were in the foreground but no agreements could be reached. A formal church wedding seemed beyond their reach because money had become really tight. Ten years out of depression and war looming in distant Europe produced a sad look in the American economy. No one was really too sure how life might change in the very near future. Martha and Waverley, mostly Martha, decided that this big church wedding was financially irresponsible and that they would be better off with a small wedding, or maybe even elope to the Justice of the Peace. They were very strongly linked to their church and using a Justice of the Peace just didn't seem right.

On the 4th of August, 1941, Waverley turned 20 and only 4 days later the happy couple met and sealed the eternal union. Together, they pledged their lives to each other. The short double-ring ceremony took place at their church parsonage with the Reverend Jack Unruh presiding over the ceremony. Miss Doris Twilley stood as Martha's maid of honor wearing a light spring dress patterned with an assortment of summer blossoms. Waverley's best friend William stood with him as best man and sported a grey suit only a slight darker shade than the groom's. It was a funny sight as the witnesses looked on. Waverley and Martha stood like Mutt and Jeff before Reverend Unruh. Although Waverley towered over his bride, William hovered a good three inches above his friend. Also in attendance were Martha's parents and Waverley's mother. Although promoted as a casual affair, Waverley Jr. wore a suit and tie with the top button buttoned and the tie screwed on tight. Martha wore a basic black dress with pearls. They honeymooned in Richmond, spending their days and evenings strolling through Maymont Park. They really made a beautiful couple but it was as if there was a sign over their heads proclaiming "NEWLY WEDS." Following the honeymoon, the couple returned to live with his parents in Petersburg. It wasn't long after their marriage when the whole world went into chaos.

The Newlyweds on Honeymoon Rock
at Richmond's Maymont Park.

On Sunday morning, December 7th, 1941 the world changed forever when the Japanese Empire aggressively, and without provocation, attacked the United States, thus pulling the country into a war that its president was trying so hard to avoid. Japanese planes, from a battle group laying just off the island chain, began their air assault on the Military Base at Pearl Harbor, Hawaii. Being caught by surprise and unprepared, the American Navy suffered a tremendous loss. Not only were ships and aircraft destroyed, but 2,400 men lost their lives that morning.

The new year dawned and news came by post that Waverley was being ordered to report for his induction physical. Coincidentally, William too received a notice. This was not really much of a surprise since the United States was now at war. But this was a new generation and war was, for the most part, alien to them. Arriving at the Petersburg Courthouse he noted that there were, as expected, an abundance of young men each waiting their turn to visit with the Army medics and doctors forming a conga line of poking and prodding. "Strip down gentlemen" was the order at the head of this madness. "Down to your shoes and shorts"—how embarrassing, but no one really noticed. He learned that day that he had Varicocele (Varicose Veins). It exhibited no discomfort with absolutely no pain, either dull or sharp. There had been no discernable symptoms of any kind associated with this non-life-threating condition. Without further examination, he was classified as 4F and sent on his way. In a way he was disappointed, but with such knowledge in hand he could begin planning his civilian career. William too was deferred from service having had a bout with Rheumatic Fever when he was younger. The Army just wasn't comfortable having men with these conditions in their ranks.

The Armed Forces were mobilizing in early 1942 and war ration books were appearing in everyone's possession. During the war, you couldn't just walk into a shop and buy as much sugar or butter or meat as you wanted, nor could you fill up your car with gasoline whenever you liked. All of these things were rationed, which meant you were only allowed to buy a small amount (even if you could afford more). The government introduced rationing because certain things were in short supply during the war, and rationing was the only way to make sure everyone got their fair share. The Traylor family kept a lot of unused ration stamps but not because they didn't need the supplies. Like a lot of families at the time, they just couldn't afford to buy all of the goods that the rationing system allotted to them. Business had been poor for Waverley Sr. With the war being fought on two fronts, no one seemed to be buying unnecessary goods or having work done on their homes that could wait until times improved.

Waverley was fortunate in the fact that his job at Dupont would stay secure throughout the war years. Actually, the war effort caused an increase in production at the plant and overtime became commonplace. On a nippy March afternoon, Waverley arrived home exhausted and was hit with the news that he and Martha were to become parents. This was good news, but shocking. Knowing that his living arrangements would not fare well with a new baby on the way, they jointly decided that they needed to find another place to hang his hat, her stockings, and plenty of washed diapers. During their off hours they searched for another place to make a home. They came across a small, two bedroom, brick home in the Colonial Heights suburb. With a great job at DuPont, and being exempted from military service, they felt safe in investing in a house.

The newlyweds (that title is good only for the first year) finished moving into their new house. Of course much of the furniture and appliances were hand-me-down articles from nearly everyone in the family. No two pieces matched or were they even the same color or style. Plates and cups were all mismatched as were the orphaned glasses and sporadic everyday dining utensils. Some were old and some were new, some were borrowed and some had turned green. After giving everything a good hand washing, they discovered that in reality, there were no designs on the glassware. The furniture too was very irregular. The dining room table had been a side table at his uncle's house and not one of the four chairs around it actually matched. They were also able to furnish the nursery with furniture from the family vault. The bassinet was once new, when Martha's older sister was a baby, unlike the crib that had been new when Martha was born. No one in the family could remember just how long the high chair had been around, it was just always there.

Responsibilities were now piling up on the newlyweds, with a new house and mortgage, a car payment, and a baby on the way. It was no wonder that Waverley began feeling a bit stressed. Add to that the longer hours working at the plant, and the stress bowled him over the edge and a slight panic attack ensued. Returning to work on Monday brought Waverley a bright surprise. He had been promoted and was being transferred to the Rayon research lab to work as a chemist assistant. This promotion could not have come at a better time, with the couples new responsibilities. His fears lessened and his unknown future became just a little bit less unpredictable.

As the brightly colored leaves became ankle deep on the ground, the time for Martha's big moment was at hand. She rattled Waverley from a deep sleep to announce that it was time to go. Immediately wondering where they were going, he began dressing when it suddenly occurred to him who he was. That was when the first panic attack set in, but he was able to finish dressing, grab her bag, and head out the door. He returned in a split second to retrieve Martha, and off they drove. At the hospital, Martha was rushed into the delivery room while Waverley was escorted to the waiting room with orders to "sit," "stay." The nurse obviously had a side job as a dog trainer. Sitting didn't last long as he found the worn path impressed into the floor and took his turn pacing the indentations even deeper. His nervousness was apparent by the way his legs wobbled with each step; his tension was noted watching his head swing forward and back through uncontrolled muscle twinges, and attempting to bite nails that were no longer there. This was a sure fire bet that there was apprehension at work. The nurse finally emerged from the hallway and informed him that he was the father of a healthy baby girl. Welcome into the world, Linda. Home life became more enjoyable each day when he had a wife and a daughter to meet him when he arrived home from work. He even went out and found a playmate for young Linda in the form of a purebred mixture of whatever breeds you might think up. "Skippy" turned out to be a great companion. He loved that little girl, and she loved him.

He was doing very well in his new position at DuPont. They had trained Waverley to take test data and check the analysis with the predicted specifications. He also was given the responsibility of testing the produced Rayon yarn for required strength. Additionally he mastered the skill to test Rayon as it was spinning and performed tests on the bath filtrations.

The war was affecting the lives of every American as the troops were keeping their feet dug into the coral rock which was the foundation for most of the South Pacific islands. They were slowly advancing from one small island to another, each hop fighting a new battle with the same enemy. The United States Marine Corps, running into a shortage of men to fill the combat ranks, once again opened up their ranks to women and made the decision to revisit previously exempted personnel for possible recruitment to replenish the Leathernecks wounded or killed in action. The first to be drafted filled the ranks needed for the assault on Iwo Jima. Those drafted later would be sent to replenish the 1st Marines or to help form the new 6th Division for a planned attack closer to the Japanese homeland. It was no surprise then that although classified 4F, Waverley was again about to be called.

April 21st 1944 brought a tremendous shock to the new Traylor family. In the mail that day was an Order to Report for a Pre-induction Physical Examination. The war had caught up with and otherwise invaded plans for living happily ever after. Waverley was to report to the Petersburg Court House at 7:30 am on the 13th of May, 1944. That would probably be the last time in the near future that am/pm time would exist. This was more of a shock than one might imagine. Only two years before, Waverley had been called to serve, but was denied and given a classification of 4F. But when was the last time a varicose vein kept anyone from serving. Thinking maybe that he would go through the motions of his previous trip, he arranged to take the day off from his job in the Chemistry Lab at DuPont.

May 13th arrived and Waverley drove their 1936 Dodge down to the Petersburg Courthouse arriving well before 7:30 am. There were, as expected, an abundance of young men waiting for their turn to visit with the Army medics and doctors who had formed a buffet line of poking, prodding, and questionnaires. "Strip down gentlemen" was the order at the head of this madness. "Down to your shoes and shorts"—again how embarrassing, but no one really noticed.

He learned that day that he was 6 foot and weighed 170 pounds in his abbreviated attire. That was amusing because for the past three years he had been 5 foot 11 inches and 145 pounds. Six foot at 170 pounds, however, represented a perfect candidate for the Corps. This made him the perfect specimen for the draft and exactly what the United States Marine Corps was seeking. They also were fantastic in their ability to determine that he had blue eyes, brown hair, and a "Ruddy" complexion. What the hell was "Ruddy" anyway he thought. Oh well, "Ruddy" it is. They took some blood which they typed to "B positive" and proceeded down the assembly line where hand prints and finger prints were taken. The blood they kept but with a little scrubbing with soap and water, his finger prints were returned.

The clerk at the small table was there to play the game of 20 questions. Have you had any previous service? Have you ever been arrested? Do you have any condition that would prevent you from serving? The questions went on, although it appeared that he was writing down the answers before he finished asking the questions. They learned a bit about him this way. He had no previous service but it was not for lack of trying. They didn't appear at all interested that he had been classified 4F or that he had a wife and young daughter at home. They didn't even raise a brow when he explained that he had a slight case of scoliosis as a child and had worn a back brace for nearly four years. He finally was able to return home around suppertime and you can believe it, he was never this tired from working a full day at the lab. He broke the news to Martha that he would be inducted into the Marine Corps Reserve, and the clock started ticking.

He had discovered that an acquaintance of his, Robert Churn, was also inducted at the same time. Although not truly friends, the two boys knew each other from school and had shared positions on the ball field. They spoke and became emotionally bonded. While waiting for their inductions to finalize, they would often sit around and talk about where they may go and how the war was going in the Pacific. They were both convinced that they would be headed to the islands of the South Pacific and often daydreamed about the exotic places they may see. They never seemed to grasp an appreciation of the horror that they would inevitably experience.

PART II
The Marine

"Some people spend an entire lifetime wondering if they made a difference. The Marines don't have that problem."

Ronald Reagan
President 1980-1988

Chapter 5
Pride of the Corps

Waverley entered the reserves at the Marine Corps Recruiting and Induction Station, in Richmond, Virginia, on 14 July 1944. He was sworn in, promising to defend the constitution of the United States, assigned a unique serial number, and welcomed as a Private in the United States Marine Corps Reserve. Four new Marines were sworn in that day, but they had not yet realized that they were, in fact, not yet real Marines. He returned home to have that last home cooked meal, to say his final good-byes, and whatever else might need his attention on his last night as a civilian.

The sun rose quickly the next morning and the trip to Richmond was slow. Final good-byes had to be said along with an extended kiss and an even longer hug. It was as if Waverley and Martha never wanted to let go for there was no guarantee that they would ever see each other again. A quick handshake from his dad, who had driven them to the big city, and a "bye-bye" from 20 month old Linda was all that was necessary for his emotions to swell and leaving became that much more of an ordeal. Waverley's mother settled on a quick hug and peck on the cheek before handing him a small brown bible that would fit very smartly into his shirt pocket. A promise to read it every day sufficiently pleased his mother and he was now ready to leave. He watched as his family drove away and a tear ran gently down his cheek.

The ragtag group of inductees was once again at the Recruitment Center to complete their indoctrination. Paperwork, paperwork, sign this, sign that, bend over, etc. The day had passed slowly and they all were getting antsy to get up and go. Gene, an inductee from Charlottesville, was placed in charge of this motley crew. The recruiters deemed him to be the most qualified of the group by virtue of the fact that he had been assigned the lowest serial number. Orders were cut for the four men and they were directed to proceed to Broad Street Station. Train tickets were provided as well as a generous allowance of cash which they would use to buy meals—one dollar apiece. Robert was there and was ordered with Waverley's group to proceed to the train station. This provided them each with a soul to cling to as they faced the unknown together.

It was dusk and the 12 block walk to the train station seemed like a real trial. Upon arrival they hunted down the correct gate for their Atlantic Coast Line ride to glory. Each grasping a small bag of personnel effects, they climbed on board and took their seats for the journey south. Waverley made sure to grab a window seat because he wanted to see the countryside through which they transited. The realization was soon upon him, however, as he remembered that most of the trip was being conducted under the cover of darkness—bummer.

The train arrived at Yemasse Junction early in the morning, and the newly sworn recruits were met by a rough and tumble Marine Corps Sergeant as they slowly emerged from the train. It didn't take long for all to realize that if you didn't do exactly as told, and faster than any of them have ever moved before, the sergeant would be directly in your face. His demands were perceived as beyond comprehension, and dare say, beyond anyone's physical capabilities. Who knew that in a short blink of an eye, all of this chaos would become entirely too clear.

They started with a short truck ride, loaded onto a Troop Carrier, and were chauffeured through the main gate and into their new home, hastily erected one story wooden barracks. The Drill Instructor (DI) ensured that each recruit left the truck,

LEGACY OF MY FATHER

entered the barracks, and lined up like a proper Marine should. Well, at least a semblance of such a pose. The new recruits lined up within the barracks and placed their feet on the painted feet that lined the barracks floor. Of course, all of this took place under the watchful mouth of the DI. They were informed that they would do what they were told to do, how they were told to do it, and when they were told to do it, without question. The most important reminder, however, was that "Yo mama ain't here to tuck you into bed no mo." By this point the new recruits were scared, confused, and totally unsure of what awaited them. The training would be tough and life as they knew it was about to change, and change it did.

> "When I first got here, I thought I would die. After two weeks I hoped I would die. Later I knew that I would not die because I had become too tough to kill."
>
> *Anonymous*
> *USMC Recruit*

Monday, 17 July 1944, a day that will live in the minds of these recruits forever. This is the day that they were formally introduced to the Corps, and the DIs that would oversee their training. The Marine Corps philosophy was to teach the recruit to perform all basic functions in life, the Marine way. Each prospective Marine must learn to walk like a Marine, talk like a Marine, shoot like a Marine, shit like a Marine, and above all, act like a Marine each and every day of his life. Of course to learn the Marine way, the recruit must first unlearn everything he had ever been taught. Amazingly, the Marine way of doing everything takes only 12 weeks to master.

They sped through what was referred to as "receiving" in just one week. There they were fitted with uniforms and if you were one of the fortunate ones, the uniform fit. The men distributing the uniforms, though, really knew their stuff and had the uncanny ability to project the recruits sizes upon completion of basic. If those uniforms did not fit well when issued, by the end of training, they fit like a sealskin glove. Basic uniform issue continued as each item was stuffed into their clothing bag. When it came time for boots, each recruit would step forward, pick up a bucket of sand in each hand, and step on the Brannock Device. This allowed for the shoe to fit while carrying a typical pack. This did make them a bit loose through most of boot camp and the cause of many foot problems resulting from blisters. Indignities of all types were suffered in those first days. None as bad, however, as their first haircut. It really wasn't as much of a haircut, as it was a jiffy hair shedding seminar. Waverley later discovered that the purpose for this particular hair style was to ensure that their issued pith helmet would not fit very well.

Waverley and his hometown friend, Robert, remained together through boot camp and relied upon each other for moral support. When they could steal a moment of free time, they would usually spend it making fun of each other's haircut or uniform fit. By the end of the first week they had been untaught how to walk, talk, dress, and stand. As a matter of fact, they were ordered to forget anything they knew coming into the Corps. One new lesson was discovering how to make up a bed like a Marine and how to sleep like a Marine. This wasn't too difficult since most of the recruits had never made up their beds when they lived at home. They then had to learn to walk like a Marine. This task was a bit more complicated, since they were all required to step out with the same foot at the same time. This took quite a bit of concentration and some real effort as they would march everywhere they went in those wavy recruit ranks. Next was mastering the standing in line maneuver. Although thought of as a really easy lesson, they all learned how important this was for the next simple task, how to eat like a Marine. This operation took skill and tactful maneuvering. The time allotted to eat a meal was fixed and the last one into the chow hall had the least amount of time to eat. It was crucial to be near the front of the line, but those with names starting high on the alphabet just had to learn to eat fast. The strictest rule surrounding the chow hall was the "you take it—you eat it" rule. This was always getting someone in trouble since their fried liver looked a lot like a steak.

The following days brought new and surprising adventures. They donated what felt like half of their blood and were then herded down the runway for shots. Every step brought a new needle in the left arm and one in the right. There was Tetanus, Cowpox, Typhoid, Yellow Fever, and Rabies. No one kept enough concentration to count how many holes were made in each arm but "many" seemed like a close enough estimate. Waverley weighed in at 145 pounds and stood 5 foot 11 $^{1}/_{2}$ inches. He stood there at unclad attention while every part of his body was examined for scars. This was assumed necessary so that the Marine Corps could not be held responsible for scars present when they took possession of the body. Next was a rest period. Waverley was seated in a nice comfortable lounge chair which was swell, at least until the dentist arrived. Thirteen teeth missing and one nonrestorable, not a good report. Lunch was interesting. They either had steak, or liver, or a pork chop. It was really difficult to distinguish, but it was definitely meat. There wasn't enough time allotted to be able to determine its true source so it was swallowed as is. This delicacy, they discovered, was what was referred to as "mystery meat" in all services.

The final day in Receiving brought exams and paperwork. Test were given to purportedly find out in what specialty the new recruit would fit. Waverley had requested duty in Aviation Ordinance which naturally qualified him for the Infantry. After all, he was recruited through a replenishment draft, which was a manpower pool for bodies where they were needed most. The Corps asking for everyone's preference was a feel-good sort of thing. His salute at this point left a lot to be desired and he still marched like a penguin on its way to a beach party picnic. The remainder of each day was spent in physical exercise testing to provide each recruit with a baseline to begin their physical transformation. They were then issued the most important piece of equipment for any Marine, his .30 caliber, gas-operated, clip-fed, air-cooled, semiautomatic M1 rifle. Along with it, each recruit was charged with learning the Corps' Rifle Creed.

The Creed of the United States Marine

This is my rifle. There are many like it, but this one is mine.
My rifle is my best friend. It is my life.
I must master it as I must master my life.
My rifle, without me, is useless. Without my rifle, I am useless.
I must fire my rifle true.
I must shoot straighter than my enemy who is trying to kill me.
I must shoot him before he shoots me. I will . . . .
My rifle and I know that what counts in this war is not the rounds we fire, the noise of our burst, nor the smoke we make.
We know that it is the hits that count. We will hit . . . .
My rifle is human, even as I, because it is my life.
Thus, I will learn it as a brother. I will learn its weaknesses, its strengths, its parts, its accessories, its sights, and its barrel.
I will ever guard it against the ravages of weather and damage.
I will keep my rifle clean and ready, even as I am clean and ready.
We will become part of each other. We will . . . .
Before God I swear this creed.
My rifle and I are the defenders of my country.
We are the masters of our enemy.
We are the saviors of my life.
So be it, until victory is America's and there is no enemy, but Peace!

USMC
Rifle Creed

Moving into the more substantial wood barracks completed the first week's events, preparing them for the next day when the real work was to begin. Here they met their regular Drill Instructors who had been charged to mold the new recruits into sharply disciplined, physically fit, and well trained Marines. By their own example, the DIs reflect the highest standards of personnel conduct, morality, appearance, and professional skills.

The days were spent continuing to teach the raw recruits how to walk, talk, and move like a Marine. These lessons projected a normal way of life far from what they had ever considered normal but now they were at the point when failure to be sharp and precise meant everyone had to pay the price. Discipline was quickly accepted and within a very short period, each company began working as a unit, just not yet well-oiled. Handling their weapons, bathing, and folding their clothes were all considered "quick learn" lessons. Failure to get it right the first time resulted in a blast of DI hot air directly in the face. Many hours of Physical Training and weapons drilling were crammed into the next phase where individual recruits were taken out to complete individual requirements. For Waverley, this meant an afternoon at the dentist where seven teeth were extracted. When the days were filled with extreme heat conditions or severe inclement weather, the training did not stop. Physical exercise, drilling, runs in full pack, and multiple mile hikes did not slow down because of weather. Where these recruits were headed had some of the worst weather conditions in the world and preparation for these conditions was a must.

Along with their physical training, these men also learned the basics of mountain climbing and rappelling, and of course, battlefield first aid. Where most of them had trouble was climbing up and down the cargo net wall. This was not a difficult task if time was not a consideration, but they were being required to transverse these nets in a matter of seconds. These time constraints led to a lot of missteps and hang-ups in the net. Even after being directed as to the importance of time, not one of them could yet fully grasp the concept of "hand vertical—feet horizontal." They were soon to realize, however, that a misstep could cost a timely delay and that each second could cost a life.

If life on Paris Island was ever considered easy, then this was an indication that maybe that particular recruit should be checked for mental instability. The afternoon spent in the gas house was so far from fun that most considered it downright unpleasant. The only upside to chemical weapons training was that there were no mosquitoes to contend with. All of the other days, thousands of these Dragonfly-size vampires would swarm around trying to make lunch out of the sweetest tasting Marine they could find. It seemed that the sweat that covered any unclothed part of the body would attract the maximum number of these unofficial "Drill Suckers." Nothing was worse, though, than marching with sand fleas invading their boots. They all quickly learned that lacing their boots tightly was for more than just looks. The sand fleas, however, would always find a way, into the eyes, or crawl into the ears and nose.

Half of a day had been set aside for completion of forms and allotments. There was an allotment to go home as well as a living allowance for the family. Insurance, death benefits, religious preferences, beneficiary arrangements, and all of the other forms of paperwork required in preparation for ones ultimate demise. Now that made everyone feel really good. Over the weeks, classes were set up to teach everything from the founding of the Corps in Philadelphia's Tun Tavern, through the history of every major battle the Marines fought. No one was excused from learning every word of the Marine's Hymn and how to sing it with gusto, like a true Marine. Near the end of July, Waverley was called out again, resulting in the disappearance of yet another tooth, leaving the exact amount of "not many" remaining.

Through the month of August, the training remained hard and furious. They had learned the basic values of the Corps which were hammered into them every day through the remainder of their time on the island. Honor, Courage, and Commitment formed the fabric of every Marines life. The traits of a Marine such as Honor, Integrity, Duty, Teamwork, and Espirit de Corps would remain with them long after they no longer wore the uniform.

Two weeks were spent on weapons and field training. There they went through intensive rifle training and qualifications on other field weapons. On "Record Day," Waverley qualified on Hand Grenades and as Marksman on the .45 caliber semi automatic sidearm. He also qualified as Sharpshooter on the M1 Carbine with a score of 295. While at Paris Island, recruit Traylor trained hard and incessantly. One of the most common break down items was the M1 rifle. They learned to disassemble, clean, and reassemble this rifle in all kinds of conditions, including the pitch dark. With its butt on the ground, the tip of the bayonet reached shoulder level. It was amazing how the weeks in boot camp reduced the weight of this piece. When he stood with rifle in hand, he stood proud. Tall, thin, and courageous was the impression he projected and near the end of Boot Camp, he actually looked like the pride essential Marine. His salute was sharp. A quick snap to attention reflected repetitive training in even the most basic of activities. The instructors emphasized marksmanship but stressed two other lessons they felt were much more urgent. Clearing a rifle jam and rapid loading of the weapon were two critical skills that could, and would, save your life. The very next day he qualified on the Browning Automatic Rifle or BAR.

For Waverley, the weapons range was a contradiction of emotion. He loved shooting and with a lot of hard work had become very good. Holding his breath, keeping the rifle steady, and maintaining his concentration became very difficult with the mosquitoes trying to drain him of his life's blood. Helping them along were thousands of sand fleas crawling under the uniform and irritating the flesh. But these were going to be the conditions at the front line and it was well worth the aggravation to become used to it now.

Nearing the end of Boot Camp in September, the time for uniform fitting had arrived. Their dress greens were issued and tailored to fit the body that they had spent weeks developing.

With their uniforms now fitting like a glove, the senior companies were allotted liberty for a day. Waverley spent the day in the local town of Beaufort. He visited the ruins of Old Sheldon Church which was originally built between 1745-1757 of brick and tabby. The church was destroyed in May of 1779 by British troops under the command of General Augustine Provost, rebuilt, and subsequently ruined by General William Tecumseh Sherman's troops in 1865. The church yard included graves dating to the 18th century. These old markers fascinated Waverley to the point that he even wrote home about this adventure.

He was called out of training again on September 17th to the dentist office where he was fitted with a top plate. This was a wonderful event for him and the first thing he wanted was a good, well done, steak. It had been so long since his last. Back to full training witnessed him qualifying in hand-to-hand combat using his bayonet. He had spent much time stabbing sand bags and being humiliated with the Pugil stick.

In their last week as recruits they went through their drill competitions. Every aspect of their drilling and every movement made was carefully watched and noted. This is where it all came together. Their long weeks of training and practice emerges to show how they can operate like a synchronized machine, this time well oiled. Each and every one of them could be proud knowing they were part of such a fine team.

Graduation day came at the end of a grueling 12 weeks of torture, performing task that were certainly beyond their physical capability. They each had learned what level they could attain and were proud of themselves for sticking it out. They received their globe and anchor and for the first time were addressed as Marine. For anyone that does not know just what that title means it has little value. But to its possessor, that title has a value that is beyond price. The title is not freely granted. It must be earned. Marine Corps training is a constant, always tough, procedure. The process is mental as well as physical, sometimes to the limits of endurance. Once the title of Marine has been granted, it forever changes the life of the proud recipient. Martha had taken a bus ride to Beaufort for the ceremony and Waverley's Uncle Edward and Aunt Margaret drove up from Atlanta. They had a great time sightseeing in Beaufort with Waverley as their tour guide. At least for what little he knew of the city. After all, he had spent only one day in town before their visit. About all there was to do included visiting historic markers. This was like reading a book on the town's history except that each large print page was bolted to a steel pole. And, naturally, being a Marine town, there were movie theatres, restaurants, and the over abundance of bars and dance halls. Not too many of these were suitable for relatives visiting from out of town. So dinner followed a walk through the park and an abbreviated tour of the camp including a visit to "Iron Mike." Not very much of the camp was available for touring. After all, there were two wars ongoing.

Waverley's Uncle Edward and Aunt Margaret attend Waverley's Marine Corps Graduation.

On September 22nd, they left for Petersburg with Uncle Edward at the wheel and Aunt Margaret riding shotgun. Martha and Waverley were forced to share a portion of the back seat for the ride bringing him home for ten days of leave. He had received orders to the Tenth Training Battalion, Infantry Training Regiment, at Camp Lejeune, NC, but didn't have to report until the second of October.

Arrival back in Petersburg meant a reunion with the family he loved. His mother and dad were a sight for sore eyes along with his little brother Allen. Although he was glad to see everyone, he was ecstatic to again hold his daughter, now almost two. He projected a genuine pride in his uniform, the Corps, and his country. He wore his uniform everywhere he and Martha traveled and it was always sharp, clean and pressed. It was really amazing how the Corps took possession of his life. At 0530 his first morning home, he was awake and sitting in the chair working up a good spit shine on his shoes. The only down side to his home reunion was the weather being intermittently warm and the only issued dress uniform was constructed of wool. It bore no medals but he ensured that his sharpshooter pin always remained shined. He was so proud of his qualification as a sharpshooter. Every picture taken at home was in his uniform. Those in the front yard, with Martha, sitting on the front steps or even relaxing with his black four door 1936 Dodge sitting in the driveway. Not so much as his family, but he did love his car. He was particularly proud of the rear suicide doors even if the engine was merely a six cylinder, flat head, in line engine, and three speed transmission. It did have something that most cars of the area did not, a built in radio. What a delight. He also loved the four-legged member of his family "Skippy," a Jack Russell Terrier sort of mix who would jump straight up and looked like a rabbit bounding across the yard.

During his leave time he could never be found without sporting a friendly smile on his face. He was genuinely happy with himself and his family. After posing for pictures, he began to release his more outrageous and humorous side. Martha wrote on the back of one picture that he ". . . looked too silly for a Marine. Ha! Ha!" They were both being playful and silly at that time. On his first Sunday home the family attended church services and there was constantly a swarm of parishioners hovering around him, although who could blame them. He looked ultra sharp in his uniform and beamed with as much pride in himself as they all shared for him. He tried on some of his clothes that had remained at home and surprise of surprises, none of them seemed to fit his newly molded frame.

Waverley Jr. home on leave from Boot Camp.

His time at home was short and precious. It was difficult to spread himself around to his close-knit family and the even closer family of Martha. There were so many people to visit and so very little time. Although he did enjoy seeing everyone, his real desire was to spend the most time with his wife and daughter. Ten days leave passes so rapidly and it was soon time to leave for his next duty station. He knew that this would not be another 12 weeks and home again. This time was truly unknown. He was in for the duration and no one was able to predict the outcome of battles yet to be fought. A year may pass before he could return home, or two, or four, or even maybe never. His bags were packed and in the car the morning of his departure. He had risen early to spend several hours playing with his daughter and wanting so much to be able to stay and watch her turn two. A final hug for Martha and a lingering kiss. There was silence between them when they held each other close, as if she knew that her husband would never be returning home.

He slid into the driver's seat of his '36 Dodge and started up the engine. As he backed out of the drive, he watched Martha pick up their daughter and they both waved as he passed out of sight. Waverley took a deep breath, exhaled, and settled in for the long drive to Jacksonville, North Carolina. Suffolk Virginia was reached in time to stop for lunch and then on to route 17 and south through the Great Dismal Swamp. Stopping in New Bern for a bite to eat, he proceeded south and checked into Camp Lejeune that evening.

The 29th Marine Regiment was the last infantry regiment formed by the Marine Corps during the war. This outfit being activated at Camp Lejeune, in May 1944. The officers and non Com's were handpicked from returning veterans and new recruits. They had been shipped out to Guadalcanal for intensive training in preparation for an undisclosed invasion in the Pacific. In November of that year training was underway for a newly forming 26th Replenishment Draft preparing to support the 1st Division.

Training at Camp Lejeune echoed his time on Paris Island except for the constant reminder of "You're Marines now, not Recruits!" The weather was a bit more moderate, warm and cool cycling through the weeks with the humidity of a whistling steam pot. One would have thought that nowhere else in the world could the mosquito population have been as thick as Paris Island, but the marshes around New River produced heavy swarms of mosquitoes the size of Hummingbirds on steroids. Not to imagine that it was intentional, but the overabundance of mosquitoes ended up being good training for their ultimate destination.

This was the place where specialties were determined. The training began with a day of indoctrination and classification. Waverley stood in line and at each station was pelted with a barrage of seemingly innocuous questions whose answers were ostensibly ignored. With no worthwhile information in hand, someone in a windowless office decided that Waverley should become a machine gunner. They spent long days training in varying conditions and in all sorts of weather. The weather won't stop a postman and will never slow down a Marine. This was pounded into the entire class every single day.

Training began at Reveille (0445) each morning when all hands were up, shaving in the makeshift barracks using a helmet as a wash basin. Breakfast consisted of Field Rations and then off to Physical Training (PT). There was endurance training (usually a 10 or 15 mile run) in the morning and amphibious landing training in the afternoon. Every other evening or so a marathon march would be called with full battle packs. The most uncomfortable situation at "slum city" was the awful water, tasting of dead fish. They drank plenty because, after all, it was wet and cool. The water they lost through hard work and sweat had to somehow be replaced.

Waverley Jr. with ammunition handler during Machine Gun qualifications on the range at Camp Lejeune.

This was the range where Private Traylor studied, practiced, and qualified on the M1917 Heavy Machine Gun. He enjoyed his time on the range because firing this monster was really swell. The gun sat steady on a low wide tripod allowing aim to be established from a completely prone position. But this monster had its drawbacks. The gun was water cooled to facilitate faster firing and the mounted tripod was bulky and awkward to handle. Weighing in at nearly 100 pounds, this was difficult, at best, to transport and usually was moved using two carts and a squad of six Marines. Fortunately the production weapon used in battle had been modified to be air cooled and could be easily handled by two Leathernecks. What they failed to include in their training was that manning this machine gun was like hanging a big red flag above your head that read "Here I Am" with an arrow pointing down.

The machine gunners all bunked in the same hut which produced an air of comradery. After all, they were not only Marines, but they were all Marine Machine Gunners. The word had been passed down to prepare for a battalion inspection at any time. This, of course, initiated an immediate "field day," or concentrated house cleaning. With the experience of Parris Island recently behind them, their quarters were very quickly squared away.

On the 6th of November, Waverley was honored by his church in their Sunday Bulletin. He was transferred to the 26th Replenishment Draft effective that same day.

> "Pvt. Waverley L. Traylor, Jr. 298526,
> Co. E. 2nd. Plt. 10th. Bn.,
> Tent Camp, Camp Lejeune,
> New River, North Carolina."

High Street Methodist Church
Bulletin 6 November 1944

The gun was the most valuable piece of equipment a Marine owned and the training provided what was needed to form a lasting love affair with the weapon. Constant gun drills and nomenclature study ate up a good portion of the training day. Continuously driven in to the machine gunner's heads was to "know your weapon, know it now, know it with the insight of its designer; be able to disassemble it blindfolded or in the dark, reassemble it without the aid of sight; recite a detailed description of the gun's operation, know the role played by each and every member of the squad, from the gunner down to the water can or machine gun box carrier."

Although designated as a Machine Gunner, training continued in other basic areas. This included qualification on the M2 Flame Thrower, a back tank unit carried by infantrymen in the field. Much time was also spent on amphibious assault landing practice and many hours on the cargo nets. Along with this additional training, Waverley had to keep up his concentrated weapons instruction. Also included in his daily routine were exhausting exercises in the New River swamp, inflating rubber boats and silently paddling them towards land, carrying out simulated missions at night, and becoming entangled in rolls of communications cable. Often Waverley's squad would disappear into the pine woods, subsisting on only C-rations, completely lost until a white flare high in the sky would guide their way back home.

On the other hand, most of the company enjoyed the famed obstacle course. The men scaled high walls draped with cargo nets, negotiated deep mud holes, dodged shell holes, and crossed a stream by running across a log suspended by ropes at each end. Waverley suffered many soakings before discovering the timing and method needed for a successful crossing. Sticks of dynamite were detonated nearby to simulate combat conditions.

Perhaps the most important phase of training at New River was the company's introduction to amphibious landings. This base had been selected in part for its closeness to beaches resembling those found in the far Pacific. Waverley's company was then marched out to the Camp Lejeune "boondocks" for the first time. After a series of very confusing and sometimes conflicting orders, the men assembled their packs and fell out in marching order. In addition to the required gear, some of the men would slip in extra soap, cans of beans, or maybe even letters from home. Ranks secured, the procession to the new training area began.

The men marched maybe ten miles; not much by post war standards, but a great distance for new trainees. They passed through the pine woods and over a dirt trail barely wide enough to allow the passing of one good sized bear. The whole battalion was on the march, and Waverley's poor squad was tucked away somewhere amongst the hoard. Clouds of red dust settled over the Marines. Waverley complained about his helmet bumping irritably against the machine gun that was making an indent into his shoulder, or else jumping forward maddeningly over his eyes by the erratic motion of his pack. A mile or two out, his uniform was saturated with sweat. His mouth was desert dry and his tongue swollen. He dared not drink any more water from his canteen but would moisten his lips with a swig of that precious commodity. With chin up and an honest attempt to straighten his back, Waverley continued with the dull plodding rhythm of the march. At the conclusion of their jaunt, the Marines encountered a amphibious landing craft for the first time, and then practice, practice, practice.

Learning about other combat jobs was also a necessary part of a Marine's training. Contrary to common thought, an engineer does not only build stuff, he also blows things up. The Marines were additionally taught how to operate radios, drive trucks, and operate tracks. These lessons were driven into their natural behavior so that all became second nature. Waverley and his team worked hard that last week practicing not only how to shoot but other, what would prove to be vital, lessons such as how to carry the weapons, clearing jams, loading the ammunition and keeping the weapons dry and clean. It was a very long week leading up to completion of their training and making preparations to ship out. And then, the training was over and it was time for these Marines to face the enemy.

Waverley's Uncle Urban (his mother's brother) came down for a visit dragging along Waverley's baby brother Allen. At the age of 15, Allen tried to discourage his big brother from referring to him as "baby brother" but Waverley had long ago determined that this was the surest way to irritate his sibling. The three of them went out for dinner that evening, courtesy of Uncle Urban. Waverley was reluctant to order any of the more expensive meals on the menu, a habit of living lean. His uncle insisted that he look at the food choices and not the cost. After all, this was a celebration of sorts. Realizing then that this may be his final big meal for a long time, he ordered a T-bone steak with a baked potato and green beans. When the meal came out, the aroma of the hot steak battled the scent of the basket of fresh baked yeast dinner rolls. How scrumptious! Following the meal, the boys continued talking while enjoying their cups of fresh brewed coffee. Waverley learned the details of their trip south on the big silver Greyhound bus. When they arrived in Jacksonville, the pair had taken a taxi from the bus station to the base. The cab they rode in was beat up but had air conditioning. The rear window behind the driver was broken out and the temperature inside the taxi was very chilled, much like the inside of an icebox with a new block of ice installed. Allen appeared to be a little jealous of his big brother. After all, he was going overseas to fight the Japs. He sure did wish that he could go too. Waverley turned his car keys over to his Uncle Urban who, with brother Allen, left the following morning to return his vehicle home.

The following morning, Waverley, now a highly trained Marine, fell out with his compadres for their march to the Camp Lejeune train depot. This was to be the beginning of their westward adventure. The United States military had taken control of all rail lines throughout the country and all passenger and commercial traffic was halted. These convoys on rails were referred to as America's "Troop Trains." The equipment heading for the west coast was loaded onto the box cars and flat cars. The Marines were herded into the Pullman cars like cattle, but single file and most smartly. The bench style seats were all wooden. Although somewhat padded, they were truly not the most comfortable of accommodations. The troop train finally completed loading and pulled away from the station. The countryside began its long journey past the windows of those brave souls on board.

The Marines in the car with Waverley found varied methods of entertainment. These included shooting craps in the aisle or poker on the floor just a few feet away. Waverley, not being a gambler, distanced himself from these activities but did find comfort in playing solitaire or some other card game with a buddy. Most often, though, he could be found sitting by the window and watching the scenery pass by. This was a part of the country that he had never seen before.

Lunch time arrived and the mess sergeants from one of the dining kitchens had spent his morning assembling sandwiches for the troops and with each was served a ladle of slightly chilled milk dipped and poured into individual canteen cups. Most everyone ate very slowly, a welcome change from their military meals served thus far during their training. Following their first meal, the men laid back, forth, and sideways in their seats for a quick nap but Waverley remained vigil to watch the farms pass by with the cattle grazing and the horses playing.

The train passed through Charlotte where an extraordinary sight took place. At each track crossing the cars were stopped and backed up to await the trains passing. People were getting out of their cars to wave at the "Troop Train" passing. Several of them had flags to wave as they watched their heroes pass by to the cadence of the clackety, clackety, clack of the trains wheels against the steel rails.

Leaving the congestion of the populated city the "Troop Train" began passing through the rolling hills of South Carolina. When they reached open ground, the clear skies allowed them to see the haze on the mountain tops further away than they should have been able to see. More cattle grazed the fields and a full contingent of sheep was spotted grazing a nearby hillside. As the hills became steeper, goats became the livestock of choice passing into Georgia.

Closing in on the "Gate City to the South," the train pulled in to its refueling depot to take on coal in the tender and much needed water for the locomotive. The engine sat directly beneath the water tower while the troops disembarked and fell in by car. Exercise was the name of the game and calisthenics were the rules. After all, the troops cannot be allowed to soften on their trip west. The men were put through their paces with jumping jacks, toe touches, and a concentrated game of Leap Frog—by the numbers. The train completed its water load and began moving away to the coal loader just a mile up line. Not to waste any opportunity, the men were set to double time march to keep up with their train for the distance. The steam from the engine filled the air alongside the procession and produced a rather effective steam bath for the men. This was supposed to have been a fun trip?

The Marine travelers were fortunate to have Pullman cars to ride in for the trip. This meant that they could expect actual beds to sleep in for the evening. There was no way of describing the breadth of the beauty of the warmth that the American people showed along the way. As they rolled through Atlanta the train slowed and temporarily paused at the Atlanta freight yard. Little children approached the Pullman cars and began dancing their hearts out. Waverley and the other Marines on board enjoyed their show and threw nickels out the window to show their appreciation. The young boys and girls quickly scooped up the nickels and began tossing them back into the open windows. "Free for the sojers, please, mister." Even from these poor children, was support. This really gave the men something solid to fight for; holding back tears was fight enough for the moment.

Resuming the journey, Waverley absorbed the beauty of the landscape with the rolling red hills of Georgia. Beyond those hills, the sun was setting with a fiery red vengeance. To him the look was of anger and fury but, strangely enough, he felt a deep down sensation of calm and contentment. Now if he could do something about the cigarette smoke that seemed to permeate from all points in the car. His best escape was to leave his window open. This in turn allowed the crisp night air to flow into the compartment and wash out some of the pungent atmosphere.

The mess servers rolled around a triple deck cart with the dinner de jour. This evening the fair was baked ham, boiled potatoes, bread, and cooked greens. The aroma of that fresh baked ham set the digestive juices stirring and with the fresh greens boiled with fatback, made Waverley remember his mother's home cooking. This fine meal was served up as each Marine held up the compartmentalized portion of their mess kit. The cup was filled with good old southern tea, barely sweetened. Waverley enjoyed his meal. It sure beat those C-rations issued on the training marches back at Camp Lejeune. Following dinner the car broke into a musical extravaganza. A couple of harmonicas surfaced and rest of the men joined in with spoons or paper & combs. Since darkness had eaten the view, Waverley too joined in with his comb during their rendition of the Marine Hymn.

The porters came around to set up the beds for the evening. The bunks were opened up two high once the bench seats had been collapsed into a bed. Clean sheets were on all of the bunks, a much welcomed luxury. And pillows, actual soft, comfy pillows. What a treat! Sleeping arrangements were decided by a three way coin toss. Odd man on top, the other two on bottom. Of course the man on top usually needed just a little help from his buddies who would most willingly toss him into his bunk. Waverley got lucky on his first night and ended up in the top berth.

During the night they had passed through Birmingham and were well on their way toward New Orleans. They were awakened early and the porters broke down the beds while each man waited his turn at one of the small sinks on board. After a morning brush and shave everyone took their seats and broke out their mess kits. This morning they were served up a mess of scrambled powdered eggs, ham, and hash brown potatoes. Hot coffee filled everyone's mess cup and by this stage of their training, they had all learned to drink coffee the Marine Corps way (black, bitter, and strong), the more caffeine the better.

Waverley now could resume his sightseeing as they passed through the thick, dark black swamps of Louisiana. The Cypress trees were surrounded by their childlike knees and their branches flowed with the long scraggly hair of the native Spanish Moss. Alligators could be seen along the banks of the canals, basking in the bright sunlight and sliding into the water as the train passed.

Pulling into the station in New Orleans brought another unexpected sight. Flooding the platform at the station were hundreds of young, and rather attractive, girls. The young ladies from all over the city were armed with pieces of paper on which were scribed their name and addresses. These were nice girls who wanted to write to a Marine and have them write back to them. They hovered around the open windows and those athletic and fortunate enough, were able to jump into the arms of a brave Marine for a great big "wish you safe return" kiss. It was fortunate that the Marines were not allowed off of the train because it most certainly would have been mayhem.

Not long after leaving New Orleans the train was found passing through the thick forest of the Pelican State. As it traveled west with the sun high in the sky the trees thinned morphing into slow rolling hills filled with Longhorn cattle. The endless china blue sky stretched forever in all directions and a lone rider could be seen in the field corralling the stock. The cooks served huge ham on rye sandwiches for lunch on this, the second day out. A generous helping of potato salad was spooned into each mess kit with milk again ladled into their cups. Calicoed hills rose up from the plains exposing the lean and athletic looking cattle of the Texas breeds.

Out across the low hills were oil wells working hard to pump up the valuable "Black Gold" so vital to the nations well being and in particularly the war effort. The palm trees and the cacti were exciting for Waverley to observe. He had never before seen such a beautiful place other than in magazines or in the movies. The sunset began to manifest behind purple hills that rose suddenly from flat plains, as though someone below had punched up into the soft tissue of the land. The view had been repeating itself through day two and activity onboard the train was repeating for the second night. That evening, Waverley wasn't quite so fortunate and was relegated to share the lower berth.

Morning brought new vistas as the troops had crossed the Continental Divide and were on their downhill run into Camp Pendleton. The landscape was baron, broken up by the occasional saguaro cactus, yucca tree, or sagebrush. The train roared through the desert kicking up the sand and encouraging the occasional tumbleweed to race them down the track. Waverley marveled at the countryside as it rapidly passed by the window and was totally engrossed by the view crossing the Arizona desert. The wide open spaces and the solitude of the desert were enough to rob him of his breath. How could anything so baron be so beautiful?

Passing over the famed Colorado River brought them into California and a significant change in the landscape. A sand storm appeared across the rolling dunes as the train passed over the desert area. When they dropped down into the East Mesa, the engineer slowed down as they went through the orange groves so that the children of the Mexican farm workers could throw fat, sweet oranges into the cars for the brave soldiers. Waverley could see that these wide valleys between snow-girthed peaks, filled with peach, plum, and apple trees. Cows here were fat and supported a thriving dairy industry. Passing through the Cuyamaca mountains, the salt air from the Pacific ocean filled the troop cars with a freshness not felt on the entire cross-country venture.

On arrival in California, (6 November) Waverley and the other recent Camp Lejeune Graduates were billeted in the Marine Tent City at Oceanside. The accommodations were suitable in that the tents were at least semi permanent with actual wooden floors. The Replenishment Draft Regiment's short time here would be spent in physical exercise, firing range practice and additional training for their Pacific island adventure. Even for November it was exceptionally warm and their typical dress around the camp was shorts, boots, and dog tags. They did get a start in working on a tan but didn't stay there long enough to notice much difference. After all, these men just spent a blistering summer between the beaches of Parris Island and New River. The Replenishment Draft Regiment was biding its time awaiting transportation to the war. Of course for a Marine, biding your time consisted of honing their skills and conditioning all day, every day.

The base at Pendleton spread out over 125,000 acres of desert, mountains, forest, and bivouac areas. Vegetation was sparse with an occasional cactus and the wildlife was plentiful, even if never seen. Of most concern were the hundreds of Gila Monsters, thousands of rattlesnakes, and the tens of thousands of scorpions and tarantulas. As it turned out, these conditions provided good avoidance training for the wildlife native to the Pacific islands. Waverley found that the training at Camp Pendleton closely mirrored the training provided at Camp Lejeune. Instruction in the wide array of weapons never ceased. The open spaces available gave them the opportunity to train with live artillery and close air support.

Amphibious landings were practiced to acquaint these Marines with beach landings while under heavy fire. The scenarios here were more elaborate and closer to real life conditions than were ever simulated at New River. The day to day training maintained a furious pace with continual trips to the boondocks for 24 hour exercises. Everyone became experts on long marches in full gear with weapons as well as blisters, cuts, scrapes, and bruises.

The final training scenario was a full-scale amphibious assault on San Clemente Island. The Marines boarded a troop transport vessel and got their first experience of the cramped quarters aboard the ship. Their compartment was a modified cargo hold with canvas bunks covering the full length and width of the compartment. The bunks were stacked five high and getting into or out of these makeshift beds really showed off their acrobatic skills as they clambered around on the ships piping like monkeys through the canopy.

Once offshore of San Clemente, the Marines climbed down the cargo nets and dropped into the flat bottomed landing craft below. While support ships maintained a steady shelling, the boats formed a circle until all craft were in position. Once formed up, the boats headed for shore across the rough water and heavy swells just off shore. The erratic movement of the flat bottomed landing craft brought forth a wave of sea sickness for the Marines and Sailors alike. Being unfamiliar with the terms "windward" and "leeward," several of the new Marines vomited into the wind and successfully spread joy to all on board. A few yards short of the beach, the ramps were dropped and a mad rush for shore ensued. Unfortunately, one squad ran directly into a cactus patch and all were immediately classified as wounded in action. From that point, the training exercise continued losing momentum. Landing craft were bumping into each other, tracked vehicles were heading in the wrong direction, and companies failed to maintain tight communications and were separated upon advancing. They returned to their transport and climbed the cargo net alongside. Being totally exhausted, the realization finally hit Waverley that in just a few days, these maneuvers would be for real.

Like himself, the other Marines did not know where they were headed. What was known was that more and more Marines were showing up at Pendleton every day. On the 13th of December the order came down to pack tightly that night because they were shipping out first thing in the morning. The entire barracks was abuzz that evening and sleep overpowered very few of the new leathernecks.

Reveille sounded just as a few of the men began dozing off. Everyone finished packing their last minute personnel effects and fell out with full packs and weapons. Following a hearty breakfast at the base mess, the regiment, about 3300 strong, were loaded onto troop trucks and transported to the docks. The "Devil Puppies," as the battle veterans referred to them, commenced boarding the transport ship for the trip west to the South Pacific. It took the full day, and into the night, for all of the Marines to board and settle. From this point on, they were classified "In the Field," a military term for heading to the front.

Chapter 6
Off to War

The USS General H. O. Ernst (AP 133) was a huge ship at over 520 feet stem to stern and over 70 feet wide at deck level. Very little of the ship could be seen from the dock. Each side was covered by life rafts and life boats, some stacked three high. It was a good bet that there weren't enough for all the souls on board. The primary purpose of this ship was the transport of troops but she was well protected with four 5 inch guns, eight 1 inch guns, and sixteen 20 mm Antiaircraft guns. Adding 3,300 Marines to over 420 sailors made things just a wee bit crowded. Fortunately everyone was on the same side in the war which held down the amount of fighting on board. The real pressure was on the ship's cooks. Feeding nearly 4,000 men three meals a day could get to anyone.

The Ernst set sail early the following morning and laid in a west southwest course. The winds had picked up making the seas a tad choppy. Little time had passed before the rails were lined by the Marines. The sailors on deck just stood back and enjoyed the show. Obviously a comedy by the way the swabbies were laughing. Days passed and time appeared to not advance as quickly as it should. The passengers on board the Ernst passed the time by playing cards, reading letters from home for the hundredth time, or watching a movie. It didn't take long though, before everyone on board the ship could quote each line of "Stagecoach," apparently the only movie in the locker.

The immediate plan on board was the preparations to be made for the upcoming holiday. For Waverley, this was his first Christmas away from home. Everyone wanted to ensure that their celebration was a good one. Christmas Eve came and the final preparations were complete. The mess hall was decorated, the makeshift Christmas Tree was up, and the mistletoe (made from green packing paper) was hanging in its place. It was now getting late and time for taps. Who knows, Waverley thought, maybe there will even be a Santa Claus. Reveille brought all hands up from their hammocks and looking forward to their celebration. A quick look though, at the ship's Plan of the Day, brought a definite letdown to Waverley and the troops. It indicated that the new day was December 26th. There were many who assumed they had slept for two days, but the truth was a little more down to earth, or in this case ocean. It seems the ship had crossed the International Date Line during the night and left Christmas 1944 sitting in the middle of the Pacific Ocean.

Local newspapers back home were also keeping tabs on their favorite hometown heroes. The Progress Index from Waverley's home town of Petersburg was no exception as it printed an update as to how their favorite son was doing. On January 14th, 1945, The Progress Index reported that Private Traylor had arrived for duty in the Pacific Operating Theatre.

"TRAYLOR IN PACIFIC

Pvt. Waverley L. Traylor, Jr., of this city, has arrived in the Southwest Pacific, according to a message received here. Before entering the Marine Corps last July he was employed by Dupont. He received his basic training at Parris Island, S. C., and also trained at New River, N. C."

The Progress Index
Petersburg, Va
14 January 1945

Waverley continued his journey south, enjoying the warm winds of the equatorial South Pacific. Meanwhile, the crew of the General H. O. Ernst began preparations for their next seafarers event known as "Crossing the Line." This was the ceremony where all of the uninitiated "Pollywogs" become fully fledged "Shellbacks." Sailors who have previously crossed the Equator are nicknamed (Trusty) *Shellbacks*, often referred to as *Sons of Neptune*. Those who have not, are nicknamed (Slimy) *Pollywogs*. The two-day celebration is a ritual in which the older and experienced enlisted crew members take over the ship from the officers. The transition of events flow from established order to controlled "chaos" of the Pollywog Revolt. The eve of the equatorial crossing is referred to as "Wog Day" and is a mild type of role reversal and a prelude of events for the day to come. All of the uninitiated are allowed to capture and interrogate any *Shellbacks* they can find. Interrogation is commonly performed by hogtying, cracking eggs or pouring aftershave lotion on their heads. The *Wogs* are made very aware of the fact that it will be much harder on them if they do anything like this.

On the morning of the crossing, *Pollywogs* receive subpoenas to appear before *King Neptune*. Neptune's court, consisting of Davy Jones and Amphitrite, officiated at the ceremony, which was preceded by a beauty contest of men dressed up as women. Each division of the ship was required to introduce one contestant in swimsuit drag. Afterwards, some of the *Wogs* may be "interrogated" by *King Neptune* and his entourage. The use of "truth serum" (hot sauce + after shave) and whole uncooked eggs put in the mouth, is a common concoction to induce the sailor to say anything necessary to win his freedom. During the ceremony, the *Pollywogs* undergo a number of increasingly embarrassing ordeals such as wearing clothing inside out, crawling on hands and knees or being swatted with short lengths of fire hose. Real humiliation is provided by having each potential *Shellback* kiss the Royal Baby's belly (the fattest sailor on the ship) coated with pure lard.

It was unfortunate that the Marine Corps passengers were not allowed to participate in the actual ceremony but the numbers on board precluded full participation. Waverley, and his fellow Marines, were allowed to watch the festivities which allowed him to experience the event without actual participation in the ceremony. The crew did bestow the honorary title of "Shellback" on each Marine on board. For this, Waverley felt honored and the kinship that was shared between the Leathernecks and the Swabbies grew.

On the day following the equator crossing, Waverley arrived in the South Pacific when the ship docked at Banika. This was the island headquarters for the 1st Marine Division which the troops were scheduled to join. Waverley was a member of the 26th Replenishment Draft in support of the 1st Marine Division. The weather was hot and incredibly humid, but on the brighter side, the smell was unbearable; comparable to the garbage dump back home on a hot summer afternoon. It was a joy for the new Marine to set foot on dry land following his bumpy ride aboard ship all the way from San Diego. Arrival by ship was a little bit safer than coming in by airplane. Occasionally a free-roaming cow, left over from the pre-war plantations, would stagger onto the runway and be hit by a landing plane. There was no waste on the island. These dead cattle would be dragged off the runway and served up as fresh burgers for the Wimpy's Hamburger Stand that sat at the end of the airstrip.

The camp set up on Banika was a Boy Scout's delight but was considered a bit primitive for the boys who had been in their own comfortable beds just a few short months back. Care was paramount for Waverley as he wandered through the row after row of tents searching for his billet. A misstep could have found him trying to balance on top of a crab as the walkways were covered by a multitude of those crustaceous foot pinchers. Of course, this wasn't the final destination but merely a staging area. At least this tent city was equipped with the latest in Air Conditioning. The sides of each tent could be lifted to reveal the mosquito mesh used to discourage the nightly raids from those insect hoards. This was an event for which Waverley had been well trained, having spent the past several months in the marshes of Paris Island and New River. It was actually kind of nice to have the warm tropical breeze blowing through the tent on a clear and rainless evening. There was never a concern about missing the evening mess. As chow time approached, the number of rats scurrying toward the mess tent would significantly increase. The men were never sure if they were trying to be first in line to eat, or if the cook had some magical method of calling them in to be fried.

The unofficial uniform of the day was a casual hat, shorts, and combat boots. The boots were protection from the varmints with pinchers. This was Waverley's first introduction to the hardships of combat. The number of troops on the island far outweighed the availability of fresh water. The navy had ensured that a healthy ration of beer was available but this was inconsequential to those who did not partake of the alcoholic brew. Rudimentary stills were set up in many of the tents for the purpose of purifying water. Coffee was also made plentiful by their Navy brethren and tea was available in smaller quantities. Heating water for these beverages was insufficient and a full boil was necessary to clean out the natural bacteria and other living organisms. Bathing was not as much of a concern. The clouds would move in and the rain would fall every afternoon around 1500. The daily schedule allotted half an hour every day for this blessing from heaven. Stripped bare, there would be dancing in the streets with a bar of soap. Speed was of the essence because the shower would normally last for only 15 minutes. Anyone a little slow lathering up might be stuck soapy, with no way to rinse. A couple of days bathing under these circumstances would make it very uncomfortable living inside your own skin.

The daily grind consisted of calisthenics and more running, followed by a dip in the big pond. That would be the one with the salt water, sandy beaches, and sharks. The married or well spoken for men could be picked out of the crowd. They were always the ones writing a letter home. The bachelors could all be found at a poker game, set up wherever they could find. In the afternoon there was usually a swim call for those who paid no attention to the rumors of sharks off the beach, while at night, there was usually a ~~good~~ movie playing in the common open area. For those who wished to take advantage of its availability, and everyone was ordered to wish so, the firing range was open all day to hone skills which would become so valuable in battle. Incorporation into the 1st Division never happened, but word quickly passed down the line that the 26th Replenishment Draft may be moving to Guadalcanal to hook up with the new 6th Division being trained there.

During their time on the island, many of the Marines became familiar with, and some friendly with, the local island natives, known as Melanesians. They lived off the land, in grass huts, and dressed sparingly. These natives were very friendly to the American visitors possibly because they rid their island of the Japanese or maybe, just maybe, the Americans brought with them money and other tradable commodities. They ran their tourist trade from their grass huts, dealing in trinkets they made from the wood and grasses found in their forest or posing for pictures. The natives wore their traditional grass skirts (both men and women) and barely anything else.

> "The censorship has been lifted so now I can tell what has been going on. First I went to Banika (Russell Islands) where we were to join the First Division, but was later sent to Guadalcanal for the 6th Division."
>
> *Letter Home*
> *23 April 1945*

The troops of the Replenishment Draft were loaded back onto the Ernst for a quick afternoon cruise of the South Pacific Islands. Finally docking on Guadalcanal, they found that a tent camp was already in place on the island with each tent berthing individual squads. Each squad consisting of 6 to 12 members under the control of a senior corporal. Each tent had Identification markings boldly displayed at the entrance which identified the unit bunked within. Guadalcanal was the point of establishment for the Marine's 6th Division. They had been formed initially by battle hardened Leathernecks. Extensive training was conducted in preparation for an important invasion. New recruits were arriving each week from the states to become members of the "Striking 6th." It soon became apparent that the troops brought in by the USS General H. O. Ernst were the last to arrive at the party. Most of the training had been completed for the early arrivals. The later arriving units were placed in a Reserve status for which no additional training was provided. They did arrive just in time to help with the load-out of supplies onto the Transport vessels.

It was doubtful if anyone in the division had certain knowledge of the units next target when the training program began on Guadalcanal, but it was clear it would be some point in the inner defense of the Japanese empire. It was evident the division could expect to meet the best of Japan's well trained, well equipped, troops. Fighting on ground with which the Japanese were thoroughly familiar, and where they had had ample opportunity to prepare for defense, would place the Marines at a huge disadvantage.

Waverley found himself physically ready to go but not so mentally. He embarked on the USS Leon (APA-48) Attack Transport with trepidation. The Leon sailed on the 14th of March with approximately 1,200 troops, a platoon of war dogs and a full quota of landing craft on board. The ship was heading to Ulithia Atoll located in the Caroline Island chain. This was the rendezvous point where 434 warships and 186,000 troops staged the final assault force. The USS Leon arrived at Mogmog island on the 18th of March.

Waverley and his buddies spent as much time as they could recreating. On the island of Ulithia, they played baseball, pitched horseshoes, listened to a Navy band, drank beer, ate fried chicken and ham sandwiches, and tried for a few brief moments to forget that the war existed.

"It was the 14th of March when we sailed from there and we arrived at Mogmog, Ulithia (Caroline Islands). There one week to the day we found out where & when we were going to hit. That was the 25th of March."

Letter Home
23 April 1945

The target for the assault was revealed to the troops on the 24th of March and it started quite a buzz. In a continued move toward the Japanese mainland, they were to take the island of Okinawa in what was now referred to as Operation Iceberg. Air and sea bombardment began devastating the island on the same day that their destination was revealed to the troops. Bombs and shells were exploding for the full length of the 70 mile long island. There were daily briefings on the battle plan, what to expect, what not to expect, tactical plans, and assignments. On March 25th the Division was briefed on the target being Okinawa. That afternoon, Corporal Biscansin instructed his machine gun squad:

"Stay alert for snipers. They love machine-gunners, dead. Don't be too anxious to get off a few rounds. The Japs will scream and yell just to draw fire. This way they can pinpoint our automatic weapons, providing targets for their mortars or artillery fire. And don't shout out anyone's name. A Nip hears a name and a short time later he shouts it back. The Marine sticks up his head for a look and 'BAM!' gets it right between the eyes. Don't lose it if they charge with a Banzai attack. Hold your fire until you see their buck teeth—then cut them all down. When you are moving up or firing, keep your head up and tail down. The GI Bill of Rights doesn't mean a thing to a dead Marine. And last—your worst enemy on that island will be complacency. You become complacent—you become dead."

Machine Gunner Briefing
Biscansin, Corporal USMC

These were truly words to live by. Those who did not heed those words did not live. Day two on the Ulithia Atoll brought more information to the troops than some of them had a capacity to retain. The lead Hospital Corpsman gave a really soothing talk as he dispersed vital knowledge of diseases which were inherent on that small hunk of coral.

> "Okinawa is known for its many maladies and diseases such as malaria, plague, leprosy, typhus, rabies, dengue, dysentery, filariasis, jungle rot, and every other skin affliction known to man. There are flies here by the millions, mosquitoes by the billions, and a climate with one of the highest humidity rates in the world. The average rainfall was about 120 inches per year. It also is home to two of the world's deadliest snakes: the Okinawan Habu and the Kufau. The Habu is greenish-yellow, about five feet long, but not usually aggressive. Be alert though and don't let one of them crawl up with you in your foxhole."
>
> *Machine Gunner Briefing*
> *Hirschman HCC, USN*

The troops then took a break for lunch and how tasty that meal was could only be found in Waverley's imagination. There were several death threats to whoever it was that planned the order of the briefings. After nearly everyone had dumped their full trays into the garbage, the Lieutenant was next on the agenda to brief the men on the natives living on the island.

> "The native inhabitants of Okinawa were very poor, most of them engaged in farming. Their cash crops were sweet potatoes, sugar cane, and rice. The only livestock on the island were kept for personnel use. Most of the natives live in small villages of thatched roof huts while the more elite had stone houses with tile roofs. Remember that the Okinawa native are citizens of the Japanese Empire and as

such may be supporting the Japanese defense and possibly even aiding them."

Machine Gunner Briefing
Bachiak, Lieutenant USMC

To finish up the evening the Platoon Sergeant gave the men a quick look at the terrain, the island geography, and intelligence as to where the Japanese forces might be hiding.

"The shorelines lay behind coral reefs which extend 200 to 400 yards out at the landing sites. They extend up to half a mile out at the other beaches. The northern end of the island has high sheer mountains honeycombed with caves accessible only over small paths too small for any vehicular traffic. In the south, hills are rolling and the terrain broken up by limestone escarpments. Many ravines and hills in the south which are also filled with many caves. The largest city is 'Naha' which lays on the Southwest end of the island."

Platoon Briefing
Sloan, Sergeant USMC

Waverley cleaned and checked his weapon. Then quietly attended religious services because Easter Sunday was about to enter with a bang. Their final briefing disclosed a little more about the invasion tactics. The 6th Division was to land on the left flank of the 10th Army. The initial objective was to capture the Yontan airfield. The 29th Marines were to be held in Corps reserve while the 26th Replenishment Group was assigned to assist in the staging of supplies on the landing site.

The USS Leon departed Ulithia on the 27th of March with a full complement of troops on board and the convoy of 434 warships and 960 cargo carriers, tankers and supporting non military boats. As they sailed for Okinawa, the ship was over stuffed with cargo, Marines and every type of landing craft they could squeeze on board. The landing craft were stored in the cargo holes and carried on deck, stacked up to three deep. Heavy equipment was lashed securely for use by the Seabee Battalion riding on board. Below decks, multiple crates were stacked in place housing the Marine's secret weapon, a full platoon of Marine War Dogs.

A typical Marine attitude swept the ranks on board ship. On one hand there was a realization that this would be one of the most difficult battles in the history of the Corps and yet there was an air of gayety. Songs were spontaneously generated such as "Goodbye Mama, I'm off to Okinawa." Men laid around, played cards, wrote letters. Many methods were used to try and relieve the tension in anticipation of the forthcoming battle.

The ships took up prearranged positions off Okinawa and began invasion preparation. Landing craft were loaded-out with supplies. On day L-1(the day before the invasion) the Marines cleaned and checked their weapons again. They were also able to attended continuing religious services. At this stage of the operation, there were no atheist left within the entire 6th Division. Easter Sunday was about to enter with a deep sigh, prayers said, weapons cleaned, and the men ready for a good night's sleep. It was seriously doubtful, however, if anyone got any sleep that night. Waverley certainly did not.

THE BATTLE WAS AT HAND!

CHAPTER 7
Onward to Glory

Easter Sunday, 1 April 1945, the 6th Marine Division arrived at the island of Okinawa. Everyone was still very tired when 0300 Reveille awakened the troops from an uncomfortable sleep, or what little sleep there was. No one on board the ship had rested well that night for the constant crash and thunder of the heavy guns of the battleships and cruisers bombarding the slopes from the beach up to Yontan Airfield, 1,200 yards from water's edge. They needed to get used to the battle noise because this was the way every night for the next two months would sound. Waverley laid in his hammock thinking about their dinner the night before, having been a real treat for him. The cooks served up steak, potatoes, and hot apple pie for desert.

On board the USS Leon were units of the 6th Marine Division, the 11th Special Construction Battalion, and a full platoon of Marine War Dogs. With the echoing gunfire ringing in everyone's ears, the troops crawled from their makeshift beds and somehow found their way to the mess deck. Their Easter Fools Day breakfast consisted of oranges, steak, eggs, hash browns, ice cream, coffee cake, and plenty of fresh hot coffee. This hearty breakfast was prepared and ready for the landing troops to *chow down* like right proud Marines. Several of Waverley's buddies had expressed a thought similar to his own. Was this just the command being nice, or was this to be the last meal for many of the troops landing this morning? The briefings that were held on

Ulithia had attempted to make everyone aware of the possible results of the landing. They were preparing to meet the toughest and most experienced fighters the enemy had to offer. The coral reefs surrounding the island made a close approach impossible. The landing craft with the Marines aboard had to be launched approximately one to two nautical miles off shore.

At 0406 local time, the order came down from the top and there wasn't a boat that couldn't hear the command, "Land the Landing Force." The landing craft were lowered into the choppy waters of Hagushi Bay. The boys finished their meal, grabbed their gear, and were topside by 0430. The troops assigned to the first wave were already loading, hundreds at a time, climbing down the cargo nets draped over the side and into their assigned landing craft.

Japanese planes had begun the attack on the fleet at the first break of morning light. Several ships had been hit by strafing fire but no serious damage had occurred. There had been some narrow escapes as a few Japanese pilots aimed their planes for the ships. Five planes had been shot down and none had yet reached their targets. Planes from the American carriers were now taking command of the airways and began firing and blasting the Japanese fortifications directly behind the landing sites.

> "I am an American, fighting in the forces which guard my country and our way of life. I am prepared to give my life in their defense."
>
> *USMC Code of Conduct*
> *Article I*

From his vantage point on deck, Waverley had a perfect view to watch the Marines in the first wave clamber down the cargo nets draped over the side, and into the LCAs. The LCA's revved their engines and proceeded to form up for the landing. The landing craft formed a line off of the beaches. They were only one craft deep, but stretching as far as they could see in both directions. This formation ensured 60,000 troops would all hit the beach simultaneously. Heavy gunfire could be heard from the ship's guns pounding the shore, but fell silent as the troops neared the beach. They watched the first wave of the 6th Division land on the left flank of the invading force onto the area designated as Green Beach. The 1st Division landed just to the south at the Red, Blue, and Yellow beaches.

Waverley watched the distant shore, even though there was very little that could be seen. His ears were trained toward land, listening for the eruption of gunfire signifying the landing was in progress. Very few sounds of combat were heard emanating from the beaches and the word filtered back on board that the spearhead troops had met with very little resistance. It was concluded that this was in fact a surprise attack. At least it was a huge surprise to the Americans.

The first wave had been comprised of well seasoned troops. These were the veterans of Guam, Guadalcanal, Saipan, and Bougainville. The troops remaining on board the ship, of which Waverley was a member, were fresh from the states and being held back in reserve. They were to be gradually introduced to the fighting, anticipated to be the most dangerous met so far in the war. Waiting topside for their turn to disembark gave Waverley time to think about what he was about to face. Thoughts turned to fears and fears turned to prayer. He had always heard that there were no atheists in foxholes and now he knew why. The roaring from the water began overtaking the noise from the shore as the landing craft began returning to the ship to pick up the next wave.

During the morning, conditions had changed drastically off shore. The sun was peering over the watery horizon with a red and angry stare. A bad omen for sure. The Japanese were launching a heavy attack by the most feared weapon in the Japanese arsenal—the Kamikaze. These planes were no more than manned flying bombs. Even if the ship's guns could take out the plane, they also had to force the plane into the ocean before it could be steered into the ship. Gunfire from the ships became deafening and the visibility was approaching zero. Heavy smoke screens were being laid down to prevent the Japanese planes from having the ability to sight the American warships. Everyone waited as their battle skilled brethren climbed the rising ground terraced by stone ridging and dotted with concrete tombs. Their advance was swift and by the time the reserves were ready to load, the beach had already been cleared and the advance wave had nearly reached the Yonton airfield.

Waverley's troop, "Fox" Company, began loading around 1430 in the afternoon. Climbing down the side of the ship on that same cargo net was a skill many of the boys had practiced but had not yet mastered. Unlike the battle hardened Devil Dogs that went in with the first wave, this soufflé of new participants to the war, didn't manage the climb nearly as well. It was really a shock to realize how many of these Devil Pups had trouble mastering "Hands on Vertical, Feet on Horizontal." Although they had been provided with months of training for this operation, on the morning of the invasion it just wasn't the same. Many of the Marines would misstep about half way down. Their feet would slip off or they would step totally through the net and end up dangling head down, feet up, about 30 feet above the water, then 20 feet, then 30 feet, etc. Waverley wished that there had been calmer seas to lessen the impact of such trivial errors.

No one was seriously injured during the disembarkment, but that's not to say that many of them didn't try. Now, Waverley didn't care much about the people who watch a film or movie and quickly assess that this action was so easy. Climbing down 50 feet of cargo net, attached to the side of a tall ship, rolling with the waves, is not so easy. The ones who he really felt bad for were the men that literally became seasick from the motion and trying to hang onto the nets. Or maybe he felt worse for the men who were already in the landing craft, directly below them.

The morning of the invasion was referred to as Love-Day. Packed tightly in a small landing craft under cover of smoke and gunfire, Waverley was unable to really feel the love right about then. Although they knew that the trip to the beach covered less than two miles, it seemed to take forever. The sea had appeared choppy when they loaded but now as they began entering the surf, the water became extraordinarily rough. This was the time for that last cigarette or maybe catching a few moments of silent prayer or maybe throwing up just one more time. Waverley bowed his head but could not distinguish his own prayer over the pounding beat of his heart. His senses were peaked and adrenaline flowed as he grasped his weapon firmly in anticipation of the gate on his LCA dropping. The landing craft churned closer to the shore, the waves broke over the sides and completely soaked the Leathernecks preparing to disembark.

> "I will never surrender of my own free will. If in command, I will never surrender the members of my command while they still have the means to resist."
>
> *USMC Code of Conduct*
> *Article II*

By the time they hit the beach, the tide had gone out and they had to disembark about 200 yards from shore. Their LCA grounded on the coral reef and the men were all thrown forward. The coxswain of this craft obviously had plenty of landing experience because as they were tossed forward, the front ramp dropped, and they were hurled out into waist deep water.

Waverley remembered back in school where he had learned that a body in motion tended to stay in motion. It had taken him six years to fully appreciate how physics affected his everyday life. But there he was, half way around the world, playing the part of the body in motion and flying head first out of an LCA. After a minor struggle he righted himself in spite of the heavy field pack on his back and 20 pounds of rifle and ammunition. Fighting the resistance of the waist deep water, he pushed the 200 yards to the shore where he fell, exhausted.

They had landed on the Green Beach near the town of Hanza and quickly recovering, sprinted over the jagged coral and twisted stumps to find cover. Luck was on their side this day as the first wave had moved inland and there were hundreds of pre-dug foxholes just waiting to be occupied. Everyone agreed in the premise that men in holes are hard to hit so everybody grabbed one and curled up for the night. Scared, that would really be the statement of the century, but not worried. The Gunnery Sergeant once told the company "if you are scared, then you are awake and alert. That is how it needs to be." By evening the 29th Regiment, which had been held in reserve and had not anticipated an Easter landing, were on land.

> "Soaking wet in a small fox hole and scared that any minute a sniper would jump in with us, this is how I spent the first night ashore."
>
> *Letter Home*
> *23 April 1945*

They were also expecting almost anything to happen as things had been going far too smoothly to suit them. The landing encountered extremely light opposition with few casualties. The battle veterans in the landing party warned the new guys not to get too over confident in the unopposed landing. This was a good indication that the Japs had dug in and a stiff defense would be encountered somewhere along the advance. As it turned out, the real enemy was the landing itself. The tide and the coral reef gave them a greater challenge than the Japs on that particular day.

Limited resistance on the Green Beach was quickly dispatched.

The first evening was quieter than expected. There was almost no enemy fire on the ground but the Japanese pilots began flying night missions to bomb and strafe the beaches. All in all, the Marines received superb support from the carrier planes during the landing.

> "The next morning we went to work early unloading supplies and have been working every day & night since then. We follow the front lines handling supplies, standing by for replacements, and setting up a secondary defense."
>
> *Letter Home*
> *23 April 1945*

As part of the SToS (Ship to Shore) company, Waverley handled the stores being unloaded from the transport ship. Success was measured in gross tonnage of supplies moved from ship to shore. They were the Replenishment Draft and their immediate job was to unload cargo from the assault ships and follow the lead group with supplies, fresh personnel, and ammunition. By the time the reserves feet were planted solid on the coral island, the lead group had already taken *Yontan* airfield. The infantry always seemed to be unaware of the big picture. They only knew what they could see or what scuttlebutt filtered back from the front line. Often they would find out more of what they were doing in letters from home. The best information came from the newspaper clippings sent from home about the battles they were fighting.

> "You know more about this operation than I do, as we only know what we see and nothing else. Your clippings are greatly appreciated and are widely read by the boys. It has gotten to be a habit now after mail call for them to want to see the clippings. We are all more interested in the ones about this operation as we don't have much news of it."
>
> *Letter Home*
> *23 April 1945*

The Marine is acutely aware only of what his fire team is doing to engage the enemy in battle, and defeat him. The actions of smaller units made possible the accomplishments of the operation plans of the higher echelons of command. In Marine lingo this is the bigger picture correlated to the actions of the rifleman. The 6th Division was managing to advance more than five miles per day over rugged and difficult terrain. The Infantry progressed across the island and had reached the Pacific Ocean by the end of the third day. This rate of advance was dangerously fast as it left unsecured holes in the covered fields and overran several caves where both civilians and the Japanese Army were entrenched. The advancing front line had quickly examined a number of caves and tunnels but found no Japanese. No one realized how deeply the Japanese had tunneled into the coral bedrock and many positions were passed over by the rapidly advancing front.

The USS Leon remained to unload cargo. Kamikaze planes made an all out effort against Okinawa island, shipping, and beach heads. The planes strafed the beaches, dropped their bombs on the fleet and aimed their planes into the nearest ship or gathering of troops that they could find. Heavy smoke was laid down across the fleet and the beach in an attempt to shield their locations from the sky. The orders were to not fire at the Japanese planes unless you were uncovered or were in immediate danger of being hit by their piloted bombs. Not fighting back was a new concept for these Marines. There was quite a bit of confusion as to how they would deal with that order. On April 4th, the Leon slipped her dragging anchor, worked her way through the crowded anchorage and set sail for parts unknown.

The 26th Replenishment Group, with its available mechanized units, began convoying the supplies up the island in support of the advancing front. The Replenishment Infantry covered the supply train while sweeping the area for any Japanese stragglers. During this phase Waverley was called upon as a sharpshooter protecting a forward flame thrower. Having himself been only marginally trained with the flame thrower, his methodology was that of point in the general direction and fire. This method served him well in battle as a machine gunner and was a harbinger of events to come later in life both positively and during episodes of regressive disturbing behavior. This methodology did not, however, work as a Marine sharpshooter and he had to do a rethink on his intentions. He had come to realize, even this early, that shooting at another human being was anything but natural. Conflict though it was, his duty was to protect his homeland and his family, and do his duty he must.

"Praise the Lord and pass the ammunition!"

Chaplin Howell Forgy Lt.jg USN
USS New Orleans
7 December 1941

Flame thrower duty was exceptionally hazardous and his sharpshooter bodyguard wasn't in a much better position. The Japanese soldiers were deathly afraid of that flaming weapon. So much so that carrying the "torch" was likened to wearing a target on your back. Even the sharpshooter assigned to guard them and the tank they carried did not help very much in placing them in the warm and fuzzy "feel good" category. They felt a little safer than usual at this point because they were on mop up duty and not on the front line. Reaching Yontan Airfield, they left a small garrison there to protect the territory while the Navy Seabees worked to prepare the field for the support planes arrival. The replenishment regiment moved to fill gaps that developed due to rapid advances by the spearhead Marine regiments. The reserve crew cleared ground up to the China Road and held positions there for the tracks to move supplies forward behind the rapidly advancing front line. This main North/South byway was more on the order of a muddy pathway, barely discernable from the surrounding jungle and open fields. When setting up their defensive positions, anticipating the invasion, the Japs had destroyed all of the bridges along this road by explosives or by burning. The enemy demolition crews were obviously unskilled in that they failed to completely destroy several bridges. The invasion force was therefore able to utilize the remaining structural members as foundations for their new spans.

The enemy attempted to impede progress of the invading force but actually caused little or no resistance. The destruction of highway facilities, during their retreat to their defensive position in the north, was for the most part inept. In many instances, the forward momentum of the 6th Division was not slowed to any great extent. The company commanders were constantly reminding their troops ". . . the enemy was in the caves, in the jungle, and in the rain, be aware." The 6th Division engineers and the accompanying Seabees kept busy making the road passable. Mines placed in the roadways had not been covered or defiled very well and created no more than a nuisance to the advancing troops. Many trails were heavily laden with sharpened bamboo stakes to impede progress. These Abatis were easily pushed aside by the tank dozers, causing no deterrence to the riflemen.

It wasn't long before the "honeymoon" was over. Waverley's company was ambushed during an attack on a Japanese position in the hills. Clambering over piles of enemy bodies, several of the platoons were sent ahead and his platoon stayed behind to protect and care for the wounded until the stretcher bearers arrived. The Chaplin had stayed and was concerned that there was no fresh water to provide for the wounded. He had remembered spotting a small ravine a ways back with a clear spring. A small contingent of the men left with the padre to find this spring. While they were filling canteens, they were hit by sniper fire about 30 yards away. The Chaplin was ordered to take three of the riflemen and get out of there with the canteens. The rest stayed behind to give them cover. When the Chaplin was clear, they opened up in the direction of the sniper fire and the bullets suddenly stopped flying.

As the convoy continued its trek north, they encountered sporadic pockets of resistance both from the enemy and the local reptiles who had taken cover under the outcroppings. The Japs' armament was limited to small arms and the many natives they had recruited. It became obvious how poorly trained these combatants really were, but even small weapons can make large holes. During the march up the main road, Waverley heard, and felt, a chink, as a bullet fired from the nearby hillside struck his helmet, knocking it off of his head. Everyone hit the ground and prepared for a short skirmish. Waverley took up a position in nearby ground cover. A quick lick of his thumb, as he set the sights on his rifle, assured him that his good luck would continue. This was one of his good luck habits which stuck with him throughout the war having been born at Camp Lejeune during his sharpshooter qualification. The company laid there in position for several minutes but additional shots were not forthcoming. He retrieved his helmet, the one with the ding in the side, and continued advancing north. As the Marines neared Mount Onna they were confronted with automatic machine gun fire. Following a short exchange of "Lead Barter," they surrounded the enemy in a cave located on a shallow ridge just ahead. Mortar fire kept the enemy occupied, allowing the flame throwers to close in on the enemy position. The Marines let loose with a barrage of flame from two sources and destroyed the Japs hideout. Enemy soldiers came running from the bushes trailing shards of burning clothing. It appeared the whole cave was engulfed in an inferno. Waverley discovered later that there were nearly 100 civilians, within that particular cave, working with the Japanese soldiers. When they had cleared several pill boxes in the area, Waverley was relieved of flame protection duty and returned to a position protecting the North bound supply convoys.

> "If I am captured I will continue to resist by all means available. I will make every effort to escape and to aid others to escape. I will accept neither parole nor special favors from the enemy."
>
> *USMC Code of Conduct*
> *Article III*

It became increasingly difficult to push forward with the supply trucks. The forward troops were advancing at thousands of yards each day and often had to pause so as not to outrun their supply dumps. Try as hard as they might, keeping up with the advance was a daunting task and on foot with full packs, the loss of body fluid to the footsore Marines was significant. No one had to remind the foot soldier to keep drinking water, but they were constantly being harassed to take the salt pills that were distributed. The supply train was constantly fighting the bad roads, extreme heat, and staggered enemy pill boxes that were missed by the primary advancing front. Causalities were very low and they were losing more men from heat exhaustion than from enemy fire. The Navy Seabees and the 6th Engineering Battalion were leading the supply train working diligently to turn the mud laden pathway into some semblance of a navigable road, widen the road for the mechanized units, and repair bridges across creeks and gullies to support tanks and artillery units. They were constantly uncovering soup can mines. Made from soup cans packed with gunpowder, shards of glass and metal, and an ignition cap. These improvised devices were easy to assemble but dangerous for those who inadvertently stumbled upon them.

Mountains rose out of the sea to form a virtually unbroken spine in the interior of the island. Japanese troops who had been cut off by the rapidly advancing line had turned to guerrilla fighting by living in the wild areas and surviving off of the land. They exploited the region and natural hiding places to attack small patrols and logistic support troops in the rear. These guerrilla forces played havoc with the replenishment troops of the 6th Marine Division. They even employed the natives to participate in the struggle. Babies and toddlers had even been booby trapped with explosive devices and left for the unsuspecting Americans to find. Their fresh troops were learning a whole new type of jungle warfare. Having been trained for more intense battlefield conflicts, they were forced into painstakingly tracking small uncoordinated units whose primary advantage was their ability to hide in caves with very small openings in the coral base of the island. The Japanese appeared well suited for this type of warfare and hunting them became an daunting task. A clear shot at the enemy occurred only when they would make an appearance to fire on a Marine patrol. The company had been briefed on the diseases spreading over the island, but none were found. The natives were dying, but from malnutrition, which never should have occurred. The fields were lush, the crops were plentiful, but the entire population was starving. This was the real paradox of the war.

By the 13th of April the 4th Marines had reached the Motobu Peninsula on the North end of the island and had finally come in contact with the first formidable defense established by the Japanese. They were dug in at Yae-Take mountain. Both Battalions of the 29th Marines were finally placed into action as the 6th Division surrounded the Japanese fortification and established the division headquarters at Nago. Word was received on the

14th of the death of President Roosevelt. The 6th Division held a brief memorial service in his honor at Nago. Coincidentally, they heard of the surrender of Germany. To Waverley it seemed like most of the men had a great bit of difficulty trying to feel sorrow and delight all at the same time, he knew he did. Following the services, they loaded onto a troop transport truck headed for the village of Itomi and with the news of Germany falling, they were pumped up for the engagement ahead.

> "If I become a prisoner of war, I will keep faith with my fellow prisoners. I will give no information nor take part in any action which might be harmful to my comrades. If I am senior, I will take command. If not, I will obey lawful orders of those appointed over me and will back them in every way."
>
> <div align="right">USMC <i>Code of Conduct</i>
Article IV</div>

The 29th Regiment made a forced march from Itomi to a position in the high hills looking down on the Itomi-Manna road. Waverley, with full field pack and a 100 pounds of weapon across his shoulders, struggled as they ascended the moderate slope of the hill. The Japanese laid down machine gun, mortar, and rifle fire on the advancing Marines on all sides. Over their heads, the artillery shells whistled past and air support was laying fire on the mountain. The ground battle became a fight of small units as hit and run tactics prevailed on the rugged terrain. Waverley and his gunnery partner, Bobby, settled into a deeply dug foxhole on the hill crest and set up their M1917 machine gun with its short tripod. The gun produced that distinctive metallic snap sound, as it connected firmly with its base, and made another as the ammo belt was locked in position. From their vantage point they could see the whole battlefield and were directed to hold their position. The fight seemed to fade away from them as again they were left in the rear. They had successfully closed off a primary escape route for the Japs but to the best of their knowledge, none of the enemy tried to escape. Laying in their rear line position, Waverley wondered if he should take the chance and clean the gun. One important lesson he learned at Camp Lejeune was to clean your weapon after every firefight. What they forgot to teach them, however, was how to tell when a firefight was over. As everyone on the island learned, there was no clear cut line.

Fox Company cleaning up after the firefight on Okinawa's Motobu Peninsula.

When the 29th Marines were diverted to the Southwest, they were mobilized and spent three days firing on Japanese positions. Constantly moving forward, the regiment was relieving the pressure of dug in enemy positions. They had closed so tightly on the Japs that the machine gunners were ordered to hold fire and the "fix bayonets" order was given. The mountain was taken by the 4th Marines in bloody hand to hand combat. Although the main Japanese position had been taken, a portion of Yae Take remained in enemy hands and the regiment was ordered to secure their position. By the 17th of April, Yae Take was completely in friendly hands and a drive North began to secure the Motobu Peninsula. "Fox" Company of the 29th Regiment was ordered to reinforce the 6th Reconnaissance Company at the town of Bise on the western tip of the Motobu Peninsula. Resistance was sporadic for the 29th Regiment and within two days they had reached the coast. Word filtered down that all Japanese had been killed or captured and the North half of the island was in friendly hands. They retired to Division Headquarters in Nago and took a three day stand down while the individual units recovered and prepared for their march south to support 10th Army operations. "Fox" Company was relieved at Bise by "King" Company and they returned to Division Headquarters at Nago. Their position at Nago was relieved by the 27th Army, breaking them free to join the 10th Army that had stalled on the southern battle line.

Before the operation on the Motobu Peninsula, they had received word of President Roosevelt's death. They now picked up scuttlebutt about the death of journalist Ernie Pyle. Reports indicated he had been killed by a sniper on Le Shima. It really put the guys into a slump but fortunately they were now able to take a short rest. The regiment was able to hold a short prayer vigil for Pyle and all of their buddies who they lost on the peninsula. They also had the opportunity to catch up with the mail wagon and a couple of pieces were waiting for Waverley. He received a letter from his mother which was dated April 2nd and a Valentine card mailed January 22nd. He was able to purchase a Money Order at the Division Headquarters in Nago to send home to his Mother for Mother's Day. Finally having the time, he was able to send letters home to his Uncle Edward, his Aunt Marie, his Mother, and Martha.

Chapter 8
Duty in Hell

The 6th Division began its track south at an accelerated pace to try and position themselves to back up the 1st Marines bogged down on their attempt to enter the Shuri defense sector. The progress of the 6th was slowed considerably as they met supply vehicles moving north. Waverley also came across an injured dog along the side of the road. This was apparently an injured War Dog whose handler had been killed. Having the Corpsman check him out, they concluded that there was no helping him so the kindest act he could perform was to fire a round into the dog's head. Although he knew he had done the right thing, tears trickled down his cheeks as they continued south. The body of the dead canine was carried to the first medical aid station they encountered for burial with full military honors.

Closing in on the Shuri Barrier, they began taking aerial strafing and kamikaze encounters. Although the Americans controlled the sky, Japanese planes would intermittently slip through the defenses. The Japanese had taken to instilling misguided honor to their young men, believing that giving their lives for an already lost cause was divine providence. Like the "Divine Wind" that saved their island from the 1274 Khan invasion, their "Kamikaze" warriors could save their nation from defeat. The Marines took special care to not only hide their unit from the ground, but more importantly from the sky. They passed the makeshift aide stations as they neared the southern line but were not allowed to camp nearby for fear of drawing enemy fire on the doctors and previously wounded.

Honor was a harsh subject to discuss among the tough, dirty, wet, exhausted, Leathernecks. Often the misguided honor of the Japanese soldier would be the topic, and some could have a hearty laugh. Their purpose though, represented a sad situation to waste a life before it really had a chance to live. But then one might wonder about the honor of the American soldier when they could be seen, most every day, running from one dead Japanese to another, removing what gold they could from the mouths of their enemy. Those actions really exhibited honor and integrity at its worse, but fortunately was not wide spread.

The first of May saw Waverley transferred from the reserve force to the main fighting force of the 29th Marines. For the remainder of the fighting, he would find himself on the front line in the middle of the action. The 6th Division was holding back to reinforce the rear of the 1st Division. On the second of May the weather began cooling the air, which was a pleasant surprise. The rain started that night and was not only a cooling event, but also a way to refill canteens. After five days of unrelenting precipitation, the 29th Regiment was finally ordered into battle. They advanced slowly along the coast and were called upon to replenish the infantry units ahead. The area they were now entering contained terrain that was very irregular with wooded foothills all around. There were also low terraced hills and tall coral mounds with steep escarpments on all sides. The Japanese troops must have been slowly diminishing, as they had no reserves to fill vacancies in the ranks, but the American troops couldn't tell because of the way steady gunfire was plummeting in on them. There was a deluge of water dropping from the sky, and a steady wall of lead coming at them from the hills. It became impossible to figure out which way to duck.

Everything was happening so fast now. There seemed to be no time for anything except shooting Japs. Waverley found it hard to do what was needed as it conflicted so much with his beliefs. He knew it was sinful to kill, but sometimes, he believed, it must be done to protect ones country and ability to live a Christian life. The small bible he carried in his pocket kept him close to his God and formed a tie to his family back home. Whenever he felt alone, he would read from his sacred book and his world would again come into balance.

> "I wouldn't worry too much about Waverley, he can take care of himself. I haven't heard from him. I don't guess he has time for writing now."
>
> *Letter to Martha from her brother Jimmy*
> *28 April 1945*

The next obstacle they faced (and every day they faced a new and different obstacle) was the Asa River. The movement down the western coast had fortunately been preceded by the 22nd Regiment. They executed a pre-dawn attack across the Asa Kawa and seized the road south of the shattered bridge. The 6th Division Engineers followed and had courteously provided a top notch Bailey Bridge for the determined 29th Regiment. The bridge had been constructed under fire, including two Japanese Human Bombs attempting to blow up the span as they ran onto the structure wearing high explosives. This had been only one of many contributions by the illustrious engineers who may have very well saved thousands of lives.

In rough, but orderly, ranks they crossed the Asa Kawa. The sounds of heavy fighting could be heard in the distance to their left flank but the near area had remained quiet as they collided against a trio of low hills dominating the open country. The three mutually supporting hills rose abruptly from the surrounding bare terrain. The flanks and rear of Sugar Loaf Hill were blanketed by discharge from extensive cave and tunnel positions in Half Moon Hill to the southeast and Horseshoe Hill to the south. These positions, named for their definitive shapes, were to be the targets of concern and one of the Marines' toughest shells to crack. The smell of the front lines bore the aroma of an uncapped cesspool. In the direction from which the wind was blowing, they could make out a tall precipitous hill. This was Sugar Loaf, the Japanese stronghold, and would prove to be more of an obstacle than anyone could possibly have imagined. This defensive position was so well fortified, an attack from any direction would be uniformly defended.

> "All right, they're on our left, they're on our right, they're in front of us, they're behind us . . . they can't get away this time."
>
> *Lewis B. "Chesty" Puller*
> *Lieutenant General USMC*

The sharp depression lying within the Horseshoe contained mortar positions which were nearly inaccessible to any form of engagement short of direct rifle fire and hand grenades. Any attempt to capture Sugar Loaf from the east or the west would be immediately exposed to artillery and mortar fire from both of the supporting hills. Likewise, an attempt to charge either Horseshoe or Half Moon would be exposed to weapons fire from Sugar Loaf. The 22nd Marines were spearheading the advance on Sugar Loaf without much success. They were overwhelmed by artillery, mortar, and sniper fire and the closer they advanced to the hill, the stronger the Japanese defenders would open up their barrage. Their first series of attacks resulted in nearly a 40 percent loss and they were quickly calling for replacements. The 22nd had difficulty holding Sugar Loaf because every time they advanced, heavy fire from the other hills would force a retreat. They had not realized at the time that the three localities were connected by a network of tunnels and galleries, facilitating the covered movement of reserves. As an additional factor providing strength to the enemy's position, all sides of Sugar Loaf were precipitous, providing for no clear avenue of approach.

The 29th Marines received orders to take Half Moon in order to cut off the Japanese's ability to protect Sugar Loaf. The orders specified this be accomplished by the 15th. The western slope of Half Moon contained the most effective machine gun nests the Marines had encountered. These positions were cited as the primary target for the operation.

They approached Half Moon and immediately came under heavy fire. Even with the close support of the four and a half inch rocket launchers, their "shoot and scoot" technique still left the advance slow and costly. Waverley noted that his fellow Marines were falling like wheat straw under attack by a sharp sickle. He thought back to his memories of days preparing the flower fields on the farm. Thinking of his comrades at arms as each straw under attack made him feel sick through and through. This line of thought made it very difficult to advance without an inner pain. The longer the attack progressed, the more difficult advancing became. The wounded Marines lay stoically along the slope of Half Moon fearful that any utterance would expose their position. Stepping over and around bodies became more difficult than maneuvering across the terrain. The air was thick with smoke and breathing became demanding. The lucky Marines were able to locate materials and fabricate a mask to cover their face but most of the troops lacked resources to accomplish this protection.

The high ground east of Sugar Loaf was the first ground which was captured in order to support the 22nd and their attack. The attack went nowhere and the group had to withdraw. They shifted to occupy the northern slope of Half Moon and the resistance there was light. As they began setting up defenses in the late afternoon the situation shifted as the fanatic Japanese launched a massive counter attack. They were supported by artillery fire from Sugar Loaf and Horseshoe. Enemy fire continued to accelerate as the evening wore on, causing their unit to retreat back down to their original line and set up a temporary perimeter defense.

> "When questioned, should I become a prisoner of war, I am required to give name, rank, service number, and date of birth. I will evade answering further questions to the utmost of my ability. I will make no oral or written

statements disloyal to my country or its allies or harmful to their cause."

USMC *Code of Conduct*
Article V

The Marines of the 22nd Regiment made the top of Sugar Loaf on the night of the 14th of May but were reduced to a mere handful under the ceaseless bombardment and counterattacks of the Japanese. Shortly after midnight their commander was killed leading a grenade attack on the reverse slope. Their reserve company was ordered in and the under strength unit moved to the top of the hill and dug in. Counterattacks and infiltration attempts were constantly hitting all along the 22nd Regiment's thin lines. By dawn, there remained less than 25 men alive on the hill, and most of them were wounded. This included one officer and eight men remaining from the 250 member reserve "King" Company.

During these chaotic days of heavy fighting, the rain had not deserted the battlefield but had turned it into a quagmire. The open fields and sharp slopes were wet, muddy, and impossible to transverse. The senses of the water logged Marines were clogged, or at the very least numb, which made it easier to consume the stale crackers and ration cans which were provided on the line. They could not see for the smoke and mud in their eyes. Smell was out of the question with the entire area smelling and tasting of gunpowder, blood, and rotting corpses. Many of the men, including Waverley, who were not smokers, took up the practice. This resulted in his breaking a pledge he made as a teenager, but under the circumstances, was completely understandable. The smell and taste of the cigarette would dampen the otherwise overwhelming stench of the war. What hearing they still had was blasted away by the Japanese mortars ahead of the line, their own artillery to the rear, and the bombs, coming precariously close, in every direction, from friendly close air support. This was something that would remain imbedded in Waverley's memory forever as many of his comrades were in tears from emotional exhaustion. Their Sergeant had instructed them to maintain their positions "come hell or high water." Well, they were already sitting in hell, the water couldn't get much higher, and where would they go anyway. Breathing was labored as it became difficult to obtain oxygen from the smoke filled air. Every snap or clank detected in the distance caused Waverley to take another deep breath as his lungs worked faster trying to prepare his body with a rush of energy potential.

Fresh water was abundant, just open your mouth and look up. Of course, one had to ignore the oily—gun powdery—taste on the tongue. Food, however, was yet another problem. What they did have was prepackaged rations and it was assumed by most that they were prepackaged for World War I. Those individuals who had not lost or traded their can openers had a fairly easy time opening the ration cans. The rest of them used their combat knife, which in truth was much easier. Some days the fair exchange of lead never stopped and a single Dextrose pill would make do for a meal. They also distributed rice to each man, one pound per. If you were considered one of the fortunate ones, the meat came already in the rice, but you had to grab it before it wiggled away. They couldn't heat the meals because on their last check, fire did not get very hot under water. The food, though, had improved over time. What used to taste like stale biscuits and meat paste, now was more of a VERY moist biscuit with cold meat soup, or such.

During the daylight the 29th Marines, besides contributing substantially to the repulse of the enemy counterattack on Sugar Loaf, improved its hold on the high ground north of Half Moon. The remnants of a rifle company from the 22nd Regiment had undergone a hazardous trek to the 29th's position to attempt a coordinated attack on Half Moon and Sugar Loaf. The seven man rifle squad fell in to support "Fox" Company and they were most certainly grateful for the help. The assault on Half Moon was quick and the lead riflemen were at the top in about 30 seconds. Lugging the heavy machine gun and ammo boxes took just a bit longer. "Fox" Company took a beating for the entire day from mortar barrages, machine gun fire and artillery emanating from Sugar Loaf and Horseshoe.

Then the good news came. Not only was the 29th Regiment charged with taking Half Moon, but also relieving the 22nd Marines of the responsibility of taking Sugar Loaf. This sounded like a good strategy to coordinate the attacks, but Sugar Loaf itself contained elaborate concrete-reinforced reverse-slope positions. This made a coordinated effort an insurmountable undertaking but at least they all couldn't become more scared than they already were. With the air of death now surrounding them, they prepared for the attack while artillery shells, Naval 16 inch shells, and 1,000 pound aerial bombs took their turn of softening up the Japanese stronghold. This seemed to have about as much effect as softening up a loaf of stale bread with an eyedropper.

"Put your trust in God; but mind to keep your powder dry!"

Oliver Cromwell
Conquest of Ireland
1649

On the 16th of May the 29th Marines began a renewed assault on Half Moon. The Japanese unleashed a barrage of machine gun and mortar fire on the Marine's position. They returned fire with the heavy machine guns but it appeared not to make much of an impact. By this time much of the ammunition had become waterlogged which caused a large number of jams and misfires. Waverley was not exactly sure how many rounds he fired off, but the pile of shell casings nearly covered him, laying there in the prone position. The tenacity of "Easy" Company brought success in reaching the summit, even though a heavy Japanese counterattack had been launched against them. Unfortunately the 29th Marines were not able to supply them with additional ammunition as it was nearly impossible to climb the hill over the bodies of so many "Nips." One Japanese soldier was laying face down in the mud with a telephone handset clutched firmly in his hand and the cord dangling in the air. With "Easy" Company unable to receive supplies, the hill was reluctantly returned to the enemy. Over 200 men died on the hill that day while only 60 survived. The wounded were brought down the slope and the dead remained laying in the rain. The day ended with "Easy" Company finishing exactly where they started. In daylight the coral hills and gullies were reminders of how a moonscape might appear. At night the sky was alive with flares and tracer rounds which gave the area an aura of flashes and dark shadows.

Daylight brought the order for "Fox" Company to divert from Half Moon to move on Sugar Loaf. It was only a short distance, but to the exhausted company, it felt like a march into hell. The real danger approaching Sugar Loaf was not so much the hill itself, but in a 300-yard by 300-yard killing zone which "Fox" Company had to cross to make their approach. From their position at Half Moon, and the Marines moving in from the north, the 6th Division suffered an estimated 600 casualties. It was a grim sight, men falling and tanks being taken out. Their battle tune became *"When I die, I'm going to Heaven, cause I done spent my time, in Armageddon!"* They dug in near Sugar Loaf and waited for the lead to stop flying. Nice sentiment, but no one ever really expected that to happen. Their foxholes filled with water as fast as they were dug. No one remembers whose bright idea it was, but pretty soon all of the Marines were digging drain holes in their foxholes. The water would run out and into the next foxhole down the slope.

They immediately set up for an assault on Sugar Loaf. During the evening, a group of nearly 50 volunteers from "George" and "Fox" companies made an assault up Sugar Loaf. For hours the volunteers underwent close-in hand-to-hand combat. When the battle was over, the volunteers retreated down the hill with only 22 souls surviving. The commanders preached that every man lost was worth it, for a just cause. Light broke through the morning clouds, another assault on Sugar Loaf was attempted on the eastern crest of the hill. They were fully exposed to raking fire from Half Moon and Mortars from Horseshoe. The noise was deafening. The clacking of small arms fire, the machine guns, mortars, artillery, aerial bombs and the constant and insidious screaming of "Corpsman!" It really became impossible to catch forty winks, or even one.

The weather cleared and good visibility returned. The entire regiment was shocked at the presence of the sun and interpreted this to be a sign from above. A squad of Japanese was spotted running from Half Moon toward Sugar Loaf and a heavy machine gun was called up to intercept. It turned out that Waverley was fortunate in that his position was out of range for that purpose. As soon as the assigned machine gunner began firing, an artillery gun opened up from Horseshoe killing the gunner, his ammo man, and destroying the weapon. More and more of the battle weary Marines were reporting to their commanders, laying their weapons on the ground, and declaring that they just could not take it anymore. They lost as many good Marines to battle exhaustion as they did to physical wounds.

The clearing exposed a sight none of them were really pleased to witness. Column after column of Japanese reinforcements were driving northward, through Takamotoji village, towards the killing field and the carnage that lay there. Orders were spread on the 17th to *"get the hell off the hill"* and stay clear. A massive bombardment was about to lay waste of the entire ridge. Soon thereafter the ships off shore began an all out barrage of the three hill defense. Artillery shells rained down on the area and aircraft from the carriers were spreading bombs like they were dusting crops. Flame-tipped rockets etched black lines of smoke against the sky as they streaked toward the Japanese positions. The Battleships, Destroyers, and Heavy Cruisers laid in a wall of fire in the attack against enemy positions. All of this commotion in support of the American infantry, what a comforting thought. This was the fifth day of the battle for Sugar Loaf. Their buddies, their friends, were falling like dominos and dying where they fell. There was no time for stopping, no time to mourn. The only consolation was a short silent prayer as they maneuvered through the field of those in agony or were fortunate enough to have died. A reconstituted "Easy" Company now prepared for a fresh assault on the defensive line. After four attempts they were no closer to a victory and Sugar Loaf Hill was not to fall on that day.

The evening of May 18th continued the pounding by the Japanese artillery which never seemed to let up. No matter how many "Nipponese" they exterminated, more kept on coming. There hadn't been any supplies moving in to the defenders so they knew that they would be running out of ammunition at any time, but this never happened. The members of "Fox" Company crawled forward through the incessant artillery and mortar fire. All attempts were made to remain quiet. Waverley could feel his heart beating as he inched forward through that insidious mud. They advanced slowly but the sound of his own heart was filling Waverley's head with an explosive beat he could hear over the artillery fire surrounding him. His volatile heart palpations were enough to release the insanity which he kept contained and the screams that hovered just below the surface. White flares were intermittently fired by the Japanese to expose the Marines' position and as each illumination faded, the darkness could be felt creeping up behind them. As they made slow progress up the hill, they were met by a terrifying Banzai charge of the Japanese infantry. Everything appeared to be moving in slow motion as the "Nips" drew even nearer. Waverley's machine gun fire group leader was shot during the chaotic firefight and died on the hill that night. "Fox" Company took a heavy toll that evening and were finally relieved and evacuated from Sugar Loaf. They were totally exhausted and hungry. All they really wanted was a little fresh water, a ration or two, and no more than 20 or 40 hours of sleep. They were afforded the pleasure of having a little food but the sleep was measured only in minutes. After all, curling up with your weapon in a muddy foxhole, with bombs bursting all around, was not considered by Waverley as being conducive to a restful sleep. Waverley lay stretched out in his bed, which he personally carved out of the hillside, on a soft mattress of sludge. He grasped tight his shirt where beneath was worn the gold cross given to him by his aunt a lifetime ago. This battle was later defined as the bloodiest day of fighting in the history of the Striking 6th. As it turned out, this was the bloodiest day of fighting in the history of the Corps.

"Dog" Company had provided "Fox" Company's relief and their continued push saw them earn the distinction of the first company to take and hold Sugar Loaf over night. They were not about to let it fall back into Japanese hands. Reinforcements arrived in the form of two tank battalions It took an additional three days of continuous fighting from the headwaters before they had full possession of Sugar Loaf which guarded the entrance to Shuri and the headquarters of the Japanese Army near Naha. This was the fifth taking of Sugar Loaf and all hoped it to be the last. As they paused for a brief rest and regrouping on May 29th, the rain opened up once again in a torrent, with water pouring down the eroded gullies and washing many of waterlogged Marines out of their dug in positions. The wounded were being recovered with makeshift stretchers using sticks and shirts. Waverley watched as one of his buddies, after having the shirt blown off of his back by a Japanese mortar, was helped off of the battlefield to a nearby aid station. Those that had avoided serious injuries worked diligently to bring their buddies back to a safe area, or at least safer than where they had lain.

"We few, we happy few, we band of brothers."

William Shakespeare
King Henry V

The regiment had been pulled back to the bivouac area for the opportunity to grab a hot meal and coffee. They had been hoping for dry clothes but they couldn't have it all. When Sugar Loaf fell, Waverley's squad managed to capture a Japanese battle flag. The squad proudly posed with it for a picture everyone could take home as a souvenir. In hindsight, Sugar Loaf lacked the physical size to accommodate anything larger than just a rifle company. But it was the bloodiest battle yet in the conflict. Ten days of fighting for the small ridge would shred a series of very good companies from two Marine regiments.

Waverley's Machine Gun Squad displays
the captured Japanese Battle Flag.

It had been a life changing experience attempting to capture that God forsaken hill. Flames had roared from the ground troops into the tiny cave entrances that seconds earlier had been blasted open by grenade toting infantrymen. Apparently igniting some weapons cache, flames and black smoke came thundering from those deep dug in positions. This had been the warm up for what had come later. Sugar Loaf provided the opportunity for the weary Marines to face their enemy close enough for eye contact. Waverley and his squad had managed to set up near a tunnel entrance and were able to fire point blank on those soldiers emerging from the inferno. Under the conditions of this attack, machine gun fire was probably the most merciful action to be taken. At times during the battle, less than 20 yards separated them from the determined Japanese. Combat became limited to hand-to-hand utilizing grenades, flame, satchel charges, and bayonets. The sounds of the flames, weapons fire, and explosions mixed with the smell of rotting corpses left an impression on the mind of Waverley as well as the other brave Marines on the hill. The sight too, of Sugar Loaf, would be forever etched in the memory of all who left the hill, alive. The slope of Sugar Loaf had been littered with bodies of those fallen brave as well as the slaughtered Japs who had been caught out in the open. Driven from their caves by fire, they had been cut down by small arms and sliced quite effectively by waiting bayonets. In order to secure this one hill, the Marines had suffered 2,262 killed and wounded. Those Devil Dogs who reported to the aid station to have their serious wounds dressed had to be forcibly restrained to prevent them from returning to the battle.

Most of the day of May 19th was required to effect the relief of the depleted 29th Marines by the 4th Regiment. Members of the 29th withdrew to defensive positions along the beach fronting Machinato Airfield, where they sought whatever rest and rehabilitation they could muster.

As they were preparing for the advance on Naha, Shuri Castle had fallen and an American flag was hoisted that could be seen throughout the entire southern part of the island. Scuttlebutt spread rapidly and the battle worn troops each got a much closer look at the waving banner. Flying over Shuri Castle was a big bright Stars and Bars of the Confederacy.

> "One of the first acts of the occupying company was to raise the Stars and Bars of the American Civil War Confederacy, which was the company's victory flag at bloody Peleliu. The American Standard was officially raised approximately 25 hours later."
>
> *The Progress Index:*
> *2 June 1945*

The twentieth of May witnessed the 22nd Regiment, in support of the 1st and 4th Divisions, move in position for their advance on Naha. By the 28th of May, the 29th Marines had regrouped and taken a position in support of the 22nd Marines in Naha. This was a monumental change in their tactical fighting moving from mud soaked hillsides to an urban theatre. As the regiments penetrated deep within the city they could see the actual destruction of the war. What once was a thriving city of 64,000 citizens now lay in ruins, a victim of systematic destruction. Everywhere on the grotesque landscape were streets filled with debris, bodies of Japanese soldiers in gutters or hanging limply from shattered windows. Smoke permeated the area as fires still burned from the incineration of the residential areas. Naha was secured and the 6th Division set its sights on their next objective, the Oroku Peninsula.

They had still not taken one of the primary objectives of the Okinawa invasion, the Naha Airfield. Located on the Oroku peninsula, this objective was one of the largest airfields in the region and a must to handle the support aircraft for an invasion of the Japanese mainland. The Japanese were dug in deep protecting the peninsula and the Kokuba River. The infantrymen didn't have a clue as to what they would do next but there was ample room for conjecture when word filtered down to prepare for another amphibious assault.

The 4th Marines took the spearhead landing on shore-to-shore amphibious assault. Landing on the Nishikoku Beaches, they were followed by two tank companies, and the 29th Marines. On the afternoon of June third, the tanks were loaded on their LCTs. The 4th Marines boarded their LCAs in the predawn hours of June fourth near the Machinato Airfield. They moved southward along the coral reef for nearly two hours before reaching their destination on the Oroku Peninsula. Dawn was just breaking with cloudy skies and a new moon. The landing area had been pounded with artillery fire for an hour before the landing craft reached the beach.

The beaches were oozy with mud, sinking the legs of the invasion force to the knees. It was like trying to march through an enormous pig pen. The Marines met with little opposition and secured a 1,200 yard beachhead. The LCAs that had effected the landing had returned to the beach by Machinato Airfield and the 29th Regiment began to embark. Within hours, the final force was in position and the advance to the objective was underway. They had moved inland, about 400 yards, when the familiar rain of Okinawa again began to come down in driving torrents. With it came a warning of a possible typhoon and the landing craft bringing in supplies had to find shelter. The supplies were never able to reach the troops now stalled near Nishikoku Hill.

Naha airfield was the primary target on the island because of the three runways, each a mile or more in length. On the advance toward their goal, progress had slowed as they encountered fields laden with mines. In the thick mud the regiment encountered more mines than at any other place on the island. There were so many mines that the disposal squads were swamped with work which slowed down the movement of the tanks and the rifle companies.

The line had reached, by dusk on the fourth of June, a point only 1,500 yards from the beach. Enemy resistance was heavy and the Marines were forced to halt and dig in. The fighting continued through the night while simultaneously a typhoon struck the island. The rain, wind, and mud made conditions near impossible for those dug in their foxholes. This was like trying to sleep in a bathtub overflowing with water and mud, but sleep was not easily coming for any of them. Winds topped out at 100 knots and the eye passed over the island at approximately 0930 the next morning. This was an eerie repeat of the conditions defeating Genghis Kahn and his army so many years before. The Japanese, entrenched in the coral ridges and caves, continued raining lead on "Fox" Company's position while the Leathernecks were hunkered down, bracing against the torrent of rain and wind.

"I will never forget that I am an American, fighting for freedom, responsible for my actions, and dedicated to the principles which made my country free. I will trust in my God and in the UNITED STATES OF AMERICA."

USMC Code of Conduct
Article VI

The afternoon of June 5th brought continued weapons and mortar fire on the 29th's position. The Marines reinitiated their barrage of fire on every movement they saw on the Japanese line. The air was filled with white flares and nearly a flattened canvas of tracer fire. Smoke filled the air and the whistle of incoming mortar rounds was near deafening. Waverley emptied his gun and yelled to his loader for another belt . . .

Chapter 9
Cheating Death

A Hospital Corpsman, covering the field of battle, came upon the machine gun nest from which Private Traylor had been operating. The edges of the foxhole had been blown away making the lair resemble a shallow soup bowl. The machine gun that had once set sheltered in the hole was no longer in one piece as the tripod stood vacant and the gun had abandoned its operators. One corpse lay silently amongst the debris and a spare set of legs lay pointing in different directions. The body, the parts, and other fragments stood out exhibiting the bright red of blood and internal body organs. Although it appeared that someone had splashed a five gallon bucket of red barn paint over the remains. He recognized the scene, he had seen so many times, where the foxhole had taken a direct mortar hit and that the two men inside did not survive. As the front line moved inland, cleanup began. Vehicles were being liberated from their muddy prisons, workable hardware was being salvaged, and bodies were being collected and identified for evacuation to the beach. As Waverley's body was being lifted onto the liter, a fellow Marine noted that he was breathing, really shallow, but he was breathing. With the number of apparently open wounds and the amount of blood covering his torso, they didn't give him much hope for survival but they quickly called for a Corpsman.

He remained unconscious while the Corpsman ripped away part of his blood soaked uniform to perform a quick evaluation in order to bandage the wounds to control the bleeding. The doc examined him from head to toe and could not locate one single open wound. It was obvious that the foxhole had indeed taken a direct mortar hit but apparently all of the blood and body parts covering Private Traylor belonged to his fellow Leatherneck who had taken the blow directly.

Traylor was immediately moved to the beach, still unconscious, and was tagged for immediate evacuation. The area was covered with wounded Marines locked in a battle with unmanageable agony with more coming in each hour by exhausted stretcher bearers. A small strip had been cleared on the beach allowing the Marine Observation aircraft to land. One was called in to pick up Private Traylor and he was quickly ferried to the 82nd Field Hospital in the rear where he was transferred to the Causality Battalion. The Piper Cub "Grasshopper" bounced around on takeoff, and likewise on landing, but he was delivered safely to the doctors and staff, set up in a previously cleared cave.

The doctors and Corpsmen at the field hospital were very concerned about the condition of the private as he had remained unconscious. They had cleaned him up and found a few minor abrasions and burns. Also found were two puncture wounds on his chest and abdomen. These had been caused by bone fragments expelled when the mortar shell had exploded point blank on his buddy.

On the third day Waverley regained consciousness but was unsure of where he was, who he was, or what had happened. He complained of a constant and severe headache with tingling in both legs and arms. He also suffered with blurred vision and was intermittently spitting up mucus containing blood. He had been stabilized and evacuated to the hospital ship Relief (AH-1).

During the transport south, the doctors and nurses worked diligently on the wounded Marines who were being evacuated. Test were conducted aboard the USS Relief and a report made ready for Waverley's transfer to the U. S. Fleet Hospital 111 located on Guam.

> "Patient was injured by a concussion on 5 June from a nearby explosion of a mortar shell. He was unconscious for two days and continues to be mentally confused. He now complains of a headache, backache, and cramping pain in both legs. Patient spitting up blood after the injury. X-rays of chest taken and showed negative. (Report not enclosed)."
>
> Medical History
82nd Field Hospital

Waverley continued to suffer with severe headaches and a significant hearing impairment. He remained confused for an additional three days. The weakness in his body was unrelenting and tremulous. His back and legs continued to ache around the clock. It was impossible to get any sleep and this deprivation was causing a number of additional symptoms. There were a large number of Marines on the ship whose injuries were not immediately apparent. These were the ones whose flesh was not torn but whose souls were frayed and tattered.

On the 19th of June, the USS Relief arrived at the Casualty Battalion, Transient Center, U. S. Hospital, Guam. Upon arrival, an examination was conducted and a preliminary diagnosis concluded that Private Traylor suffered from an Atmospheric Cerebral Blast Concussion. Thousands of wounded Marines have been pouring in from that "Hell Hole" called Okinawa. The hospital was filled with a wide variety of injuries and ailments. Without substantial physical injuries, he was assigned to the psychiatric ward. He witnessed Marines who constantly babbled to the air in front of them and those curled tightly against the wall, never speaking a word. Most of the men there were just tired; tired to a point far beyond what a reasonable man would consider total exhaustion.

Although he was treated as an exhaustion case, there was never even a consideration that such a close blast could possibly have caused any brain injury. Because of the extreme number of cases, a conclusion of battle fatigue would never be questioned.

His doctors were playing the odds when they diagnosed his circumstance, looking into his past for a pre-existing condition. His records indicated he had a history of trouble with back and leg pain in childhood and had worn a brace for several years. To the overworked doctors, this was a good indication that his pains may have come about from prior diagnoses. He was otherwise determined to be a well developed, well nourished, white male age 23, who does not appear acutely ill. The General physical examination is negative. With no evidence of there being anything physically wrong, he was referred for a Neurology consultation. It was a real discredit to the medical establishment when they declared that he had no internal injuries based on a chest x-ray and his problems had to be mental because a mortar blast within feet could not possibly cause injury the brain.

Once a determination had been made that his injuries were not life threatening and the patient was fully ambulatory, freedom on the base was granted. On his very first trip to the base exchange, Waverley found and purchased a pair of oriental handkerchiefs. These were the perfect little souvenirs to send home to Martha. He mingled with other ambulatory patients but conversed with them very little. He really wanted to just be left alone. It appeared that battle exhaustion and battlefield enuresis were both very common ailments among the evacuated combatants of Pacific campaigns.

By the 25th of June, Waverley's Neurological test had been completed. They reported that all of his reflexes were equal and active but a general impairment of the sensation of the left leg was still a hindrance. An x-ray of the lumbo-sacral spine was ordered with negative results.

> "27 June 1945—Fleet Hospital #111
>
> Please transfer this man to N-P ward 9-B for study and treatment. I strongly suspect hysterical features."
>
> Dr. D. C. Brown
Lieutenant Commander
USNR

Within two days, the clinic transfer had taken place along with a complete summary of his injuries and the history leading up to the injury.

> "This man was a machine gunner under intensive action for three days. A near miss by a mortar shell apparently produced shock for a passing Corpsman had taken him for dead. He was confused for three days, was weak, and tremulous but not panicky. He suffered from severe headaches for two weeks with gradual defervesence but his back and legs have continued to ache and fall asleep. He has Varicocele for several years. This caused him to be classified as 4F for 2 years. There is no disturbance in the progression of ideas or orientation or grasp of time relations.
>
> It is felt that the long standing headaches marked symptoms from a very moderate Varicocele, the Anesthesia of stocking type, justifies the change of diagnosis."
>
> C. Brown
Lt. Cmdr (MC) USNR

This was the very beginning of a poorly handled, misdiagnosed case of a brave and honorable veteran injured in one of the world's greatest atrocities. With obvious signs of internal injuries such as spitting up blood, a negative chest x-ray report supposedly provided proof of no such internal or brain injury. It was unimaginable for doctors to believe that laying within feet of an exploding mortar shell and remaining unconscious for two days would not be the cause for headaches or hearing loss but could in fact be caused by a minor case of varicose veins, identified when he was inducted. His final diagnoses was Psychoneurosis Hysteria, a clinical term which defies a sensible definition or explanation. This diagnosis was used extensively in post combat cases of battle fatigue or shell shock. With the high number of these cases being processed, it was common place for

Marines suffering with brain injuries to be classified as mental cases.

Meanwhile, a letter had been received by Martha notifying her of her husband's injury.

> "My dear Mrs. Traylor:
>
> A brief report has just been received that your husband, Private Waverley L. Traylor, Jr., USMC, sustained a concussion in action against the enemy on 5 June, 1945 at Okinawa Island, Ryukyu Islands.
>
> Your anxiety is realized, and you may be sure that any additional details or information received will be forwarded to you at the earliest possible moment. Please notify this office of any change in your address.
>
> Sincerely Yours,"
>
> D. Routh
Lieutenant Colonel
U. S. Marine Corps

The mismanagement continued, for the day after this letter was sent another was generated from the US Fleet Hospital, via San Francisco, CA. This letter was never received by Mrs. Traylor but a copy was placed in Private Traylor's permanent service record.

> "Dear Mrs. Trazler:
>
> I wish to inform you that your husband, Private Wareby Trazler, 978526, U. S. Marine Corps Reserve, who was wounded on 5 May 1945, is making good progress. His wound consists of a blast concussion.

His present condition is good. Please be assured that he is receiving the best possible medical care at this hospital."

C. E. Prewitt
Chief Pharmacist USN
Casualty Report Officer

The efficiency of the Naval Hospital administrative department ensured that the letter was addressed to the wrong person, at the wrong address, in the wrong state. Of course it was the difficulties within the Postal Service that would make sure this letter would have difficulty being properly delivered. Based on the content of the letter, it was fortunate that Martha never had a chance to read how Waverley's name had been butchered. This would have really set off her worry alarm as to how accurate such a report could be.

"Mrs. Martha E. Trazler
711 Hamilton & Colonial Heights
Petersburg, New Hampshire"
Address of letter never received.

C. E. Prewitt
Chief Pharmacist USN
Casualty Report Officer

Waverley was now awaiting a transport back to the States. He was improving slightly and had more freedom on the base at Guam. A lot of the indigenous personnel had discovered the souvenir trade and were making a fortune from the Marines who transited through the area. Most of these Americans were on their way back to the States and therefore were perfect marks for the natives' business. Waverley became acquainted with one particular family and parlayed with them for a teak wood sword. The sword was very unique and short enough to be crammed in with what personal things he packed in his duffle bag. It was a heavy piece and a perfect replica of an ancient Melanesian War Club. This club was now the closest thing he had to reality. Back at the hospital, nothing appeared to be based in the here and now. Reality had only become a state of mind.

His treatment on Guam continued as did his increasingly frequent headaches. The doctors treated these with increasing amounts of pentothal. Rather than continue their effort to find the cause of his afflictions, they noted that he was unfit for continued duty in a forward unit and recommended he be evacuated to a naval hospital in the continental United States for further observation, treatment, and disposition. His treatment would probably have been more effective if they had given him two aspirin and sent him back to the front, but understandably, he preferred to be homeward bound. As he waited for his transfer orders, he had time to reflect on what had happened to him. He became more aware of his situation and realized now how war can drive you to release your hidden feelings.

He was received on board the USS Newberry (APA-158) for transportation to a U.S. Naval Hospital. The ship left Guam the next day, Friday July the 13th. The sailing was fairly smooth that first day and the evening was uneventful. When the wounded warriors were awakened the next morning they discovered that Friday, 13 July was playing on the main stage all over again. It seems they had crossed the international date line during the night.

CHAPTER 10
Recovery

On the 27th of July, the wounded Marines from Okinawa arrived at the Navy Dry Dock at Hunters Point, San Francisco, California aboard the evacuation ship USS Newberry. They were a motley looking bunch as they dragged themselves and their bags down the gangplank and onto the pier. A long line of ambulances and busses were waiting and drove onto the pier to gather up their broken bodies and spirits. A few of the passengers were carried from the ship on litters to the waiting ambulances while many more, with less serious injuries, were ambulatory and proceeded to the waiting busses. The remainder suffered from Battle Fatigue, Shell Shock, Guilt Complex, and even a few syndromes which at that time had no names. Then there were those suffering from all of the above and the Navy Department had not figured out what they were going to do with them. These were the majority and would end up living their lives without treatment. These were also the true victims of man's inhumanity to man, often referred to as "war."

> "Virginia War Casualties: Traylor, Waverley Lahmeyer Jr. Pvt USMC, Wife Mrs. Martha E. Traylor, Petersburg."
>
> *Richmond News Leader*
> *6 August 1945*

Waverley was moved from Hunters Point, to the U. S. Naval Regional Hospital in San Francisco. There they began testing and diagnosing all over again. They couldn't seem to get away from the ridiculous diagnosis which was fabricated in Guam. This diagnosis was reached partly because of Waverley's statement that shortly after his brother Allen was born, his mother had just reached her breaking point and had a genuine full-bore hissy fit. Being unfamiliar with such technical southern medical terms, the navy doctors classified her episode as a "nervous breakdown." This was obviously another injustice in the making and the record was never cleared of this grievous error.

Admitted to the hospital, Waverley still complained of headaches, backache, and severe cramping in his legs. These symptoms, like those of many other infantrymen, persisted despite the insistence that there was no physical cause for these pains. This, however, did not lessen the fact that these symptoms were very real and caused much discomfort to the afflicted combatants. Although the fleet hospital in Guam found no organic cause for his symptoms, he was evacuated to the mainland because of his persistence of these complaints.

The results from the mental examination at this hospital generated the "Psychoneurosis Hysteria" diagnosis and revealed a tense, tremulous, and shy individual. This really wasn't over the hill for an individual who had just gone through the stressful events on Okinawa. The psychologists believed these symptoms represented a method of escape from an environment inimical to his personality. Although it was a fact that he did want out of that environment, he had not consciously attempted to escape. The truth be told, he was *blown* out of the environment he disliked so much. He had decided long ago that he would stick to his commitment and fight to protect his family, his country, and his honor. This he did even while many around him were walking off of the battlefield and declaring that they just could not handle it anymore. His frustration lay in the fact that the military doctors had decided to lump him into that category.

The second week in August saw an end to the mental poking and prodding at the San Francisco facility. The fix was in and he was being transferred to Casualty Company, Marine Barracks, Naval Shipyard, Charleston, South Carolina. Orders from Charleston, however, had already been cut for a temporary assignment at the U. S. Naval Hospital in Dublin, Georgia. This was to be his next battleground and, hopefully, his last.

The doctors at the hospital in Dublin subjected him to the same battery of exams and interviews he had previously undergone on the west coast plus a new treatment where they attached electrodes to his body, generating a shock each time they didn't like the answer they heard. This was medical torture in its finest sense. The proof of a mental condition was the doctors insistence that the symptoms had abated following psychotherapy. This torturous procedure found its basis in the fact that following sufficient treatment, the patient would no longer complain of his persistent symptoms and would say whatever was necessary to make the shocks stop. A medical board was to be convened to interview Private Traylor but he remained hospitalized until such time.

Meanwhile, Waverley had written Martha of his assignment in Dublin. Leaving Linda with her grandmother, Martha caught the next bus to Dublin to see her wounded husband. Even before finding a place to stay, she paid him a visit at the hospital. The changes he had undergone were shocking both in appearance and in attitude. Waverley saw in her face the confusion as she stared into his eyes. It was as if she was staring into a strangers eyes. Martha learned from him that he would have a hearing in a few days to decide his fate in the Marine Corps. Following the hearing, he would most likely be granted leave while the board pondered his fate. This was good news for the couple but the atmosphere surrounding them was thick with apprehension and uncertainty. She immediately wrote a card home to his brother telling him of the intelligence she had gathered.

> "Am having a swell time and getting a nice rest. The way it looks now Waverley might come home with me for a few days. Love, Martha"
>
> Post Card Home to brother-in-law
25 August 1945

Waverley's Uncle Edward drove up from Decatur to visit with his nephew and arranged for Martha to have a place to stay, covering all expenses. This had been an unexpected godsend but Uncle Ed always had a habit of showing up at the right time in the right place.

The first Medical Board met and took Waverley through the ringer. It was a wonder he did not have a breakdown being forced to relive his last weeks on the island. He did, however, hold his composure and finished strongly as he felt any Marine should do. When the "Inquisition" was finished, the board concluded that "This patient warrants rehabilitation leave. He has received maximum benefits from hospitalization at this time. Leave will be of therapeutic value." Leave for Waverley would also be advantageous to the government. With 20 days leave on the books, this move would preclude the government from providing financial compensation for these days upon discharge. "He is to begin 20 days of leave on the first of September." For this decision, if for no other reason, he was grateful. He was going home.

It must have been like an unimaginable dream as the couple stepped off the bus and had their first glimpse of his parents waiting at the bus terminal to meet them. There were hugs enough to go around twice and then some. Everyone was talking, no one was listening, and then another round of hugs, on the house. His bag, and Martha's, were loaded into the automobile and they all took their seats. Mom and Dad were in front, with Waverley and Martha in back. Little Linda, of course, was clinging to Daddy with a headlock that was surely going to take a locksmith to remove.

The party that ensued was small and held at his own home. There were signs "Welcome Home," balloons, and bright colored ribbons tied around the porch columns, trees, and even the bird bath. Festivities went on into the night as the "Welcome Home Hero" party finally wore itself down. Waverley had given quite a convincing performance reflective of his limited acting career. He actually was having no fun and silently wished everyone would leave. He loosened his tie and graciously thanked everyone for coming as they paraded out the front door. Finally he and the family were alone, he tiredly slumped onto the couch and quickly drifted off to sleep. He fell into such a deep slumber that the smell of morning coffee and the fresh bacon and eggs passed over without stirring him.

He was awakened in the afternoon and immediately changed to much more comfortable attire. As he unpacked his bag, removing the oriental kimonos he had purchased in the hospital exchange on Guam, he pulled out a wooden sword. Waving it around in the air, his thoughts wandered back to his pals who had been evacuated with him and wondered what they might be doing now. The sword was laid softly on the dresser and he carried the kimonos to the other room to show Martha. She fell in love with the gift but was even more pleased with the smile pasted on Waverley's face. It had been so long since she had seen his smile, and for it, she had waited so long. Grabbing the gift from his arm, she ran into the bedroom to try on her souvenir. She called on Waverley to come and try on his, but the only response she received was "later." When she came out modeling the robe, he was sitting in the big chair in the Living Room and seemed uninterested in talking or even listening to the radio. He seemed to be completely self absorbed when Linda bounded into the room and climbed up into her Daddy's lap. This was a comfort but he had no interest in playing games. Just holding her was satisfying for him but not for little Linda. She finally climbed back down and meandered back into her room to hide amongst her toys.

Martha had been waiting for this day for a very long time and she had so many plans as to what they would do. His condition, however, was not conducive to these plans. The couple now silently decided that it might be better to lay those plans aside and let the days pass as they may. Severe headaches would plague him each morning when he would awake from a less than restful sleep. The tossing and turning combined with his incoherent speech were good indicators of not so pleasant dreams. The sheets on the bed needed changing each morning as they would become soaked from his night sweats. It was apparent that his assimilation back into civilian life was not going to be easy. He was slowly coming a little out of his shell. Opening the newspaper, he read the headlines where a formal surrender ceremony was performed in Tokyo Bay, Japan, aboard the battleship *USS Missouri*. America had brought the Japanese empire to its knees. His thoughts drifted back to the killing fields on Okinawa and his buddy who was blasted directly into the hereafter, literally from right under his nose. This depressed him even more, and he had no interest in celebrating Victory in Japan (VJ) day. After all, there was no celebrating for those left behind on the island. And strangely enough, he still remembered to include the War Dog he had found in his daily prayers.

His 20 days leave at home had not gone as well as Martha had anticipated and surely not how Waverley had wanted. He was not able to get the rest that the doctors had hoped for and would become agitated by the slightest little comment. Waverley noticed how Martha seemed to wander away from the happy homecoming as if confused about what was happening. She never expressed her thoughts but they were so very obvious to the man that had once loved her so dearly.

He uneasily made it through his leave time and returned to the Naval Hospital in Dublin on September twentieth. The hospital placed him in the records office to keep him busy while he awaited his medical review board. His personnel record was noted that he was making a good adjustment in his job and his previous symptoms had lessened.

The preliminary report summary submitted to the medical review board indicated that ". . . this 24 year old private participated in the Okinawa campaign, was admitted to this hospital with a diagnosis of 'Psychoneurosis Hysteria', with symptoms of headaches, back aches, cramping pains in both legs, which developed following a close explosion of a mortar shell.

Upon physical investigation it was determined that this patient was knocked unconscious by a close proximity explosion of a mortar shell, which killed his buddy. He spit up blood at that time but chest x-rays were negative. He also complained of headaches, back aches, and cramping pains in both legs. A stocking type anesthesia was present at that time. X-rays of his spine were reported as negative. Therapy had failed to improve his condition. Since he has been at this hospital, he has slept better, his headaches less frequent, and backache and legs aches less severe, and anesthesia of limbs has disappeared under shock therapy. Family history indicated his mother and father are living and well. Mother was nervous and once suffered from postpartum depression. One brother is living and well with no nervousness."

"This patients physical history shows he was unusually excitable, irritable, and timid. This was not a good mixture and he did not like meeting people who had claimed more success in their lives. He bit his nails only occasionally and had no history of temper outburst. Started school at six and graduated from high school at 18 after repeating several subjects (mainly foreign languages) which necessitated his repeating one year. His industrial history started while still in school, working with his father in construction work, which he continued one year after graduation. He then worked with DuPont as a textile machine operator and was transferred to the lab as a chemist assistant working in rayon research. Worked there two years before entering service. His past medical history is normal except as a child (about six) when he had symptoms of leg pains. He was treated by an orthopedist by a back brace which he wore for two years and his symptoms disappeared permanently. Social adjustment in the service has been poor with few friends. Patient disliked meeting new friends for fear of losing them in battle. He had no civilian or military altercation with authorities and no nomadic tendencies. Service record has been good and he has had no disciplinary actions.

A recent mental examination indicates a strong sense of inferiority, tepidness, and a fear of new situations. The patient appears friendly, cooperative, and sincere. Previous evidence of hysteria is no longer present but a return to duty may precipitate new symptoms. The physical examination by systems is essentially negative."

On the 17th of October, Waverley appeared before a medical review board with the diagnosis of "Psychoneurosis Hysteria." Somehow, the board determined his disability was not the result of his own misconduct and was *not incurred in line of duty*. His condition existed prior to enlistment but may have been aggravated by his service. They had alluded to the fact that by his own admission, he had an acute anxiety episode in 1942. What the record failed to show was that this episode occurred as he waited alone in the expectant father's waiting room for the birth of his first child. Presently he is unfit for further duty resulting from what is probably a permanent condition. It was recommended he be discharged from the U.S. Marine Corps Reserve. The final report from the medical board was released on 18 October 1945.

> "This 24 year old patient with 7 months overseas duty and participation in the invasion of Okinawa was admitted with the diagnosis of Psychoneurosis Hysteria complaining of headaches, backache and cramping leg pains.
>
> He has always been timid, shy, passive, easily excited, and felt inferior to other children because of his poor health. He complained frequently of pains in his legs which disappeared when he wore a back brace. In the service

he made a borderline adjustment, but states that his work 'fell to pieces' under observation. On June 5, 1945 he was rendered unconscious by a nearby shell blast, following which he complained of many somatic pains for which no organic cause could be found. He had a stocking type anesthesia which was removed by therapeutic suggestion, but he was evacuated for persistence of his other complaints.

Mental examination in this hospital reveals a tense, tremulous, apprehensive, passive, shy individual who was occupied by many somatic complaints. It is felt that these symptoms represent a method of escape from an environment inimical to his personality. Following psychotherapy his symptoms have abated, but it is felt that further retention in the service will aggravate his condition. He has received maximum benefits from hospitalization. The admission diagnosis is hereby retained. Physical, neurological and laboratory examinations were essentially negative. No disciplinary action is pending in this case.

It is the opinion of the board that this man is not likely to become a menace to himself or others and that he is not likely to become a public charge."

J. J. Eberhart, Commander MC, USNR (senior board member)
L. E. Villant, Lt Commander MC, USNR
M. N. Retridge, Lt junior grade, MC, USNR

Additional misnomers crept into the record from the medical board. The report had stated that by his own admission, his work fell to pieces under observation. What the report failed to consider was that this was a post injury condition. Had this been true in his initial training, he would have washed out of boot camp or at the very least, failed to qualify as a sharpshooter. It was further noted in his record that he was informed of the board's findings and indicated that he did not desire to submit a statement in rebuttal. Now, being a draftee, who in their right mind would want to rebut that decision. The board recommended Private Traylor be discharged from the U.S. Marine Corps reserve. He was immediately transferred to the Marine Barracks at the Navy Yard in Charleston South Carolina to be discharged from the USMCR.

As has always been typical of military service, it takes forever for anything to happen. Waverley sat at the Marine Barracks in Charleston through October, Thanksgiving, Christmas, and New Years. He was finally separated on the 5th of January 1946. His discharge was Honorable and his designation was officially listed as Designated with Physical disability (psychoneurosis hysteria). He was issued a USMC ID card certifying satisfactory service, a discharge by reason of report of medical review for disability, and awarded a total of 43 points for his service. Upon discharge, Waverley was awarded a ten percent disability for his injuries but the payments stopped within the year and all efforts to get the payments reinstated were futile.

PART III
The Survivor

"You say you understand me, but if you do you must be able to hear the screams of days gone by.

You say you understand me but if you do you need to let my story touch your heart in a way that you can feel the pain I feel, see what I have seen, hear what I have heard.

Live with what I went through, and then—and only then—will you understand me."

Anonymous
Combat Survivor

Chapter 11
Rebuilding a Life

Returning home after the war was one gigantic shock to Waverley's system. Reveille no longer played at 5am, standing in line wasn't a requirement to secure a meal, and there was quiet at night which made it very difficult to sleep. The feeling of an enemy out there with a bullet engraved with his name was still an ever present thought. Try as hard as he might, stepping away from the war was not as easy a task as he had hoped. The thundering of the guns and screams of the wounded continued to invade all aspects of Waverley's life day and night. Trying to take a nice quiet walk could be interrupted by a car backfire which would send him head first into the nearest ditch. A simple afternoon nap could immediately transport him back to the killing fields where the mud and the stench were overwhelming to the senses.

He never understood just how much Martha was trying to comfort him and keep his mind in the here and now. Nothing within her power though, could prevent his mind from reliving the events he left behind on that North Pacific island. Just as progress was being made, something would occur to set him back. Shortly after his discharge a letter was received in the mail which undid all of the families progress and set him back to where he never had wanted to be.

"To you who answered the call of your country and served in its Armed Forces to bring about the total defeat of the enemy, I extend the heartfelt thanks of a grateful Nation. As one of the Nation's finest, you undertook the most severe task one can be called upon to perform. Because you demonstrated the fortitude, resourcefulness and calm judgment necessary to carry out that task, we now look to you for leadership and example in further exalting our country in peace."

President Harry Truman
1946

Waverley learned that while he was on the ship, waiting to be landed on the island, Martha had been going out to concerts and dances at the high school and swinging to the big band music. This really angered him but he couldn't comprehend why. It was okay for her to enjoy herself, but to realize such enjoyment while he was on his way into battle; it just wasn't fair. But then again, who ever said war was fair; to either those who fought it or those who remained back home.

He remained plagued by nightmares, which prevented him from obtaining a good rest. He would wake up in the mornings exhausted from the battle he refought the night before. Headaches dominated his waking moments and the daily stress of dying, felt during the intense fighting in the war, had turned into a daily stress of living. He pondered what he wanted to do with his life now and how his family was to be supported. His younger brother Allen was in his last year of high school and had focused on college and maybe a career at Dupont to follow in his brother's dreams. College was not, however, in his future since finances were not readily available to further his education. He urged Waverley to return to his previous position in the lab and continue with his pre-war aspirations.

Waverley's concern was the residual effects of the war that plagued him daily. Would he ever be rested enough to work in the lab? Would the constant headaches prevent him from concentrating on his job? These were unknowns which he didn't want to face. He was so tired of having to face the enemy, head on. It was time for him to take cover, any way he could. He tried to lose himself by digging deep into his Christian ethics and working to serve others through the church. He felt that he had done his hitch in Hell, and survived. It was time to serve the Lord and his fellow man.

> "How unfriendly is war to domestic happiness."
>
> *General Nathanael Greene*
> *Continental Army*
> *December 1780*

Waverley's father remained in the contracting business specializing in painting and wallpapering. His health, however, was not good and the long years of smoking, paint fumes, and lead exposure had taken its toll. To stay away from a boss looking over his shoulders all day, Waverley offered to help his father and join him in his contract work. This decision had upset his brother but young Allen never knew, or even suspected, the true reason for his abandonment of his Dupont position. It was likely he could never really understand.

It felt right returning to work with his father even though the paycheck was no longer steady. Compensation for their jobs were collected when the work was completed and his share helped to pay the medical bills for his dad. He also had problems of his own, but having them treated could always wait. He placed the well being of others above his own, always. He was no longer "Junior" as he had been before the war, nor did he refer to himself as "Wave" as he did during the war. He was now living his life as "Waverley" and trying his hardest to put everything else behind him. Even at the most inopportune times, the smell and taste of the battlefield, with the gunpowder and rotting corpses, would return and ruin a meal, an afternoon, or an evening. Whenever this occurred he would become violently ill but unable to explain to anyone why. Great explosions of temper would erupt with no apparent cause and often focused on hurting Martha emotionally as though she was at fault for all his misery. Linda too would feel the brunt of these episodes in the form of unreasonable punishments or disappearance of her favorite toys. Fortunately, these episodes would not last very long. If they could place themselves out of the direct line of fire, the girls could wait out the paroxysm. Emotionally though, the pain would last a lifetime.

The spring of each year was again a busy time for the Traylor family and this meant Waverley too. April showers brought the flowers, and in the Traylor household this meant work for everyone. The daffodils blooming on the farm would be ready for harvesting and Waverley would spend several afternoons with his dad picking these flowering bulbs and trucking them into town. But before this could happen, the fields had to again be cleared of the invading grasses and Waverley Jr. had been conscripted to share in this effort. Tired of the backbreaking cutting done by sickle, this year the Senior Traylor bought a World War II surplus flame thrower. This way, with a little pressurized gasoline, he could clear those fields quickly and efficiently without having to utilize his son's valuable time. This was not a healthy chore for young Waverley's psyche; he already had enough stress in his new life.

Waverley's slow return to civilian life was a longer road then he had ever imagined, with plenty of twists, turns, and potholes. He loved his family very much and he would do whatever necessary to make them happy. For Linda's fifth birthday there was a very special present waiting. She was led into the back yard and there stood a beautiful white and brown pony with a giant Red Ribbon attached. There was no way a five-year-old could have been made any happier. The pony's name was Mickey and his previous occupation had been pulling an ice cream cart through the streets of downtown Petersburg. This was so typical of Dad. When he could afford to give his child what she wanted, he would surely do so. But he was just as quick to take the gift away.

He would sometimes show his temper when Linda would misbehave. Maybe a hand to the butt or banishment to a corner, but this was being a father. He had been progressing into tantrums which were unpredictable and lacked apparent cause. During this same time frame he started becoming very controlling and protective of his family. With these unexplainable outbursts, he would exhibit a type of guilt which appeared very bizarre. He seemed to blame himself, yet he would take out his anger on the women in the family, or at least their possessions.

Shortly after Linda celebrated her fifth birthday, Martha announced to the family that she was pregnant once again. Martha was glowing, Linda was all ready for a baby sister, but Waverley, although feigning joy, was worried about the extra expenses. The couple also talked about their new living arrangements because the small house they owned was not sufficient for an expanding family. He had discussed the matter with his parents and his mother offered him a plot of land on the country farm if they wanted to build a house. The prospect of this was exciting to the young couple and Waverley began spending his evenings drawing plans for this dream home. Finally the industrial arts training from high school was paying off. When it became time for a break, the family would take a trip, all the way across the street, to watch this new device they called television. It was a large cabinet radio with a screen at the top, six inches round, on which you could watch the performers as you heard them. First they made picture movies with sound and now they had radio sound with pictures. Technology was just growing all too rapidly.

During the spring, Waverley had been having trouble with his left foot and the pain became excruciating. He had become unable to climb ladders and could barely work considering that this placed him on his feet all day. But no work meant no income and Martha was in no condition to work. After already having been out of work for nearly a week, the pain grew to such an intensity that he was now even unable to drive. He felt that he could not handle not working so the time had come to break down and visit his doctor. Since Martha did not drive, he convinced his brother to drive him to the doctor's office. Now Allen was not of that age where he willingly did favors for other people but he did love his big brother, so for him he would make this exception. Following a substantial period of time in the waiting room, Waverley was called in and examined. The nurse took a little blood from his arm and the doctor withdrew some fluid from his big toe. Not being one to complain about pain he normally handled procedures like this very well, but that stick in the toe really hurt. He wondered at this point what was worse, the ailment or the treatment. The doctor finally had the results for him and announced that he was suffering from a form of gout. This was caused by a buildup of uric acid in the blood and caused joints on the lower extremities to become crystallized and very painful. Best advice, watch your diet and it should ease up in a couple of weeks. This, at least, provided Waverley with the information he needed to live with—get back to work and to hell with the pain.

The year sped by and the pain from the gout eased up. He was able to return to a full work schedule and return his pay back up to a nearly acceptable level. This was extremely important since baby number two was getting close to showing his rounded little head. July sweltered in and the big day finally arrived. Martha was rushed to the hospital and Waverley woke up his parents at home to care for little Linda. He rushed back to the hospital only to be told to have a seat and wait, and wait, and wait. This was the first time in years that he had felt like he was back in the Corps. Hurry up and wait, the famed military motto. The nurse came into the waiting room about 4 am to tell Mr. Traylor that he was the father of a 7 pound 8 once baby boy. She didn't have to wake him up because who could sleep under the circumstances. The hospital staff was concerned, though, that they may have to replace the carpets. For the first time in forever, there was a genuine smile on his exhausted face. A boy!

He got his first glance of his new son while standing in the hallway, looking through a huge glass window. The nurse held the boy up so Waverley could get a better look and he placed his arm around Martha as they both stood there admiring their contribution to the world. He looked so tiny all bundled in a soft blue blanket with a small tuft of light blond hair protruding skyward from the very top of his tiny head. In due time, Little Waverley followed his parents home from the hospital and took up residence in their small two bedroom home in Colonial Heights. An old family basinet had been set up in the master bedroom and a family hand-me-down rocking chair was available in the living area. This was the same rocker that had lulled Martha and all of her older sisters to sleep.

Waverley Jr. proudly presents his new son to the world.

Waverley also broke down and bought a television for the family. This gave Martha and himself something to watch for entertainment while rocking the baby. The RCA set didn't have a built in radio and only a ten inch screen, but it was capable of picking up the one television channel available in the area. Entertainment was limited.

Waverley had managed to purchase a book from the Government Printing Office in 1949. The "History of the 6th Marine Division" had just been published and he wanted to be one of the first with a copy. His unwillingness, or perhaps his inability, to talk with his family about the war led the girls to think that he wanted to forget about his time in the Pacific. His constant reading and viewing the pictures in this book, however, offered an entirely different conclusion. He may not have wanted to discuss the war with the women but they had their role in the family to fill. He now had a son and with him he would be able to share his buried memories. Becoming aware of that fact, Waverley spent two days searching the house for a mystery box. What was in the box, he never shared with his girls, stating that ". . . it was none of their business." The box was not in the house so an inordinate amount of time was spent at his parents' home searching all of his old secret hiding places. The box was never found and the contents had apparently vanished from the face of the Earth.

Although Linda had really wanted a baby sister, a brother was the next best thing. She did have the opportunity to help care for him when they stayed with their grandmother. The time the children spent with their grandmother was becoming increasingly longer and more often, since Waverley and Martha were spending nearly every evening, and all weekends, in the country working on constructing their house.

One of the first procurements on their agenda was the purchase of a surplus World War II weapons carrier. With a ten cylinder engine and six wheel drive, this vehicle could deliver whatever task was necessary. They used this vehicle to take down and clear trees. On the weekends, brother Allen would help as they pushed over trees and hauled them into a log pile for burning. What couldn't be pushed down by the "Green Monster" would be cut and the stump ripped from the ground by a squad of chains attached to the weapons carrier and working in unison with one another.

To facilitate a more rapid construction undertaking, Waverley and Martha discussed setting up a camper in the country to spend the weekends on site. Allen had come across a deal for a 30 foot camping trailer at a good price. The only real downside was the fact that the trailer was in Arlington. Martha got to sit out a weekend and stay home with the children while the Traylor boys took off on the "Green Monster," which by now had more than earned its name. They struck out for the wide open spaces of urban Washington D. C. and gathered many looks on the highway north as they trucked up the pavement in their six wheel drive convertible. It was amazing that clear skies traveled with them the whole way and for that very fact, they were thankful.

Upon arrival at their destination they spotted the trailer sitting in the yard and it didn't appear to be in too bad of condition for a 1932 model. The cabin on wheels had two doors and all of five windows. The outer skin was brown canvas with surprisingly no leaks that were obvious. It was outfitted with two beds, a table, and a small kitchenette which would serve the purpose for weekend stays. The problem though, and there always seems to be a problem, was the smell. The boys had difficulty discerning whether a skunk had crawled in there for the night, or whether it had died and was still there. The price was right, however, and Waverley figured that Martha could scrub the dwelling to remove the smell, she was good at those type of chores.

The return trip was uneventful save for a minor incident with a flat tire just outside of Fredericksburg. Fortunately the trailer tire only lost the air from one side which made its repair an easy task. They were able to jack up the trailer and remove the tire. Then by disconnecting it from the engine (The Green Monster), they were able to take the tire into town for repair. They had the repaired tire back on the trailer within a matter of only three hours and they were once again cruising down the highway. This did put them home late but they still hauled the trailer out to the site and drove Waverley's car back into town. Job done, mission accomplished, and not once did the creek rise.

With the camper in place, Waverley made arrangements for temporary power from the electric company and built a comfy little outhouse directly over the latrine he had dug. Another valuable educational gift from the Marine Corps. During their preparation for construction, they had come across a number of snakes, primarily Water Moccasins and Copperheads. Waverley purchased a World War II vintage 22-caliber training rifle for protection but never once fired the weapon. He was no longer comfortable with a weapon in his hands. They were now set to begin, but the first job was one that they themselves could not accomplish. They hired a gentleman with a backhoe to dig the full basement and the septic tank hollow. The excavation turned up unexpected results indicating that the ground below this property was just about pure red clay. This made the digging difficult and the working environment a mess of enormous proportions. The digging also uncovered a treasure trove of Indian arrowheads and other artifacts. Waverley collected all he could find and washed them off for later use.

They continued construction on the house through the winter. At first it appeared that progress was not forthcoming at an acceptable pace but slowly the foundation was laid and the cinderblock walls of the basement were in place. As the wooden supports and frames went up, the building began to really take shape. When summer rolled around, the house began to look like a house. When the weather was good they would bring Linda with them to the worksite so that she had an opportunity to play in the country with the bees, the poison ivy, and the mosquitoes. Summer passed, the house progressed, and the time came for Linda to begin her long journey through the state's education system. She had spent the entire summer anticipating her first day of school but as the big day approached, she became a bit more apprehensive. Dressing Linda in her prettiest summer dress, Martha walked her daughter the two blocks to Flora Hill

Elementary School and said her goodbyes at the door. Linda was on her own.

Waverley had been using the Richmond Veteran Administration Hospital for treatment of a few minor ailments. His dental problems, remaining from the war, still required some major care and he had been referred to the Medical Center in Roanoke. In November of '49 he had taken the time off to travel to the hospital and there had the remainder of his lower teeth removed and a lower plate made. This completed the full set of dentures that he sported for the remainder of his life.

As work continued on the house, expenses built up and the stress was beginning to become a little bit overwhelming for Waverley. They decided that for the remainder of the time that it took to finish the house, they would sell their home in Colonial Heights and move in with his parents on High Street. This was obviously not the most pleasant solution to their predicament but it was the most sensible. The first movement to that end was finding a home for Mickey. This in no way made a hit with Linda but certain concessions had to be made by all. The children never knew what happened to their pony and the subject was never broached. One afternoon when Linda came home from school, the pony was gone and no mention of it was ever made again. The family moved into the second floor of the family house on High Street in January of '51. Without her pony to ride, Linda found enjoyment riding down High Street hill on a single steel skate topped by any magazine she could find laying around the house.

The elder Waverley's condition worsened. He was now suffering from Asthma, Bronchieltasis, and Emphysema. He had filed for disability under the new Social Security system that was put into place by the late Franklin Roosevelt but he quickly learned that this was not a simple or rapid process. Doctor Jones in Petersburg had examined Mr. Traylor and provided a qualifying statement but acknowledgement of the submission was never received.

"To whom it may concern:

This certifies that Mr. W. L. Traylor is disabled and unable to work and to earn a livelihood because of a chronic illness which appears to be bronchial asthma, bronchiectasis, or emphysema. I have just taken his history and made a physical examination at my office this P.M."

C. T. Jones, M.D.
Jan 18, 1951

Worry over his father's condition added to the melting pot of stress that was building up in the pressure cooker of Waverley's mind, but still the house must be built. The roof was completed and work began on the outer brick walls. The family would be out on the home site at nights laying the brick for the shell. Waverley would stay up on the scaffolding laying the bricks and Martha would heave the bricks up to him and mix the mortar as it was needed. They worked together in perfect unison and the speed at which the walls went up was fantastic.

The house was finally 80 percent finished and Linda had just finished the second grade at Flora Hill school. The Traylor's packed the furniture they had stored at the High Street house, all of their clothing and personnel effects, and of course all of the children's toys. Most of these had already been moved out to the homestead as the children played when mom and dad worked. Linda would always play in the room that was to be hers, and Little Waverley would play in his. (As it happened, his room was never finished up until the day he had grown up and left home.) The big day had finally arrived as they officially moved into the country house.

Chapter 12
Building a Family

The move had taken place in the late spring and the atmosphere was that of a whole new beginning. Everyone had wished this to be the case but the past has a nasty habit of sneaking up on you. Even after five years, Waverley's sleep patterns had not improved enough to allow him any restful sleep. His legs remained a problem and were intermittently plagued with numbness and pain. He was visiting a local doctor but she found no physical cause for his afflictions. His sleep patterns were disturbed primarily by nightmares of war which led her to recommend seeing a psychologist. Suggesting this type of treatment was taboo in the south during the '50s. He therefore never mentioned this to anyone in the family. This became the first of many secrets he would eventually keep to himself and become more fuel to flame his psychological pressure cooker.

Although several rooms in the new house remained unfinished, the accommodations remained livable, but a slight bit crowded. The bedrooms in the new Traylor "mansion" were all huge. Linda had a room to herself that gave her more space than she had ever imagined. The bedroom for Little Waverley remained unfinished so he temporally shared space in his parents lair. The master bedroom had its own full bath which remained unfinished, a large walk in closet, and a door that led to a balcony the size of its own room. The furniture fit well into the room and consisted of three dressers, two double beds, a single bed, and an assortment of night tables, lamps, etc. There was still plenty of room remaining for an impressive array of toys, teddy bears, and games strewn about in an organized chaos.

Martha and Waverley had decided on each having their own beds. This became necessary due to the ferocity of his frequent nightmares and the occasional severity of night sweats. This was one of the family secrets Little Waverley had become privy to by bunking in the proximity of their occurrence, but was explained away to other family members as a snoring problem.

The unfinished bedroom upstairs began its life as a storage room with two closets of its own. In the closet on the outside wall were kept many of Waverley's and Martha's keepsakes from an earlier life. Included in the paraphernalia was Waverley's Marine Corps uniform along with his ribbons, medals, buckles, and boots. There were many occasions growing up when Little Waverley would take out and try on his daddy's war duds. Surprisingly, with the exception of the pants length, it fit him very well. The coat only barely touched the floor and the hat was a little big but it stayed up well when propped up on his ears. His combat boots? Well that was a whole different story. They were a size eight, his father had small feet, and were a perfect fit. Little Waverley's feet were large for his young age. He was so proud of his father, and wearing his uniform seemed to bring him much closer to being a man.

Timing for the move was perfect since the summer had just lifted its sweltering head. Fortunately the house had been designed and built with comfort in mind. Several large Oak trees had been left around the house along with a few very large pine trees. These provided plenty of shade on the dwelling when the limbs were filled with full green leaves. To the west of the house were hundreds of acres of open fields and as luck would have it, this was the direction from which the weather fronts approached. By opening and closing particular windows, there would be a constant cool breeze passing through the house. Particulars such as this were prime examples of the intelligence and planning skills Waverley possessed and why he would have made an accomplished engineer.

The summer was enjoyable on the farm. Living across the road was a family with several kids. A girl the same age as Linda, with two younger sisters, and a boy the same age as Little Waverley. The children spent the summer playing in the yard almost every day with their new tire swing, a metal swing set, bicycles, a pedal car, and a front yard big enough to play a game of ball. One of Linda's favorite pastimes was swinging on the old wooden swing that her father had tied to the ancient oak tree in the yard. This would cause her long dark hair to flow to and fro as she swung higher and higher. She also enjoyed lying quietly in the grass picking familiar objects out of the clouds in the sky. Little Waverley passed his time by trying to stay at least two paces in front of their big red rooster or three paces in front of his sister. The rooster was a great teacher to the newly displaced city boy. He was instrumental in teaching young Waverley how to run fast and gave him the motivation to learn the art of quickly climbing a tree. His sister also played an important role in his education that summer. He quickly learned that he should duck whenever she swung a baseball bat at his head, and that large lumps on the head will eventually dissipate. The kids survived through to the fall when Linda had to return to school. For the first time she had to wait by the road and ride the big yellow bus. She was very fortunate in that her new friends from across the road could show her around her new school and make her assimilation more comfortable.

The children playing with their new friends from across the road.

Waverley had worked hard that summer. His commute to his jobs became longer, which made his hours away from home a little more each day. He also compensated by working nights and weekends. Often he would spend Sunday afternoon on a job to keep the household finances flowing and almost always took along Little Waverley to help him. While only four years old, his dad felt that it was time for him to start learning skills which may come in useful one day. He would take this time to show his son the way to prepare a job for painting including scraping, sanding, and laying covers. He also showed him how to apply masking tape for trimming, but it wasn't long before the boy's trimming skills precluded this step. The biggest lessons were actually simple; apply the paint on smoothly and evenly, don't spill the paint, and don't waste too much time admiring your work by watching the paint dry.

As war was again raging across the world with a whole new generation of warriors, Waverley had managed to spend enough time at home to build pig pens down by the swamp that encompassed the back half of his father's farm. He stocked the pen with two sows who very shortly gave birth to many piglets. A large chicken coop was built with an oversize chicken yard, fenced to eight feet high. This still did not prevent that damn rooster from escaping. Somehow Waverley still managed time to build a turkey pen, and a rabbit pen. Next he obtained a real honest-to-God tractor with which to plow the fields; a replacement for that all steel monstrosity his daddy had bought many years before. He had wanted so much to lead a quiet simple life on the farm, but taking over the contracting business from his dad had gotten to be a real stress builder.

His brother Allen had wisely concluded that Waverley was just too honest for his own good. He complained that he would bid a job so close that if something went wrong, he would lose his shirt. This was actually very true but that was the way Waverley was raised, honesty above all else. This quality of Waverley's character often kept the pot boiling from stress because of clients pushing to finish jobs or debtors calling for payment before he could collect on a job. With his father now unable to work, the stress grew tighter and tighter until he would blow a gasket and to all appearances, for no good reason.

The farm he was trying to fabricate also became a stressful endeavor as Martha was left to slop the pigs, gather daily eggs, feed the chickens, turkeys, and rabbits. Her day also included cleaning house, fixing meals, washing dishes, and laundry. Meals were not as simple a chore as one might imagine. Often the chicken for dinner had to be caught, killed, plucked, and dressed before meal preparation could begin. It so happened that the most stressful chore was the laundry since the washing machine was in the unfinished basement. Being so far out in the country, and backed right up on the swamp at the bottom of the hill, the basement was shared with a variety of critters such as mice, lizards, frogs, and snakes. On one particular afternoon, she carried a load of laundry into the basement and found a large snake skin draped over the water pipes directly in front of the washing machine. She dropped the basket of cloths where she stood, and with a muffled scream, took no time in removing herself from the basement. She had to wait for Waverley to come home so that he could remove the skin and search the rest of the basement for the critter that had shed it. The buildup of stress she endured resulted in a stubborn resistance to the controlling efforts of her beloved. Waverley, however, was merely attempting to control at least one aspect of his life. The other aspects remained in total disarray.

Christmas that year brought joy and an easing of all the tensions throughout the household. Santa Claus was good to everyone but none any more than the whole family. Sitting under the tree, or beside it, was a brand new Zenith, 17 inch, black-and-white television set. But this was no ordinary, run of the mill, 1952 television. This one reportedly had the very latest in advance technology, an actual remote control. This way the channel on the magic box could be changed without rising from the comfort of the easy chair. Of course there were only three channels available for viewing. The remote buttons were attached to the set by a cable and pressing the channel button would cause a motor to rotate the mechanical tuner forward or backward. There were also volume buttons which caused the volume control to rotate up or down. Another control would turn the set on or off and rounded up what was a technological wonder in the world of electronic home entertainment. The children fell heir to the television set because their father was always too busy except for the news broadcast every evening. He always watched and kept track of the news concerning the war. He never, however, let his interest in the war replace his pledge to the church.

On many Sunday nights, Waverley would lead the prayer service in the sanctuary and the senior choir, including Martha, would sing. Martha singing for her husband to hear was now an isolated occasion since this was now never allowed at home. The couple was also selected to attend the Young Adult Weekend at the Randolph Macon Women's College in Lynchburg. These were always trips where they could get away and enjoy each other. During these trips Linda would spend the weekend with a girlfriend in town and Little Waverley stayed with his aunt and uncle. This way he always got to keep under observation the movies that were playing in town. At this particular conference,

Waverley was elected president of the Virginia Methodist Conference, Young Adult Fellowship. A proud position for a proud man. At home the couple would together visit parishioners who were homebound, hospital patients, or residents of local nursing homes. These were the activities they had in common and they were happiest when they shared these experiences.

Although "Old Man Traylor" remained too ill to work on any contracted job, he still liked to visit the country and his precious flower farm. Here he still grew acres of daffodils of nearly every variety imaginable. Whenever he paid a visit to the flower fields, Little Waverley would find his way over to see his grandpa. Sometimes the two of them, with grandpa sporting his brown fedora, would sit for hours on the running board of his Hudson pickup truck. Little Waverley was often treated to tales of adventure and intrigue from the Civil War, World War I, and the Roaring Twenties. These were stories, similar in nature, to those told to Waverley Jr. by his grandpa George on the back steps of his High Street home. His brother had never had the privilege of hearing these tales of adventure because his grandpa George passed when he was only nine months old.

Waverley Sr. sporting his infamous Brown Fedora.

    Linda had missed Mickey but had hatched a scheme to get herself another pony. The Bluebird theatre in town was holding a contest to promote a new movie they had playing. Linda entered the contest by submitting an essay entitled "Why I Want a Pony." She did a really fine job with her entry and ended up taking second place, not the pony. She had won a brand new 24 inch Schwinn boys bicycle. Since it was a boys bike and since she already had one, she gifted her prize to her little brother. He was really grateful to his sister for winning the bike for him and would be happier once his feet could reach the pedals.

It wasn't very long before Waverley's brother Allen had announced his intention to marry and the wedding was set for January of 1953. Eleven-year-old Linda was asked to be a junior brides maid for the formal church wedding. Despite a minor bit of friction between the siblings, Waverley accepted the request to stand with Allen and serve as his best man. The boys' mother was present for the ceremony but their father was now too ill to attend. This seemed to bring the boys closer and they began doing more projects together.

Waverley and Allen were conducting repairs on the house at 226 High Street, when they uncovered an artillery shell they believed to have been buried there since the skirmish between the Rebels and those Damned Yankees. It was unexploded which made it a possible hazard to those who dug it up and to those who so carefully carried the shell on a pillow to the Fort Lee Army Base for deactivation. Each turn and pothole in the road would trigger a strong gasp from everyone in the car. Crossing over the bumpy railroad tracks into the fort brought pale faces to the vehicles inhabitants as they held their breaths for what seemed like an hour. The Explosive Ordnance Device (EOD) team at the fort wanted to explode the shell but Allen wanted it handled a bit differently. He talked to one of the EOD technicians asking if they could defuse the shell and return it to clean up and display. But the shell was over one hundred years old and as they were leaving the area, a loud explosion was heard in the distance behind them. Everyone seemed glad that the shell was gone and were happy that circumstances had decided against Allen keeping it.

They had also unearthed, on that day, a skeleton of what was believed to be a native Indian. Buried with arrowheads, bundled as though they had been attached to wooden shafts in a quiver, and dressed in deer hides. This discovery was a little freaky for the likes of the boys and they immediately reburied the remains in the same location where they were found, but quite a bit deeper, just to be safe.

Waverley's father continued to suffer from asthma and emphysema brought on, primarily, by his long term heavy smoking. He was now confined to his bed at home and treated with a continuous reliance on a massive oxygen bottle. He no longer visited the work sites with his son or tended his precious flower farm. This work had fallen to Waverley and, on the farm, Little Waverley was becoming a valued assistant. During the spring of '54, "Old Man Traylor's" condition deteriorated and he was admitted to the Veterans' Hospital in Richmond, where he was diagnosed with severe bronchial pneumonia. He never returned to his home and passed away on Independence Day of that year. Although a family tragedy, his passing was a relief for Waverley, and a major liberation from his roller coaster ride with stress. The funeral was held in Petersburg and Waverley's friend William served as one of the pallbearers for his interment at Blandford Cemetery. This was the first time Waverley had seen William since the war and it would turn out to be the last time he ever saw him again.

A short time following his grandfather's funeral, Little Waverley was with his dad while getting ready for bed and noticed the rather awful condition of his father's feet. He inquired into the trouble and his dad explained that he had caught a case of "Jungle Rot" while serving in Okinawa. He expounded on the story explaining how the Marines had been bogged down in a sea of knee deep mud during heavy battle on Okinawa and the rain would not stop. He described how they were sleeping in water, walking, eating, and fighting in water and how this caused his feet to suffer the affliction for which there was no cure.

Without medical intervention, Waverley discovered his own treatments that helped, but did not cure, his troubled mind. He recalled how much better he felt as a young man when he traveled with his aunt and uncle. He would now strive, at this stage in his life, to use this same method as an escape from his problems at work. He also retreated inward and found an escape in his church. Leading a Christian life had taken a priority in his behavior and abstaining from tobacco, alcohol, and foul language had now become an obsession with him. He dedicated himself to service in the church and felt this obligation because of a promise he made a long time ago in a fox hole on the other side of the world.

It became apparent that Little Waverley loved those stories that his dad related to him. His only sorrow was that they were very few and far between. He had now turned six and the time had come for his father to teach him another skill. When he worked with his father was when he had the best chance of hearing another story. Waverley was working a job in Stony Creek, which was the perfect opportunity for lessons in wallpapering. He began by teaching his son to spray down and remove the old paper and to patch the cracks in the plaster. He then set him up to mix the paste that would be used on the wall. As his son watched, his father spread the paste, folded the paper, and applied it to the wall. Advancement was step by step as Waverley taught his young son to cut the paper, spread the paste, and properly fold the paper. The boy handled these chores for a while until he was finally let loose to actually hang the paper. When placed properly into position near the ceiling the paper would drop ever so gently to the floor. Waverley emphasized the importance of lining up the paper with the adjacent run and brushing it down to ensure all of the air bubbles were removed. After trimming top and bottom, the job was done and time to move on to the next section. It only took an hour to prepare and install one piece. His father did a whole room in three. Little Waverley discovered later that learning to paper was actually a lesson in patience and keeping a vigilant eye for detail, the mark of a professional. That evening, at home, Waverley had praised his son on how well he did with the wallpapering.

Waverley went to his closet and pulled out an old cigar box and presented it to his boy. Inside the miniature Treasure Chest, were handfuls of old Indian arrowheads. His dad explained that he had collected these when they were digging the basement for the house. He had wanted to give his boyhood collection to Little Waverley but after the war, he had been unable to find his hidden treasure. This had to be the greatest gift the young lad had ever received. He showed his reward to everyone he could trap, his mom, his sister, his neighborhood friends, and anyone who stopped in for a visit. But he would never let that box leave his grasp other than when he hid it under his bed.

That summer Waverley took the entire family on a church retreat to an isolated lake resort nestled in the Great Smokey Mountains of Western North Carolina. Overlooking the quiet and serene Lake Junaluska, the retreat focused on training for those wishing to work with the youth of the Methodist Church. It was here where he learned crafting, games, and dancing to pass on to the young church goers the same way he had enjoyed the fellowship as a teenager. Returning from the retreat saw Waverley in a rather pleasant mood. He had thoroughly enjoyed himself on this venture which, of course, pleased his family to no end.

Summer was nearing a close and time for one more day trip to one of family's favorite destinations. They all loved fishing but as a family would only fish in salt water. This was due to Martha's taste in seafood. Her favorite ocean fare was a pan full of fresh Spot or Croaker. Knowing this, Waverley would often head to the coast to one of many fine fishing piers, but this year Waverley wanted something a little different. This was the right time of the year since the croaker were running. They got an early start and headed for Norfolk. Near the fishing pier that protruded from the beach at Ocean View, there was a boat rental facility for those brave enough to tackle the Chesapeake Bay on their own. They rented a small wooden boat, but renting one of their fancy outboard motors was cost prohibitive. Luckily, oars came with the rental. The family crowded into the vessel and Waverley stoked up the oars and began traveling out to sea. The day was enjoyed by everyone and the fishing was great. Waverley and the kids all had poles but he knew that Martha would insisted on her reliable hand line. The cooler was nearly full of spot and croaker when they noticed dark clouds gathering in the west.

They had drifted quite a way out so Waverley began rowing while the others began packing up the gear. He rowed for all he was worth and that little boat was flying through the water. Waverley never quit rowing and he exhibited to his youngsters just how strong he was. They were impressed.

The rain began coming down, lightly at first. The precipitation grew heavier as they approached land and had become a deluge by the time they reached shore. The children were still bailing when the boat hit the sand. It took only a fraction of a second as everyone jumped or fell from the craft and had their feet planted on wet land. No time was wasted in packing everything back into the car but it didn't help them get any dryer. Since no one had thought about bringing a dry set of clothes, towels on the seats and towels wrapped around their shoulders was the best way to be partially dry, and at this point warm. The heater in the car helped until they arrived at the Wayside Picnic Area on the bank of the Elizabeth River. This was an integral part of every trip to the beach as a convenient stop for supper. Fortunately the picnic tables sat in covered shelters which kept the rain out of the food baskets. Running the heater in the car for the rest of the way home was now very comforting. The car pulled into the driveway at home after midnight and everyone was exhausted. Waverley had driven all the way in the rain and the trip home left him highly stressed but so tired that he never really noticed. He had been the only one awake when they pulled into the yard but stopping the vehicle caused the family to rouse. Little Waverley was the only one that had to be carried into the house and carefully laid on his bed. Waverley exchanged his wet clothes for a warm pair of pajamas and fell into his bed. His head had hardly hit the pillow before he was asleep, and slept right through the next morning. This was one of the very few Sunday mornings the family had missed church services.

With autumn came school and Little Waverley entered the first grade. His sister, now in the sixth grade, took charge to ensure her little brother rode on the correct yellow bus and found his way around the school that she knew oh so well. During this first year of education, Little Waverley participated in the first of his dramatic roles on stage. He played the "Third Little Pig" as the leading role in this thespian showcase. His mother was present since she had been cast to participate in the after show party in their first grade classroom. Unfortunately, Waverley was unable to attend because of his need to work six days a week. He was working now 12 to 14 hours a day, six days a week, and often on Sunday afternoons. He always made time to attend church on Sunday mornings and occasionally on Sunday nights. He also ensured that Martha had transportation to choir practice on Wednesday nights but she often had to find a ride home with one of her choir mates. Activities with the church became Martha's release and helped keep the peace in the family. She belonged to a church Circle that was always performing good deeds to the community. They had a special place in their hearts for the armed services and would often sponsor activities at the United Services Organization (USO) in Petersburg. Little Waverley continued his thespian activities. He was a member of the school chorus and had been cast in an operetta entitled "Cinderella in Flowerland" where he portrayed the handsome prince. His father was proud of his son's accomplishments remembering back to his own days on the stage.

Warmer weather was trickling into the air and the flower fields had come alive with the arrival of spring. There was just about every color in the rainbow peppered amongst the yellow background of the daffodils in bloom. The flower farm was now 20 years old and the original bulbs planted by Waverley Sr. had multiplied many times over. Little Waverley would retreat to the fields when he arrived home from school and begin picking the bright and sweet smelling flowers. He picked until his hand was filled with the yellow blossoms and he could hold no more. A rubber band was placed around the stems, the bunch was carefully laid on the open space between rows, and picking would continue.

By the time that his father arrived home, the field would be covered by a multitude of these bunched flowers. Big flat pans with water would be loaded into the station wagon and the picked flowers collected and set into these pans. The next morning, Waverley would take the flowers in with him on the way to work and drop them off at his mother's home. Here, she would prepare them in select bouquets for sale on the upcoming Saturday.

Come the weekend, Little Waverley would ride into work with his father to be dropped off at his grandmother's house. He and several neighborhood boys were given the task of venturing into downtown Petersburg with a basket filled with springtime joy. They would march out of the house with full baskets and return empty but with a full pocket of change after selling the bouquets on the street the way his father had done at his age. The money would be counted and the baskets refilled in time to make another downtown run. At the end of the day, Mrs. Traylor would tally up each boys sales and pay them the commission that they had earned. This was a fair deal for all of the boys who participated. Little Waverley did manage to make just a little more pocket change than the other boys. After all, he did participate in all aspects of the business. He picked, bunched, and sold. This was his early education to commerce, covering all phases of a small business venture to earn the money.

His lesson in spending economics came later on Saturday afternoon. These flower sales always occurred around the Easter holiday and this particular Saturday was the day before. As a gesture of love for his mother, he had bought her an Easter Lily with the money he had earned. When his father picked him up after work, Little Waverley told his dad about the flower and why he had purchased it. Waverley blew the emergency relief valve on his steam vessel. All of the way back out to the farm, he lectured his son on the difficulty in earning a living and the consequences of wasteful spending. Meanwhile, the pot with the Easter Lily ended up in a nearby trash bin. The punishment for this error though, had really been subjected toward Martha. She was the one who didn't receive the Lily, but she never became aware of the incident.

Waverley had arranged that summer for Little Waverley to take Red Cross swimming lessons at Lakeview Park. He felt that it was an extremely important skill for the young man to master and wanted him to begin as soon as possible. As it turned out, this proved to be a most valuable skill that served him well in his later life.

Chapter 13
Jekyll & Hyde

As seasons passed, Waverley's manner was being shaped into a typical two-way circuit. His good days were exceptional and his bad days were horrendous. He literally was mutating into the proverbial Jekyll & Hyde. In his case, Doctor Jekyll was a fun-loving comedian, always with a joke, a pun, or a prank. Mister Hyde was filled with anger and fear. He was the embodiment of the resentment, the jealousy, and the need to control the women in his life. No, this was not fair but merely a manifestation of the chaos in his head from a traumatic brain injury suffered so many years before.

During the winter of his discontent, his restless aspiration for recovery had not been realized. Things were not going well in the Traylor house. Martha had informed Waverley about a problem with the kitchen sink backing up and nearly overflowing. He became upset because he thought she should know better than to stuff food down the drain. He mumbled about how much work was involved to clear the pipes. As he gathered his tools and prepared to attack the sink, he opened the cabinet beneath and found it full of pots and pans that would be in the way. The mental pressure cooker began to boil as he reached in and pulled all of the cooking gear out onto the kitchen floor. He should never have continued with the repair in this state of mind, but then again, he was not thinking clearly. He ended up placing too much pressure on the fragile drain pipe and it snapped in half.

The wrench hit the water line and broke it loose. With water flooding the kitchen and Waverley falling over the pans as he tried to stand up, he grabbed the sink, ripped it from the cabinet, and heaved it outside through the double window. Every pot and pan on the floor followed the sink out of the window and it was obvious his pressure cooker had exploded.

Little Waverley ran from the kitchen and hid in the upstairs bedroom. Martha, in tears, proceeded outside, in the snow, to collect the pots when Waverley loudly explained that she was not going to bring those pans back in the house. When he went to work the next day, she was able to collect the pots and pans, wash them in the tub, and carefully pack them into the utility closet in the hallway. It took several days, but eventually the sink was replaced and the piping repaired, all without further incident.

Although totally losing control of his temper was becoming a more common occurrence, Waverley's relationship with his son remained rather unique. On several occasions, the pair would retreat to the woods on the back 10 acres of the farm with the 22-caliber rifle that was kept in the house. Waverley was teaching his son how to shoot and passing on what he had learned as a Marine sharpshooter during the war. Along with the lessons came a few tales of the war, but these were never mentioned outside the environment of the quiet forest. These "School of the Forest" adventures always left Waverley feeling calmer and relaxed. After several lessons in handling the weapon, Little Waverley was allowed to continue his target practice unescorted.

It appeared that following any of his high pressure mental explosions, Waverley would become relaxed and calm within a matter of a day or two. This would sometimes lead to a few weekend day trips during the summer. In the early summer of this year the family was treated to a trip to Virginia Beach. The outing would usually start by packing the night before and leaving around six am. They could always tell when they were nearing the beach because of the smell of salt air permeating their senses. The southern beach was their favorite spot with rows of sand dunes covered with beach grass. Not too many people traveled past this point because driving further south meant crossing an old rickety one lane wooden bridge over Rudy Inlet. The family would truck their supplies over the dunes and set up a makeshift tent using four poles and a blanket. When it was time to get wet, they could retreat into the dunes and change into their bathing suits. As the sun began to sink low in the sky, it would be time to leave. This meant packing everything back in the car and heading for a popular wayside for an evening supper. The children would then fall asleep as the car started for home with their arrival at the usual midnight. These were always very relaxing days.

Independence Day 1957 brought sorrow again to the family. Martha's brother Gurney had passed away at the Portsmouth Naval Hospital. He had been a long-time patient at the hospital and his death was not unexpected. Even so, his passing placed a cloud over the Ellis family that lasted past the Christmas season.

Spring brings about the sound of songbirds in the air and each night wakes to the sound of Cicadas, frogs, and owls. The new year had also brought a time when the animals begin nesting for the "baby season" ahead. As the elders of the church were attending night services, they heard, and noted, the "whoo whoo whoo, whoo whoo—whoo," of a Great Horned Owl. They had wondered for days where this owl was located and finally realized that she was nesting high within the church steeple. Of course, whenever they had an unusual problem at the church, they always seemed to call on Waverley. He had been the one to call since, even as a teenager, he was always willing to tackle the difficult problems and showed the intelligence to figure a solution. For this particular problem he brought in his long extension ladders to make the ascent. He first placed a ladder from the street to the roof of the church and then, hauling up a second extension ladder, placed it in position to reach the very top inside the steeple.

After having disturbed the bird, Waverley waited for the owl to return and fall asleep on her nest. Waverley, with heavy gloves on his hands, climbed slowly and quietly up the ladders and gently wrapped his hand around the legs of the creature. It woke with a start and raised its long wings, nearly throwing Waverley off balance and knocking him off of the ladder. He was able to regain his composure and his footing without losing his grip. He ran his other hand smoothly down the owl's back, grasping her wings and legs together. With this hold he had the bird totally under control and he began his descent out of the steeple. By this time a crowd had gathered on the street along with a reporter and a photographer from the local paper. This was a great human interest story and shared the front page with the latest news on the great Greyhound Strike. He seemed to take pleasure in saving the bird, since he was able to box her up and release her in the open country on his farm. He did not, however, take to the attention and the remarks about him being a hero for saving the animal. He really wanted none of that.

Summer arrived and the children were finally out of school for the their annual vacation. It was past time for Waverley to get a little relaxation so a summer trip south was planned. A Florida trip was a common occurrence since Martha's sister and family owned a motel on Florida's west coast. With free lodging, this made for an inexpensive vacation. They also started their trips in the evenings when Waverley returned home from work. Driving through the night meant a smaller number of meals on the road and less expenses to deal with. On this trip the Traylor's were taking along their "brand new" used station wagon. A 1953 two tone flamingo pink and white Ford wagon that ran good but looked experienced. Well, in outward appearances it ran good. As they were passing through Georgia the red GEN light on the dash illuminated and would not extinguish. They pulled the car into an all night service station along the road and fortunately, there was a mechanic on duty. The engine was checked out which resulted in the determination that a new generator was needed. There was no way of getting one until morning, so they had to wait out the evening. Waverley and Martha slept sitting up in the front seat while Linda stretched out in the back, and Little Waverley had the rear all to himself. The next morning proved that a better day was ahead. The sun came up right on schedule, the part was delivered, the car was fixed, and they were once again headed south. But first, breakfast on the road. Another expense not planned. Normally a night like this would have been enough to send Waverley over the edge, but the calming effect of a vacation seemed to help hold the pot below boiling level.

They stayed with their relatives for about a week and decided to head home by way of Miami. On the leg of the trip south, they pulled over in Fort Meyers and stopped at an ice cream shop by the side of the road, it was a Dairy something-or-other. Waverley took everyone's order and, with Linda, left to order the treats. As he made it to the head of the line, he spoke for a moment with the girl inside and then stepped away and walked back to the car. Martha rolled down the window and Waverley leaned down and stuck his head inside the car very seriously asking, "Do you want 'nuts' on your Chocolate Nut Sundae?" They all broke into laughter and he returned, carefully holding in a well earned snicker, to finish placing the order. This encounter had really dissolved any tension that may have been brewing and they all had an enjoyable afternoon.

When the family arrived in Miami, it was difficult to see anything other than a large, overcrowded, urban environment. Waverley decided to take a drive along Miami Beach since he had heard so much about that place in the movies and on that strange new picture box back home. Riding along the rows of elegant homes, it was difficult not to notice the number of limousines in the drives and along the streets. With each shiny new limousine Waverley saw there stood a highly polished chauffeur. Not to appear out of place, Waverley asked his son to hand him his child's size yachting hat that Little Waverley had purchased at a roadside stand on the Tamiami Trail. He placed the hat on his head, which almost fit (or not), sat up straight in his seat, and most convincingly portrayed a chauffeur driving his employers around in that slightly experienced 1953, two tone, flamingo pink and white, Ford station wagon. The entire family could not help but laugh and continued to do so for miles after departing Miami

Beach. This was a bit of adlib fun for the family and it did draw some curious stares from the local populace. The incident was a product of Waverley's unusual sense of humor which made for many unforgettable family stories which were told for decades following their occurrence. The remainder of the vacation was fairly uneventful and was primarily a straight shot from the beach of Miami to the woods of Matoaca.

    Back at home there was one adventure that was etched in stone for each and every Sunday afternoon. After church, the family always went out for dinner. The choices were always the same. It was either the Rainbow Room in Colonial Heights, King's Bar-B-Que in Petersburg, or the Log Cabin Restaurant in Dinwiddie County. The Rainbow Room had a sweet waitress that always seemed to have the family table. She provided excellent service and the food was great. King's Bar-B-Que was owned and operated by an old family friend and the food was out of this world. The Log Cabin was a long drive, the food was kinda okay, but the owners were another of Martha's sisters, along with her husband. The "Ye Olde Log Cabin Restaurant" was a favorite spot for the people of Petersburg to dine on Sunday afternoons but unfortunately did not fare well the other days of the week. When they finally closed down, Elizabeth gave Martha the piano that had adorned the dining room at the Log Cabin. Other than needing tuning, it was a great gift. Martha loved to play the piano as much as she loved to sing. She was a highly talented lady both as a musician and as an artist. Waverley, on the other hand, no longer enjoyed music or art. He had difficulty watching anyone else enjoy themselves while he never had the time or the energy to do anything enjoyable for himself. The piano stayed, and was tuned, as long as Martha never played the instrument when Waverley was home. It stayed mainly because Linda would be taking piano lessons as any up and rising young lady should do.

    Waverley was certain that his God given talents, of math and science, were being wasted. He would not allow her talent to blossom and his talents were not being properly used. This became a wedge between he and Martha that drove deeper as time passed.

The new year was beginning and hopefully 1958 would prove to be a better year. It was time again to burn off the flower fields to remove the grass and broom straw that had permeated the land since last season, but this season felt different. No one could really put their finger on it but it was there. Waverley took out the old flame thrower he had learned to operate so effectively in the service, filled the gas cans, pumped it up and began clearing the flower fields as he had done each year. Little Waverley found a good position to plant himself to watch his dad at work.

The flames shot out of the wand with a roar as fire tore through the straw and the field became ablaze, smoke pouring high into the sky. Waverley had performed this ritual many times before and knew that short burst would effectively burn off the field while keeping the fire under control. He had even explained to his son last year why flaming this way was so important. For some unknown reason, this time, the chore was not progressing the same way as before. There were no longer any short burst. The flames were now being fanned across the field with a nonstop motion. The flames began extending out further than ever before and Waverley's eyes were staring, unblinking, straight ahead as if transfixed on some object, or some place, that was not really there. It was really scary as the flames danced across the field, seemingly unnoticed, and racing toward the wooded area to the rear of the property.

A scream from his son apparently shocked Waverley back to reality. As he looked around, he realized there was nothing he could do now except call the fire department. The volunteers did respond but not until about five acres of woodland had been burned. By the puzzled look on his face, it was apparent that Little Waverley did not understand his father's mental state at the time. That far off stare and body posturing made it difficult not to notice how upset it had made the former Marine.

The spring of 1958 arrived and Little Waverley was completing his year in the fourth grade. The time had come to plow the fields for the season and this year was particularly exciting. His dad has promised to teach him how to drive the tractor. He showed the boy the gas lever, the brake pedals both right and left, the clutch, and the gear shift and gear positions. He started the engine, with the transmission in neutral, depressed the clutch, set the gear, released the clutch, and turned up the gas—he was driving. While standing on the lift behind the driver's seat, Waverley let his son have free rein and drove around the fire roads that ran from the house, to the fields, and back around to the house. The boy was having a wonderful time. As he was passing by the open field, he glanced back toward the house and, standing by the family car, was his dad. The fear swelled up inside as he realized he really was driving the tractor—all by himself. He thought to himself how great a day this was as he spied his father standing there, arms crossed, smiling at him.

Summer brought an end to the school year and Waverley decided to observe a "take your son to work" summer. Little Waverley helped his dad with painting and wallpapering in the years past but this became a season of new skills. He helped his dad with small plumbing and electrical jobs. In doing so, he learned the skills necessary to handle this type of work. It didn't take him very long because, like his father, he could watch, listen, and become proficient at a task in mere days. Waverley was really proud of his son and was reminded each day how much alike the two of them were. This was believed to be the reasoning behind the fact that he wasn't nearly as strict with him as he was with his wife and daughter. The two of them working side by side, for most of that very busy summer, helped to form a very special bond between them.

The Florida cousins had planned a vacation that year since the Traylor's would not be traveling their way. They arrived and found quarters at Waverley's house in the country. It was a pleasant visit and on Sunday there were two cars filled with Traylors and Deakins that went to lunch at one of the family's favorite restaurants. Everything went well until the bill arrived and it was like two cats after the same mouse. Waverley and cousin Bob both attacked the miniscule piece of green paper. After a little snatching back and forth, Waverley ended up with the bill and paid directly in the waitress' hand. Waverley rushed to his car with the family and rolled all of the windows up with doors locked. Bob, in the meantime, was doing his best to stuff the money through a window but was having no success; that was until Little Waverley opened a window. The money came in the window, Little Waverley got pulled over to the front seat, and a firm hand laid waste his little tender bottom. That was the first, last, and only time his father had ever laid a hand on him.

The family vacation that year was to be short. Waverley was working hard and he had several jobs active. Leaving, even for a week, was out of the question so a weekend jaunt would have to do. They headed for the mountains and spent the weekend riding along the Skyline Drive. Often they would stop and hike along the trails to see the waterfalls along the mountain ridges or pull over on an overlook to enjoy a picnic lunch. One afternoon was spent at Luray Caverns exploring the depths of this natural wonder and wandering through the antique car museum on the site. The adventure was very enjoyable and relaxing but nowhere near long enough.

This had been a difficult year for Waverley as it came near a close. The family was worried that the trip they had the past summer had not been enough to defuse his stress. Waverley too felt this buildup and with the Thanksgiving weekend approaching he felt he had to release this pressure. The Wednesday before the holiday, he came home from work and directed the family to pack their bags, they were leaving on a trip. He would not disclose where they were going, although it may have been because he also had no clue. The only hint he gave was that they were leaving in an hour. Waverley could see that this kicked the stress level up for Martha since she had a fresh turkey ready for roasting and pies in the oven. Coming through like a trooper, however, she rearranged the refrigerator contents and found room for all to pack within. When they departed from their home, Waverley had only one question for his family; "Which way—North or South?"

The family arrived in New York City around four in the morning on Thanksgiving Day. Already the streets were lined with people in anticipation of the annual Macy's Thanksgiving Day Parade. They were passing a hotel with off street parking so into the entrance they pulled. Waverley signed them into a room for the weekend, parked the car, and the entire family retreated into the hotel coffee shop for a bite of breakfast. The shop was crowded but there remained one table open which the four of them tightly occupied, but not particularly comfortably. After a quick breakfast, they filtered out onto the street and took up a position where they had a good view of the parade route.

The morning extravaganza led off with a bright new convertible carrying the Grand Marshall of the event—Hugh O'Brien. What followed included an array of marching bands from all over the country playing the very best of Sousa as they marched proudly through the streets of New York. Additionally the bands were interspersed with elaborately decorated floats depicting a wide variety of scenes and occasionally huge balloons shaped like familiar cartoon characters such as Mighty Mouse, Popeye the Sailor, and Woody Woodpecker. These were really a hit with the younger crowd, many of which were perched high upon their father's shoulders. The parade finally came to a close with a band playing the old favorite of children everywhere, "Here Comes Santa Claus" which preceded the actual big man in his furry warm red suit. He sat on his Christmas throne which had been placed atop a shiny red fire engine with its big bass horn and sharp high pitched siren blaring its way down the street. Every light on the truck was operating basting the crowd in a layer of pulsing red light. Then it was gone. An eerie silence blanketed the street where the only sounds came from the muffled siren disappearing around the corner and the near silent shuffle of the people as they cleared the streets.

The Traylors left the street and retired into their hotel room. Waverley really needed to catch a nap since he had driven all night. Actually everyone dozed off for a while to combat their four am start on the day. The rooms at the Plymouth Hotel were small but the beds were comfortable, sort of. Everyone was up in time for lunch and by chance, there was an Automat just a couple of blocks up the street. Entering the establishment was walking into a virtual collage of delicious aromas. The odor of steaming hot vegetable soup collided with the dish of hot roast beef and gravy, sewn together with that wavering luscious smell of fresh hot apple pie. This was a strange new method of eating to the Traylor family obviously unique to the big city. It was similar to a cafeteria except each item was on a small shelf, behind a glass door. Coins were inserted at each position. Then you could open the door and take out your food. Of course the next selection to be placed in the window always looked more delicious than the one sitting in your hand.

After a quick visit and tour of the United Nations building, the family found themselves on Broadway and passed by a grand theatre showing the premier of the movie "Around the World in 80 Days." This could be a real experience since it was being shown in the all new Todd-AO format that had been introduced for the movie "Oklahoma." The process of using 70mm film had been updated for this motion picture as it was only the second movie ever made in this format. The film opened with an animated title sequence seven minutes long followed by a three hour feature. Fortunately an intermission had been placed in the middle of the action which led to nearly four hours in the theatre seats. The seats were comfortable and the movie very entertaining, especially for anyone who chose to participate in "spot the star." Forty-Five top Hollywood stars appeared in the movie such as Red Skelton, Frank Sinatra, Buster Keaton, Andy Devine, and many, many, more.

Following the four hour extravaganza, they discovered that evening was approaching and concluded that they should start heading back to the hotel. Passing nothing of interest along the way, they stopped back by the small hotel coffee shop for dinner. Their waitress took their orders but felt compelled to add a more complete introduction. "My name is Ann, just call me if you need me, my name is Ann. Just call if you need anything, just call out Ann and I'll hear ya." Naturally, everyone contracted a slight snicker once she left the room as they found her rather amusing. She brought out the orders. Where they got the impression was unknown, but it seemed likely that she had cooked the meal herself. "My name is Ann, just call me if you need me, my name is Ann. Just call if you need anything, just call out Ann and I'll hear ya." She had repeated her introduction just in case we had missed it the first time. But then she added, "Do you like pickles? I sure do. In fact I just finished making a batch. You guys wait here and I'll go back to my room and get some." Now it was getting a bit more difficult to hold in the laughter until she left. They knew this was going to be a real story to be passed down with the family history. She returned just a few moments later with an old, gray, beat up saucepan filled with small green cucumber looking things. She sat it on the table and told them to take all they wanted, she had no one to share them with and she certainly couldn't eat them all. That admission had hit a cord with Waverley which resulted in a generous tip, but needless to say, they had no more meals at that establishment.

Friday morning came and Waverley had left an early wakeup call. He wanted to show his family all he had learned from his visits with his Aunt Marie back in the '30s. He also wanted to experience new things himself such as the wide screen theatre and television. They were up and out early and lined up on the street to watch the Today Show live. As they stood in the crowd and watched, they could see their second favorite commentator Dave Garraway and of course their favorite television star, J. Fred Muggs, a chimp above chimps. While standing outside of the NBC studio, they were given tickets to see a live game show being broadcast that morning. This was a new experience, even for Waverley, so the tickets were graciously accepted.

In the studio, the whole family sat down for a half hour of "Treasure Hunt." It was exciting to see Jan Murray live with the Treasure Girls; they were cute. The family did discover several details of the show which the TV viewers at home never got to see. For instance, they had a staff member holding up signs telling the audience when to applaud, when to laugh, and when to Ooh-Ah. They also learned that the safe guarded by an actual security guard, had no back and was open all the time. What a disappointment.

That same afternoon the Traylors walked up to Radio City Music Hall to catch the matinee featuring the world famous Rockettes. The dancers put on quite a show for the crowd that had gathered to see the movie "Rally 'Round the Flag, Boys." They decided to take a subway ride to Brooklyn for dinner and took in a little shopping amongst the bright lights of the big city streets. After a very full day, everyone was extremely tired and returned to the hotel for a good night's sleep.

Saturday began a little later than usual. They started off with a ride up the supersonic elevator in the Empire State Building, all the way to the 102nd floor. The outside catwalk was open and the view was breathtaking. The whole of Manhattan could be seen from that one point in the city. This was followed by a ride on the Staten Island Ferry, first over and then back. Who could ever turn down a great boat ride. Then off for another boat trip to Liberty Island to see the famous Stature of Liberty. This was an exciting adventure because they were able to walk up the winding stairs to the very top. Martha gave up about half way up and sat down on a convenient bench that she was sure was placed there just for her. The rest of the family made it to the top and gathered up mother on the way back down. This had completed a very full day on Saturday and all were ready for some rest and an early bedtime. The trip home on Sunday was uneventful and all seemed ready for the homecoming. Christmas that year was absolutely great and Waverley really enjoyed himself. The whole family realized the New York trip was the greatest medicine for what ailed father.

What helped make a wonderful Christmas that year was Rusty, the half hound and half boxer canine that was still just a puppy, a 120 pound puppy. Little Waverley received his most wonderful gift of all, a 10 speed English racing bike. Now honestly, who in their right mind would want an English bike, living on a farm. It turned out that the bike didn't really ride very well in the field and through the woods. Rusty got a ball and a fresh chew bone, and that made the holiday all okay. As the New Year arrived, it became obvious to everyone that dad had become *very* relaxed on the New York vacation and all the way through Christmas when Martha announced she was again pregnant. Happy New Year!

Martha was further along in her pregnancy when she began having trouble with the stairs in the house. Waverley moved her bed and dresser into the downstairs dining room and installed doors to close the room off. Although there was another established room on the first floor, Martha's mother occupied that space. She was also concerned about the family dog Rusty because he had a habit of jumping up on everyone and she feared getting injured by his unintentional welcomes. Waverley found a home for Rusty on a farm in another county and it became lonely around the homestead. Little Waverley cried for his pal because he loved that big bruiser so much. Before very long, Martha received a phone call from her sister living in the city. It seemed that Rusty had found his way to her home. This was highly unusual because, even though Rusty knew and liked her sister, he had never been to her house, or even off of the farm for that matter. Waverley picked the dog up from the city and returned him to his new home. Poor Rusty was never heard from again.

Waverley spent a lot of time working with his son and teaching him the trade during the summer. He taught his son the lessons needed to be self sufficient in life. By the end of August, the boy could lay block and brick with the best of them. He even learned the skills in cutting, welding, and installing sheet metal gutters on homes. After all, the most important part of the lessons involved installing them on a two story home. Dealing with long ladders was a treat for Little Waverley but not so much for his father having to deal with bouts of Gout and Arthritis.

Near the end of that summer, Waverley rushed Martha off to the hospital during the night and by morning the Traylor family was up by one. Linda finally got her wish for a baby sister and everyone just ogled over Cindy, the new family member. After the standard warranty period, Cindy came home and moved into the mansion farmhouse. Martha kept her room downstairs for a while and Cindy slept in the same basinet that had been used by Little Waverley, Linda, and Martha.

The next month saw a crisis hit the family when Martha's mother suffered a heart attack and the rescue crew was summoned. They arrived at the house and transported her to the Petersburg General Hospital. Unfortunately, there was nothing to be done and she passed that evening, comfortably in her sleep. There was much grief to spread around the family and the incident put a real damper on their lives. She was a sweet and well loved lady and she was missed very much.

The school year was just beginning and Little Waverley announced that he wanted to join the band forming at his school. His dad was supportive, but they had to decide which instrument he was to play. Naturally, the musical instruments his son had selected were unavailable because with his braces, he would be unable to blow any of the brass instruments. Percussions were out of the question because, well just realize hours of practicing at home. It came down to the woodwinds. Little Waverley wanted the saxophone but ended up with the clarinet, for economic reasons. He played in the band for two years but barely made third chair. Needless to say, he had not inherited his mother's musical talent. He was though, an excellent singer and was featured in several school programs and on occasion featured as the premier soloist. Unfortunately, his father was only able to attend the night programs. Having his father attend any of his performances was a thrill to the young crooner.

The holidays that year brought surprises all around as Cindy celebrated her first Christmas. The area beneath the tree was filled with baby toys, Martha received a beautiful Mouton stole from Waverley, Linda found a new phonograph just for her, and Little Waverley received a rifle. Admittedly, this was not a high powered rifle but merely a single shot pellet gun. This was the really big surprise since the girls in the family always believed that there was a hatred of guns by father.

Chapter 14
Rough Times

The new summer rolled around and the walls of the "temper vessels" were wearing a bit thin. It was fortunate that both time and money were available for another Florida adventure. This trip was a little different from most of their past Florida excursions. Instead of heading directly for relatives on Florida's west coast, the family traveled down the east coast. Little Waverley was now into his rocket and space travel stage, never missing a televised satellite launch and reading all he could find on the subject. It was, therefore, mandatory that a trip to Florida contain a stopover at the famed Cape Canaveral.

The other interest which the whole family shared was wild animals. This, of course, meant a stop at Marine Land to witness for themselves the antics of the trained seals and porpoises. Waverley really enjoyed watching the water born antics of the aquatic performers. His favorite was the porpoise trained to pull a water board with a poodle along for the ride. The wildest stop occurred in Miami at an attraction called the Serpentarium. This facility was a research site for snakes run by Bill Haast and had tours to show the various species and the handling of the deadly creatures. Why in hell this family ever stopped there was beyond the comprehension of anyone on this planet. With the exception of Waverley, everyone in the family was terrified of snakes far beyond reasonable caution. They all couldn't get out of there fast enough. They then stopped at a real adventure site outside of the city called Africa USA. This suited the children better as no one left the comfort of the car when they drove through the grounds where the animals roamed free. Waverley kept the children pleasantly entertained with his menagerie of animal imitations as he spoke directly to the inhabitants of the park.

Leaving Miami behind they traveled up nearly the full length of the Tamiami Trail to visit the Landrum family at their motel and introduced everyone to the new family addition. The little curly blonde haired Cindy, of course, just reveled in the attention and enjoyed the game of "pass the baby around." Not much time was spent on Florida's west coast during this trip because of the time involved with travel up to this point. They shot straight home, nonstop, and arrived early in the morning. Waverley only had time for a short nap before he was off to work. Let the stress resume.

The apples were at their peak and the leaves had all abandoned their home as cold weather began freezing the creek. Winter was approaching and Waverley had started construction on a large shed/workshop behind the house. The entire construction was done using hand tools, since Waverley was more comfortable with them than power tools. Little Waverley was with him every night as they built the shed, learning his carpentry skills. When they were done (and they never were really done) the pair laid on a roof and completed the paper and tarring process. Waverley was pleased with the work that was done by his son and he could see, in the boy's face, that his son admired him. By the time the work was finished on that cold roof, summer was approaching.

This was to be a busy summer and a summer vacation was just not in the cards. Waverley had bid on, and been awarded, a contract for the summer to paint the High School in town, inside and out. The catch; it had to be completed, cleaned up, and furniture back in place before school started the day after Labor Day. He worked day and night through the summer and took a break only to give Linda away in marriage. She wed her long time boyfriend Ken and, although held in the church sanctuary, it was a rather informal wedding. Little Waverley, with a little egging on by his father, made sure that their car was rightly decorated to ensure they drew plenty of attention as they left on their honeymoon. This was a deed they were never to have the opportunity to repay. Waverley took great joy, though, in walking his eldest daughter down the aisle.

When Linda moved out following her marriage, her brother wasted no time in moving into her spacious studio. He finally had room to collect all of the junk so common for a preteen boy. This was the opportunity for him to buy those pet Golden Hamsters he had seen at Ritchie's Hardware store. His big mistake was when he named the critters Elizabeth, after his mothers sister, and George, after her husband. Of course this signified that one was a male and the other female. The lesson he learned from this venture was to be sure and read up on an animal's natural behavior before getting a pet. Waverley had taken an old cage (his father had used when he raised canaries) out from one of the old farm buildings. He cleaned it up, painted the whole enclosure and bought a wire wheel for the rodents to use for exercise. All went well for about the first week and that was when the exercise wheel began to squeak as those damned hamsters ran and ran ALL night. It took a while until everyone in the house learned to sleep through the racket. Waverley had come up with a plan to place a couple of drops of vegetable oil (safe for the little rats) on the wheel where metal met metal. This helped to quiet it down, but now every time the hamster stopped running in the wheel, it would keep going around and around and around.

On a Saturday morning, Little Waverley called to his dad to help him in his room. Apparently Little Waverley had discovered that George the hamster was missing. He and his dad searched all over the room for him but had no luck. That afternoon, while watching television in the downstairs living room, a scratching noise could be heard. When the TV was turned down and everyone was listening, the scratching noise would stop. Pretty soon the scratching noise started again and the sound was followed to the outside wall of the house about half way down the wall. Waverley tracked up to his son's room, into the front cubby, and with a flashlight looked down into the wall. As he looked down, he spotted two little beady eyes staring back up. There was George trying to climb out of this hole in which he had fallen. It appeared the only way to get him out of the wall was going to be to cut an opening and then patch the hole. Waverley, however, being the highly intelligent and resourceful father that he was, proceeded to his closet and gathered up a handful of neckties. He tied several of the ties together and lowered them down into the wall to the hamster. Little Waverley learned that day how intelligent a simple creature like a hamster could be. George jumped onto the tie and held on tight while he was pulled slowly up the wall and back into the hands of his caretaker. The young boy was shocked at what he had just witnessed and his father, in his mind, had just moved one more step toward sainthood.

There was a strong feeling in the household that these hamsters might be attracting snakes into the house. However, up until this time none were ever found venturing past the basement. Martha did spot a snake one afternoon in the well pit that was beside the house with the opening to the basement for the water pipes. She was outdoors by herself with Cindy in the house and Little Waverley was off playing in the woods. Martha screamed so loud for her son that he heard her across the field to the wooded area. For her to have called him that loud, he figured maybe he should high tail it home real quick like. It only took what seemed like a few seconds until he reached his mother, but she was busy hyperventilating and couldn't speak. She did manage to point into the well and there was the obvious problem. They both had the same opinion of snakes at that point in their lives: the only good snake is a snake that is somewhere else. But since neither of them was going to climb down and carry the snake away, a two by four was the next best thing. This worked just fine as a long enough stick to smash the head on that little bugger, and that he did.

Although Martha's fear of snakes had led her to dread going into Little Waverley's room with those hamsters, she honestly never saw a snake there. Her son, though, could not make the same claim. While preparing for bed one evening, he put on his pajamas and pulled the covers back on the bed to climb in. He froze as a glance to the bed reveled a small snake coiled under the bed sheet. A quick yell for "DAD" brought Waverley running up the stairs and the snake was captured and removed from the house post haste. Martha helped young Waverley change the linen on his bed but sleep in that bed, for the night was restless for sure.

Somehow during this time period Waverley's brother Allen, for reasons unknown, began referring to Little Waverley as "Brother." This didn't seem to make much sense but it caught on. His sister Linda picked up the term and baby sister Cindy began using "Brother;" that is as soon as she could pronounce the word. Everyone then began using this nickname including his aunts and uncles, except for Aunt Elizabeth who had coined "Butch" for her nephew.

When the first litter of baby hamsters were born it became a problem because they were small enough to climb out between the wires of the canary cage in which they were raised. Waverley took Brother back to one of the old sheds on the farm where his father had stored several old cages he had used when he raised canaries. These particular cages were built three to a section and assembled with hardware cloth, just perfect for little hamsters. The cages were set up on the side porch and that musty hamster aroma was removed from the house, not to mention those damn squeaky wheels.

Once the hamsters had been removed from Brother's room, it had become at least a thousand decibels quieter and the sounds of the house were again apparent. One sound that wasn't quite right was a scratching noise appearing to be coming from the wall. This was a sound they had all heard before and they couldn't help but wonder if a baby hamster had escaped unnoticed. Brother spent days tracking down the sound because it only came out at night, again making it appear like a hamster on the lam. The source of the noise was finally located in one of the front cubbyholes of the house. Inside, Brother found a nest filled with baby something's. Upon examination, his father identified them as Flying Squirrels. They were returned to the nest and monitored, but after two nights the mother squirrel had not returned. That was when Waverley appointed his son to become their mother because of his experience with his hamster hoards. It worked out well. Brother successfully raised the squirrels and they were released into the woods that summer.

Waverley had a great deal of difficulty getting through the summer with the pressure of that major contract. Although he knew a number of painters who had done work for him over time, many were committed to other employers and could only work part time or nights and weekends. This really left no time for the family and losing his temper for no explainable reason became a common occurrence. He even had Brother on the payroll for six days a week and the kid learned a great deal about painting and working with ladders, scaffolds, and drop clothing. Even for him, this was quite a summer. Although Brother had been working with his father part time on holidays and weekends since he was four years old, this summer offered the opportunity to put his knowledge to practical use, and get paid in the process.

Waverley had been able to find relief and enjoyment in working with the youth groups for several churches in the area. He worked well with the kids. He also profited from teaching them games and good ole' down home country and square dancing. He could call those dances with the best of them. He would visit the Methodist Youth Fellowship Camp at Pocahontas State Park and lead them in dances a couple of nights a week. Time was even taken off for up to a week for the youth programs and retreats held at the Blackstone College. Fortunately, Brother was a proud participant in all of the events and would participate in each one just to be with and learn from his dad.

With his son, Waverley imparted wisdom through words and actions while for the girls his wisdom took the form of demands and anger. With positive feedback and negative feedback, it became increasingly difficult to keep straight who was being affected. This again, caused a buildup of stress which always seemed to be released toward his girls. Time in his workshop, or a project outside the house, gave him the opportunity he needed to relax and talking with his son seemed to always help vent the pressure.

Brother had great faith in his father and trusted him with his life. When the lights in the church sanctuary needed changing, he and his dad would always be called on to handle the job. Waverley had a 40 foot wooden extension ladder that he used in his work and he would bring that into the sanctuary. They would extend it full length and Waverley would hold it straight up in the air, while his son climbed the ladder with a fresh light bulb. He would wrap his leg around the balanced ladder and change the lamp and then climb back down, all 40 feet, with the burned out bulb in hand. There was never any fear involved and the trust was true and honest.

During the spring of 1962, Brother was finishing up his first year of high school. Having attended the same high school as his older sister had offered him no advantage as it had in the last school he attended. This was primarily because she had graduated the year before. It did help, however, that Brother still had classes with the same classmates that had started with him in the first grade. This was also the first year that he was attending accelerated classes in math and science. He had a real aptitude for these subjects the same way that his father had at the same age.

Summer came and a summer vacation was way overdue. Waverley was beginning to have some trouble with arthritis and the prospect of 18 hour drives no longer appealed to him. Although the vacation would not be quite as long, he decided a trip to our nation's capital would be enjoyable and a great education for his son. The DC excursion included many of the standard sites such as the Lincoln Memorial, the Capitol, and the Washington Monument. Brother climbed all the way to the top while Waverley, Martha, and Cindy stayed comfortably at the base. The Capitol building was interesting as they joined a guided tour of the House and the Senate. The next three days were spent wandering through the maze known as the Smithsonian Institute. This was 300 years of American History wrapped up in one gigantic complex of buildings along with the natural history of our great nation.

When the family returned home Waverley received a message concerning an important meeting at the church and they needed him to attend. This, of course, meant they wanted him to do a job for the church, gratis, and that was precisely the case. He agreed to paint the classrooms in the church and the heavy oak doors leading into the sanctuary needed a new coat of paint. While he and his son were painting one of the classrooms, the new pastor of the church ventured in to inquire about the sanctuary doors. The new pastor was not a well liked individual by most members and he could be a real pain without trying very hard. It appeared to many of the parishioners that everything always had to be done his way. Trying to add a bit of humor to the conversation, Waverley told him he was going to paint the main doors a bright fire engine red. The pastor fell right off the sanity line. There was no way that he would allow that to ever happen. This was how the doors on the front of High Street Methodist Church became bright fiery red. The church membership fell in love with those doors and praised Waverley for his bravery and ingenuity. They jokingly asked him if he could paint the chairs in the classroom polka dot, and that was how this particular church led the district in liberalism with bright red sanctuary doors and polka dotted chairs. Moments like this were so typical of Waverley when he was in his Doctor Jekyll persona.

Waverley's mother had been in ill health for some time and was no longer able to care for herself very well. She moved in with the family on the farm, suffering from advanced diabetes. Her feet were in terrible pain day and night and walking was a major chore for her failing body. Being the ingenious man that he was, Waverley devised and built a rack which fit under the sheets on the bed which kept them from laying directly on his mothers feet. This gave her relief from the pain she had suffered for so long. This postponed but did not stop the inevitable. She was admitted to the Medical College of Virginia resulting in the amputation of both of her feet. The family found that the situation back at home would be impossible in her condition and admitted her into a nursing home. Here they would be able to care for her needs.

Throughout his own life Waverley had been plagued with many maladies. Some had affected him as a young man but most followed the action he saw in the Pacific. With the exception of his problems with control and temper, most of these ailments had been fairly minor and manifested with short term flairs. From this point in his life, his conditions became chronic and increased in severity from day to day.

The spring of 1963 brought out the love in the world and Brother received an invitation to a birthday party at the home of his girlfriend de jour. The young Traylor looked forward to the event and on the afternoon of the social gathering, he stared in the mirror and decided to eliminate the fuzz that was stuck to his face. He asked his dad to borrow his soap and razor and was making a blind attempt at shaving. Waverley decided that he had better give his son some help. He was sure the boy did not want to attend the party and try to impress his girlfriend with little bitty Jap flags all over his face. Guidance was provided, the shave was clean and another hand-me-down lesson was complete.

Martha had been talking with her nephew in Florida. He had made a comment, half joking, about Brother spending the summer with him in Florida and before the light even flickered, the trip was on. June came around, school was out, and Brother was on the train headed south. This was his first real independent adventure. While he was in Florida, his parents decided to set up a room just for him on the first floor. They cleaned out and painted the room and began preparing each piece of furniture very carefully. One piece at a time they painted the double bed, side table, room table with air cooler, wardrobe and a desk with chair. All of the pieces ended up the same color as if they were all a matching set. When Brother's room was complete, Cindy moved into the upstairs bedroom that had been her brothers.

Waverley 3rd was being given a lot more freedom since now he would be able to come and go as he pleased without disturbing the rest of the family.

When the summer was winding down, the family drove to Florida to pick up Brother and piggy-backed that on top of another Florida vacation. They spent time at the beach, fishing, and generally just hanging out. This had made for a relaxing summer for Waverley. Between his efforts in preparing the room for his son and the Florida vacation, his pot never reached more than a low simmer for the entire summer. Brother had spent the summer working two jobs and diligently saved his salaries for the purpose of buying himself a car. When he returned home, he was anxious to begin his search for that perfect car. Understanding his excitement, Waverley insisted on helping him locate a good, clean, safe used vehicle. He looked at several but father kept insisting, ". . . too much power." After all, a first car should not be a high powered Hot Rod. They finally found a suitable car and the purchase was completed.

Brother was now the proud owner of a faded red 1959 Renault Dauphine. This four cylinder, rear engine, beauty was a proud little Lady Bug that settled well into the family. Brother did not have his driver's license yet but was sporting a shiny new learners permit. It was difficult to obtain his license since he did not yet know how to drive, but he had seen it done. Every afternoon after school he would take his vehicle and practice his driving around the fire roads on the farm. By the time he was ready to test for his license, his car had a burned out clutch and many dents and dings. Waverley and Brother towed the car to Ettrick for a visit to Schrum's Auto Repair for a new clutch. The advantage of this shop was that Brother could watch closely as the repair was made. Waverley sat down in the shop with several acquaintances who were all World War II vets. They discussed their time across the world with each other and Mr. Schrum invited Waverley to join the local Veterans of Foreign Wars (VFW) post. He politely turned down the offer because he knew what went on at the meeting. There was widespread drinking, smoking, and cursing. This was not an atmosphere that Waverley wanted to be around.

The winter of 1963-1964 was very lean for the Traylor family. Work was slow in coming and a good number of days were missed for medical reasons. Waverley had never let pain or illness prevent him from working before but as he was stricken with severe flairs of gout, his perfect attendance record was in jeopardy. Money was tight and the stress was building. He was becoming very testy. He knew that he had to do something and giving up working for himself had to be the key. His medical condition was deteriorating and he still carried no medical insurance.

He began searching for job openings but was finding difficulty in counting all of his skill while self employed as experience. He located a position available in Maintenance at the Defense General Supply Center in Richmond and applied for same. All was looking good but the points that he earned serving his country were not enough. The personnel office wanted to see his Purple Heart medal or proof that he had received the award. He provided the evidence in the form of the Marine Corps 6th Division history manual which listed him as a Purple Heart recipient. This, however, did not suit personnel and they insisted on seeing the actual medal.

Following his injury in WW II, he was processed for discharge and was never actually presented with the medal. Thinking that this would be an easy error to rectify, he began writing letters and making phone calls to see how quickly he could obtain his medal. The response to his inquires was not as he anticipated. It seemed that the minor comment on his medical review board summary, "Pre-existing Condition," was coming back to haunt him. It had seemed inconsequential at the time because he had been bombarded so hard with paperwork to effect his discharge. Feeling that this was unfair, he continued efforts to obtain his medal even long after he had missed his opportunity for the civil service job.

His job search was temporally placed on hold with the passing of his mother. She had fought a tough battle but had finally given up the fight when a major heart attack took her last breath from her. As she was laid to rest in the family plot, Waverley's emotions let loose and his tears drained the built up stress which, in the long run, was a healthy release.

Brother was now deeply engrossed in activities outside of the home. He was involved in a school play where he played an aged character named Simon Stimson. Thornton Wilder could not have written the lines better for the local drama club. He also was active as a member of the National Junior Academy of Science and taught scuba diving at the local YMCA. A lot of trust was given him by his parents. On most weekends he would be off with the dive club scuba diving in mountain quarries, the rivers of Virginia, or shipwrecks off of the Outer Banks of North Carolina. He had also become a devout numismatist and had collected an impressive collection of old and rare coins.

One evening after returning from having dinner out, Brother discovered that a majority of his rare coin collection was missing. While performing his own investigating into the theft, he discovered who he suspected as the perpetrator. Discussing the details with his dad, the senior Waverley thought carefully and hatched a plan; as he always did so well. It involved a county detective, who Waverley knew very well, and the owner of a local coin shop, an acquaintance of Little Waverley. Several valuable coins were loaned to Brother and he made sure that the alleged suspect knew of his valuable acquisition. He also ensured that the suspect also knew that the family would be out all evening. Waverley picked up his detective friend and brought him back to the house being sure to enter the back door unseen. The house was locked with all of the lights turned off and they left for the evening. The plan was for the detective to wait inside the house and if the suspect made an attempt to steal the newly acquired coins, he would be caught and the front porch light would be turned on. Within an hour, Waverley drove back by the house and observed the light on. The thief had been caught. All of the coins were returned but had been removed from their individual display containers and by directly handling the rare coins, had diminished their value considerably. As a personnel favor to the young man's mother, charges were dropped. Brother never received reimbursement for his losses but a long time friendship had, in an instant, been vaporized. This was unfortunate, but a valuable lesson learned for the young collector.

Waverley, not being one to give up, continued his search for steady work. He caught wind of a construction job in Emporia where a new Georgia Pacific (a company founded by his great Uncle Bob) plywood plant was being built. It seemed a long way to travel for work but it may be a back door into the company. He took a day off and traveled to Emporia to discuss a job possibility. He returned home with a smile. He had been hired by The Austin Construction Company out of New Jersey. This was a union job as a carpenter and afforded him the opportunity to draw union wages. Traveling this distance to work every day was a "pain in the rump roast." This was the closest thing to swearing that had ever crossed his lips. The exaustion involved with being on the road two hours a day was telling on his stress. In addition, working each day at physical labor was difficult with the level of chronic pain that he suffered.

After being there only a few months, his dedication to detail and his strong work ethics paid off. The company drew weary of his stopping work every five minutes to answer questions and help the other workers. He was told to "put down his tools and get the work done." From this point on, he was no longer union labor but a supervisor and part of the management team. He was extremely proud of this advancement and couldn't wait to return home for the evening and spread the word. For some reason, that evening, he seemed to stand a little taller and his chest and shoulders appeared just a bit broader.

Although he was spending extra time on the road each day, Waverley seemed to be spending more time at home. This wasn't so apparent to his family as he was now spending a lot more time performing chores for Aunt Marie. She had become worried about the old pier at the pond on her property although Brother was the only one who ever fished from the dock. Big Waverley spent several months, working weekends, driving the poles and building a new fishing pier. It was a sturdy and well styled structure which made his aunt extremely pleased for his effort.

The entire area around the Pamplin and Traylor farms was changing rapidly and drastically. A new small subdivision had been built that backed up to Aunt Marie's property. To make matters worse, they had put in a road that ran right up to the Pamplin farm and stopped. This gave the impression that it would someday be extended, but not if she had any input on the matter. Because of this standoff, she had asked Waverley if he would errect a fence along the back property line. There was no hesitation in his acceptance of the job and weekends for the next couple of months were tied up. He was suffering so bad from arthritis and gout that Brother volunteered to help him with the fence. He delivered the fence post to the site, dug the holes, and erected the fence post with the assistance of his sister Cindy. Their dad strung the wire and fastened it to each post. They all felt good about this job well done. It was great to have the family all working together.

Waverley had noticed every time his aunt had asked him to do a job for her, Martha became quiet and a little withdrawn. It appeared to Waverley that she was not feeling very good about these jobs for Aunt Marie. He realized that she knew the pain that he was suffering and this was the the root cause for them to no longer go out or share any interest. Her interests though were stifled unless Waverley was not at home. He now would not allow any activity in the house from which Martha drew pleasure. She was unable to paint, sing, play the piano, or even listen to the classical music that she loved so. This was really working hard on her stress levels and the friction between the couple was increasing each day.

This became a special time for the family in that Brother was grabbing for his independence. He had his own car, he had purchased himself, and never seemed to be at home. His mother didn't worry too much because each morning she would check the refrigrator and see that there was food missing. This was a sure sign that her son was alive and well. He also decided that the time had come for a nickname of his own chosing and began calling himself "Wave." Unbeknownst to him at the time, his father and grandfather had used the same name, at approximately the same age, for the same reason.

Spring proved to be a busy time for Wave. Finishing his senior year of high school, he had been taking advanced college classes in math and science and had taken first place at the science fair with gold medals in Physics, Biology, and Chemistry. He had been selected to take the test for the National Merit Scholarship Program. His high Scholastic Aptitude Tests (SAT) score of 1420 was sufficient to earn acceptance at a number of top engineering schools around the east coast. He, with the push of his family, accepted a scholarship at Virginia Polytechnic Institute and would be heading there in the fall. He had obviously inherited the intelligence of his father in these areas. Even other areas of academia showed inherent traits of his father; he failed Spanish his senior year.

When the summer of 1966 had arrived, Wave had graduated high school and was preparing to attend Virginia Polytechnic Institute in the fall. He had been seeking a summer job to earn money to start college and his dad came to the rescue. He had arranged for his son to go to work at the plant as a laborer for the summer. Although he was only 17 at the time, and the minimum age requirement for the union was 18, what's a little white lie made up by father and son. His first day on the job was meeting the people, filling out the paperwork, joining the union, and getting a feel for what was required. The next day, Wave rode to work with his dad and wonders of wonders, the union was on strike. Things were a little awkward because he was labor and his dad was management. He was dropped off at the main gate and Waverley proceeded in to work. At the end of the day, he was picked up at the main gate for the ride home. He never did find out why he was on strike, but the next day all was well at the site.

Chapter 15

The Agony

Summer was over with no major blowups higher than two on the Richter scale. The time had come for Wave to leave for school and the whole family tagged along for the ride. The station wagon was packed with all of the requirements for school including a large trunk of clothes, a stereo system, and a brand new 26 inch cruiser for getting around campus. Stuck underneath the necessaries, were his golf clubs, scuba equipment, and tennis racket. All of the instruments needed to obtain a well rounded education.

As war was again raging across the world with a whole new generation of warriors, Waverley had secured a position with Georgia Pacific and was being sent away to Alabama for a month of training at one of their operational plants. This left Martha at home alone with Cindy for a month and fortunately Linda was at her beck and call for needed transportation. When the training was over, Waverley returned home and went to work as a front line supervisor to help get the plant up and running. The time had come for the Traylors to implement a move to be closer to the plant since his plan was to work there until retirement.

Waverley was never one to hire anyone to do what he could do himself, and he could do it all. His only problem was that his car had no hitch to tow the trailer he and Allen had built seven years before. Wave's car had a strong hitch but it was with him at school. When he came home for the Thanksgiving holiday,

Waverley talked his son into swapping cars so that they could move their household to Emporia. Wave drove his father's car back to school at least until Christmas. Waverley sold the house he and Martha had built to Linda and her family. They moved into a small (by comparison) house which they rented in Emporia. Martha and Cindy each had a bedroom on the main floor and Waverley took a small room in the attic that had space for a single bed and no more. This was not at all the way he had pictured his later life when he married, but the war had changed a lot of people and ruined many families.

In the spring, Wave had called home from college to inform his parents he was going to New York City for spring break. He was told that they wanted him to come home for the break and not to go north. Being the independent and rebellious son that he was, he loaded his car with his buddies and left to spend spring break in Greenwich Village. The weather was cold and snow covered the ground for the boys return trip to school. As they traveled down the turnpike of New Jersey, the engine on Wave's 1955 Chevy gave out and was towed into a small town near Trenton. Fearing the worst, Wave did not want to call home, but there they were, no car, no money, and no place to get in from the cold. Even though he expected to feel a seismic tremor, he placed a call home to his dad, and cried "Help!" Unexpectedly, his father did not blow a gasket. He calmly asked what had happened and where they were. He then told them to sit tight and he would be there in the morning.

Morning came as the boys waited for dad to appear. They finally spotted his station wagon and prepared themselves for the lecture of the century, but none came. Now, Wave's car was a green 1955 Chevrolet station wagon with black spots covering what had been a bad case of rust acne. In the center of the roof was an antenna for the Citizens Band radio he had installed. Because of this odd appearance, each front fender had been conspicuously labeled "The Whale." The entire vehicle was covered with dust, dirt, and road salt residue from the winter travel. When Waverley had, with difficulty, installed the tow bar between the cars and all were packed to go, he quietly walked back to the broken car and on both front fenders, beneath "The Whale," he used his finger to inscribe "Is Dead." This was most unexpected but fit naturally with his comical character. After returning home, Waverley never said another word to his son about the incident.

Wave returned to school and the family thought that all was going well until he showed up at home a few weeks later. He had been undergoing a period of extreme perplexity and had even changed curriculum, but this had not helped his mental confusion. He notified his mother and father that he had left school and had decided that he was going to join the navy. This was another opportunity for Waverley to have a major blow up, but again, nothing occurred. Wave was beginning to worry about his dad. He did dread his decision to have a talk with his dad to expose any and all secrets he had been holding onto for years. He announced to his father that he did in fact smoke and drank. This is something Waverley had never tolerated since the war and he always maintained his distance from those that did. He accepted his son's confession and showed no anger or animosity to the situation. This was not a normal reaction for Waverley and it made Wave suspiciously concerned. He had accepted Wave's decision to leave school, his life style, and his desire to join the military. That decision had been based on the ongoing draft for service in the Vietnam war.

Waverley took a day off from work to drive Wave into Richmond to visit the Armed Forces Recruiting offices. He did insist that they talk with the Marine Corps recruiter first. Although he talked little about his time in the Corps, it became obvious that he had been proud of his service and was still very much a Marine. After all, "Once a Marine, Always a Marine." The best that the Marines could guarantee would be in the field of aviation. This was a career path that didn't interest Wave in the least. By the end of the day, they had spoken to recruiters from all of the armed services. They returned home that evening because the kid now had a lot of thinking to do. Since Wave had finally started taking responsibility for his own decisions, Waverley stayed out of the mix and allowed his son to make this commitment on his own. For this attribute alone, his father was very proud. In May, Waverley drove his son to the recruiting station and said his goodbye, remembering the way he felt when he left home for Marine Corps boot camp. Wave was on his way to Navy Boot Camp; he was now a man and completely on his own.

Now living in Emporia, the family was separated from their church in Petersburg but did not join another house of worship. This was primarily because of their health and their inability to venture out unnecessarily. They had regulated themselves to commune with God privately at home. Supporting organized religion no longer played a large part in their lives. This decision was fully understandable, given the circumstances, but without their active role in church activities, they had no common interest to hold them together. This was the beginning of the trouble that pried them further apart and the agony that consumed the rest of his life.

Although they had taken a lot of summer vacations over the years, all of the travel had been more or less random. That is, the trip was made up as they went along. Now that Waverley was doing better in his new job at the plant, he made it a year-round pastime to plan out the vacations. He would collect maps, write to tourism departments for information, and collect brochures from destinations all across the country. Hours and days would be spent on the kitchen table, or spread out on his bed, going through all of the information, until he had a complete plan, itinerary, schedule, and had mapped out the entire trip.

That summer was the perfect time for a family vacation. Waverley loaded up the station wagon, including Martha's sister Hettie, her sister Kitty, and her brother-in-law Samuel. They hit the road and headed for the 1967 International and Universal Exposition in Montreal, Canada. Everyone had a wonderful time there riding on the monorail (Hettie hated heights) and visiting the multitude of exhibits from around the world. Any stress that had accumulated over the year was quickly vented. They really had such a great time there. So much so, in fact, that they returned the following summer. Although the Expo had closed, the exhibits remained as the "Man and His World Exhibition." The route taken home was nowhere as direct as the course taken when they traveled north. Other than Cindy, none of the vacationers were able to get around too well so they visited places where they could see the sights from the car. The return trip carried them through Quebec, Nova Scotia, and the Bay of Fundy.

Later in the summer, while Martha's sister Hettie was still visiting from Florida, they loaded themselves into the car and drove to the airport in Richmond to pick up Wave, returning home on leave after completing boot camp. They were really glad to see him once again. Waverley was now working nights so he had become a day sleeper. His son used the car and drove his mother and aunt to Roanoke Rapids to do a little shopping. He dropped them off downtown and set a time when he would pick them up. In order to fritter a few hours in town, Wave dropped by a local bar for a brew or two and an afternoon of shooting pool. He picked up his mother and aunt on time and returned to Emporia. That evening though, the boom was lowered. His father had been told about their day and he wanted to have a little heart to heart talk with Wave. Expecting his father to have a full blown conniption fit, he sat down with his dad and surprisingly received a rather calm and controlled discussion. He expressed his disappointment with Wave's actions that afternoon and gave him the fatherly lecture about drinking and driving. But he did not explode, passing up a most pristine opportunity.

Wave returned to Great Lakes for electronics school and the family settled back into what could be called their semblance of a routine. In September Waverley's Uncle Edward passed away at his home in Georgia. Being his all time favorite uncle, Waverley took the news really hard as he prepared for their trip south. The families traveled to Atlanta for the funeral and gathered at his uncle's house with Aunt Margaret. She had decided to move and needed to dispose of some of the antique furniture that the couple had accumulated over the years. Waverley and Allen got into some really deep discussions, the way brothers do, about this furniture and who was going to get what pieces. The disagreements were not fully settled when they arrived home and continued when the boys returned to Atlanta with their trailer. By the time they were back in their own homes, they were not speaking with one another and it took several get-togethers to finally work out their disagreements.

Wave, in the mean time, had completed his school and was transferred to Key West, Florida. For Christmas that year, Waverley, Martha, and Cindy made a winter trip to Florida to visit Wave in Key West. He had also taken leave and the whole troop proceeded to Sarasota to visit with their cousins. They had a wonderful holiday and a fantastic meal for Christmas. The entire herd traveled to Key West for a short visit, which included a day of off coast fishing. Waverley was having a very relaxing trip and was able to calm his temper throughout the stay.

Waverley Jr. on the piers in Key West when visiting his Navy son.

February brought colder weather to the north, that being Virginia, but in Key West the day temperatures still peaked at around 80°. Wave, although engrossed in his school, became very lonely. Enough to ask his long term, part time, girlfriend, Peg, to marry him. She fortunately accepted, which resulted in his immediate notification to his mother and father about this recent turn of events. Plans were soon underway for a July wedding. Wave was unaware of how upset this had made his mother and his sister. Dad, though, was wearing a big smile, one of the few that he ever allowed his face to show.

Wave returned home for two weeks leave but did not stay with his parents. Instead he moved in with his older sister's family so that he could be close to the girl with whom he would share the rest of his life. The wedding went off with very few snags. This was the first formal wedding in the family since Allen's in '53. Although Waverley had met his new daughter-in-law well before the wedding, on that day the world seemed different. He stood and watched as young Peg slowly walked down the aisle with her father and couldn't help but notice how beautiful and grown up she appeared. This really made him realize that his little boy had become a man, a man with excellent taste, a man of which he was very proud. The wedding reception was held at the Officer's Club at Fort Lee. The two families were so different that it was a wonder that Waverley agreed to attend. There were two areas for the reception. One for the Traylor's and one for the Roark's. The Roark's area had an alcoholic punch where smoking was allowed and the Traylor's area with a nonalcoholic punch with a strict no smoking policy. Everything worked out great. There were some Roark's in the Traylor area and some of the Traylor clan in the Roark's area. An innocent bystander could not tell that there were actually two areas since there was a lot of mingling between them. Waverley did well at the reception, mainly because he was gone for a while. It seems that Wave had dressed at his sister's home and left his pressed uniform hanging in the closet. He was wearing a rented tux that had to be returned so having his uniform was imperative. Waverley left the reception, drove to Linda' house and retrieved the uniform. He returned to the club just in time for the happy couple to change. They left the reception among a flurry of rice and were chauffeured to the airport where they boarded a flight to Miami Beach. After a one night honeymoon, they caught an early flight to Key West. It was absolutely amazing how much consideration was given to Wave by his father. He had done so much to prepare his son for a life building his own family.

Peg and Wave just minutes after vowing to Love, Honor, and Respect.

Wave and his new bride, Peg, had become pregnant and the baby was due in April. In March, she returned to Colonial Heights to stay with her parents for a short while. Wave was due to be permanently transferred around the same time when the baby was due. Their daughter was born the day after Peg's birthday and that same morning Wave arranged for leave, left Key West, and drove straight through to Virginia, the same way his father had driven all night on their Florida trips. He arrived at the hospital the next day to see his new daughter and after three days, mother and daughter were allowed to go home. She was staying with her mother and dad but within a couple of days they ventured out with the new baby to visit the Traylors in Emporia. Even though this was not their first grandchild, it was their son's first child and they both ogled over her appropriately.

Baby Christine met her grandparents for the first time.

On the moon, Neil Armstrong was out for an afternoon walk. But more down to earth, Peg and Wave were out for a walk with their young daughter. Wave had to return to Key West to attend one more school before his transfer. He then received his orders to a Nuclear Fast Attack submarine that was in the process of being built in Newport News. With his arrival to the area, they found an apartment and prepared to move into the dwelling. The one minor detail that had slipped through the cracks was the fact that they had no furniture. Peg's father found them an old German style bed. The fear of it being too small abated as they realized when they rolled into bed, they <u>rolled</u> into bed. They learned that they had to both sit on their own side of the bed and simultaneously fall over, sinking well into the mattress. They would meet somewhere near the center, but it worked. They were still newlyweds and liked to sleep cozy. Waverley provided the trailer and let Wave and Peg wander through an old tobacco barn on the farm and select any old furniture they had stored there. Their apartment was furnished in an early American attic motif and Waverley helped them move the family furniture. In spite of the severe pain from which he suffered, he still helped load the trailer, towed it to Newport News, and helped carry the pieces into the apartment and even up the stairs. What a great father he was. Of course he had done the same for Linda when she was married. Some of this furniture had even been used by her in her first apartment. Now, however, Waverley's chronic pain had significantly worsened and that made his help all the more special.

CHAPTER 16
Sunset

As the decade of the seventies moved in, the headaches, back pains, and leg pains worsened making it difficult for Waverley to get up from a chair. When he did though, he had to endure the pain of walking. Every step was an accomplishment and every step was severe. The stresses he now built up inside came more from pain than from outside sources. The pressure releases remained with no forewarning from his injuries during World War II. Even more now than in the past 20 years, he felt as if he had no control over his life and was losing more of a grip as each day passed. This resulted in his grasping at anything he could control, and this meant Martha and Cindy. It seemed nothing Martha could do was right and what Cindy did was good only if it met his approval. He became completely intolerant of drinking, smoking, swearing, or illegal drugs. At least intolerant for everyone except his son.

Wanting to move out of town, Waverley looked for another house further out in the country. They eventually located a suitable dwelling and moved the family, with all their possessions, to a rental house on a farm outside of town. This was the perfect house for them. There was plenty of living space with a plot of land where Waverley could prepare a garden for Martha. There was also a small barn out back with a huge series of scuppernong vines growing wild. Feeling in really good spirits about the new house, Waverley bought his daughter a horse, or so it appeared.

The real motive behind the gesture may have been a little more obscure. This was an animal that he had always wanted to own since he had been a young boy. "Missy" was a great horse and Cindy was on her every day riding around the fields surrounding their new home. Not long after obtaining the animal, Waverley was found riding tall in the saddle and taking "Missy" for a walk. This was a shock to the mind to see him atop the animal. Not because he could ride, but that he was participating in a diversion for the enjoyment of himself and the family. The real shocker came when Waverley watched Martha take her turn upon the mighty steed. It appeared both Waverley and Martha were enjoying each other's company and recapturing a bit of their youth together. The mood around the home lightened and Waverley was falling back into his more enjoyable comedic persona. Within a couple of years, the family's attention became centered on "Missy." She had taken ill and the vet had recommended she be put down. To help ease the pain, Cindy's father found a new horse for her, "Smokey."

Waverley Jr. taking "Missy" for a ride.

Shortly after Christmas that year, the family received word that Martha's sister in Florida had passed away and the funeral would be held on the thirtieth of December. Waverley, because of his job with Georgia Pacific, was no longer able to take off on short notice. This being the case, Martha and her sister Katherine decided to fly south for the funeral. Upon their return, Waverley picked them up at the airport in Richmond and headed for home. All the way back to Petersburg, Martha and Katherine were laughing about an incident that occurred on the plane. It seemed they had ordered Seagram's Ginger Ale to drink but the stewardess had brought them each a Seagram's whisky. Of course looking like ginger ale, Martha took a sip and sprayed the liquid all over the seat in front of her and herself. This left her smelling of liquor and she retired to the restroom to clean herself off. Meanwhile, Katherine tried to convince the stewardess that they had wanted ginger ale but she found it difficult to understand why they hadn't wanted the whisky, after all, everyone drinks booze on her flight.

In the car returning home, Waverley couldn't catch very much of the conservation but had picked up on the laughter and the smell of booze on Martha. He remained very quiet for the whole trip. After dropping Katherine at her home, they continued on in what was becoming heavy traffic which demanded all of Waverley's attention because he never spoke another word all the way home. Martha hadn't noticed his mental pot was building pressure for the entire trip. At home, Martha would randomly giggle as she thought of the plane ride but it only took one more giggle to push him over the edge. He told her that if she had to drink when she traveled then she just wouldn't travel. Upon that note he proceeded to her closet and began ripping her clothes from top to bottom, his way to keep her at home. It was obvious to him he was losing control of the family and had to rely on more extreme actions to maintain power over his home environment.

This left Martha unable to do much more than read which now took up a lot of her time. She had read an article explaining how to make Dandelion wine at home. She, at one time, had sampled several wines but this was before she was married. She dare not have any whenever Waverley was around. Martha deemed this a good opportunity to exercise her cooking skills and at the same time found another use for the over abundance of dandelions growing wild in the yard. Cindy picked a big bucket of the succulent blossoms for her to brew up a small batch of wine. She followed the directions precisely and sealed her concoction with a paraffin cap on the bottle. The directions called for a cool dark place to store the elixir while it cured, so under the sink it went. The family had fried fish for dinner that evening and the smell of the flowery brew was undetectable. Within a few days though, while playing a selection on her piano, there came a loud explosion from the kitchen as the bottle of homemade refreshment turned into a glass jigsaw puzzle. Martha panicked as her only thought was Waverley coming home to a kitchen smelling of wine. Fortunately for her, she was not a skilled wine maker because she realized the kitchen now reeked of vinegar. The day was saved and she swore she would never again try anything so foolish.

But accidents will happen and it seemed maybe a little too often for the Traylor clan. When Wave resided in Hampton, his wife had been involved in an accident whereby the front fender on their Corvair had been crumbled. She had not been injured but the same could not be said for the car. The right headlight had been adjusted by the collision to scan for snipers. The car, however, was otherwise fully roadworthy and continued to serve them well. The time was approaching for the car to be inspected and there was no possibility of it passing. Wave was out to sea for several months and this left Peg in a bind, but not one she couldn't handle. She bought a new car, or at least a new old car. Waverley, who kept in close contact with Wave's family when he was out playing on his submarine, offered to tow the injured Corvair to the farm. This was the official family car graveyard where recently passed auto-mo-vehicles were laid to rest.

Unfortunately the most direct route to the farm required a short piece on an interstate toll road. Waverley was obviously in good spirits that day because as they approached the toll booth, he told his daughter-in-law to "watch this." He pulled into the toll booth and handed the toll taker the correct change for his car—only. As he continued through, the toll taker reached out to receive the toll from the next car but there was no driver, and it kept right on driving through the booth. The look on the toll taker's face was priceless, as though he had just seen a ghost, or maybe he didn't see the ghost that wasn't there. It was imaginable that he remained confused for the rest of the day and never told anyone about the incident.

While still residing in the house out on the farm, Waverley purchased a dishwasher to help Martha with the chores. This was a wonderful gesture on his part except he never quite got around to hooking up the appliance. At the time, it was thought this was another purposeful action to maintain control. But the truth he kept hidden was his inability to crawl under the house to work on the plumbing. This was where the skills he had passed on to his son paid off. Little Waverley, who had now turned 23, was able to jump in and complete the job at the request of his father. He conferred with his father on details such as what pipe to use, where to place the washer and where to tap into the water line. This wasn't actually necessary but he wanted to make his father feel as though he was contributing and not being totally replaced. This small gift of Psychology, learned during his college days, was paramount in keeping the steam pressure low. The dishwasher worked very well and saved Martha time and wear and tear on her arthritic hands. This helped her control her aches and pains which allowed her to enjoy her trips to Petersburg much more.

In April of 1971, the family went off on one of these Petersburg visits. Martha and Cindy were spending the day with her sister and Waverley was helping his aunt with maintenance problems at her home. He had been working on the roof and while coming down he fell off of the ladder He was unaware at the time, but had cracked two ribs. Shucking off the pain, as he always did, he picked up the girls and headed back toward Emporia. Waverley heard on the radio of a fire at the Georgia Pacific plant, in Emporia. He wasn't really worried because it wouldn't be a big deal. He had confidence that the workers would have the fire quickly under control. As they neared Emporia, they could see a bright orange glow in the sky in the direction of the plant. When they drove up, the plant was totally engulfed in flames and the entire factory was burning to the ground. Georgia Pacific had brought an economic boom to the region where most people farmed or worked as unskilled labor. Over four million dollars was being pumped into the area each year by wages at the plant which, in only 45 minutes had been reduced to ashes.

This immediately caused him to drop into a deep depression wondering what he was going to be able to do now because he was physically unfit for any other career. If he was having control issues up to this point, the fire, and the stress it brought, were enough to push him over the edge once again. He began a period of total control of Martha and being unreasonably strict with Cindy. At the same time, Waverley observed Martha's attitude showing an increasing jealously toward Aunt Marie. Waverley was paying more attention to his aunt while spending less time with his wife. He took Martha and Cindy on numerous trips to New York but never really spent any time with them. The purpose of these trips was always something to help Aunt Marie. They visited the grave site of her husband and spent time with her relatives through marriage. It seemed like Waverley's wife and daughter were just tag along passengers with no input into their activities. On one of these fallacious trips, Waverley stumbled upon, and purchased, a book entitled "Okinawa: Touchstone to Victory." He obviously read this book numerous times as was apparent by the cover being broken and worn. This told about the period in his life where he had served honorably for his country but was unwilling to talk of it with his girls.

Fortunately during his short layoff time, Waverley's Aunt Marie helped him financially to keep his head above water. She originally had written Waverley into her will to inherit the Pamplin farm, the houses, the land, and enough money to cover all expenses on the property for decades. But his health deteriorated so rapidly, his aunt became concerned that she might survive him. Weighing in on this prospect, she began feeding a living inheritance to him, which kept him comfortable. When the plywood plant began reconstruction, Waverley was brought back on the job to oversee the construction and use his knowledge and experience to ensure the construction was to the companies' liking.

During this same time, Wave had been having a difficult time with their motor vehicle. This was the same automobile that Peg had purchased several years back to replace the Corvair. This V8 Super Sport had a little problem with gas mileage. It was running on only five cylinders. During a monthly phone call home to his mother, the subject of his car came up and immediately his father was on the line. It seemed Waverley had only one question for his son, "Can you get the car up here?" Thinking maybe that his father was going to have the car repaired, Peg and Wave wasted no time in making their way from Virginia Beach to Emporia. After exchanging their how-de-doo's, Waverley asked about the car and its obvious under-the-weather condition. When enough of the details had been conveyed, he instructed Wave and Peg, "Let's go downtown." Martha assumed the duty of watching the grandkids and off they drove. When they pulled into the car lot, Wave was heading back to the repair shop when his dad told him to stop, and led the couple into the new car showroom. Once inside, Waverley turned to his son and said "pick one." Both Wave and his wife practically fell out of their shoes, hardly believing what they had just heard. Obviously amused by the reaction, Waverley smiled and offered to help them pick out a new car. A check was stroked and they drove off the lot in a brand new 1974 Plymouth Duster, slant six, four on the floor. This had turned out to be a marvelous day after all for the young Traylors.

By this point in Waverley's life, all of the ailments with which he had been afflicted, were dragging down his body as well as his mind. Trying to keep control over every little thing was a chore in and of itself. The girls had to be really careful with what they did and what they said. It was difficult to anticipate just what might set off an anger episode. It became obvious, but not to his family, that he was suffering from Traumatic Brain Injury. This was a condition which affects the emotional state of a victim and, if left untreated, can worsen with time. It was unfortunate that the knowledge and tools to diagnosis this condition were unavailable in 1945. It was easier back then for the doctors to diagnosis his condition as "mental" and discharge their responsibility.

Another big impact of injury to that region of the brain, controlling emotion, was the ease of frustration. When a true cause of frustration existed, the injury would compound its impact tenfold. This became evident as he became more and more frustrated about his life. For a man who his whole life had done everything for himself and his family, his pain levels and physical constraints proved to be a clear foundation for his depression. He was unable to go out and enjoy himself any longer. His physical inability to move well, even disregarding the pain, kept him from participating in any activity. Martha and Cindy would often go out and really enjoy themselves at a show or a concert, while Waverley would sit at home, or wait out in the car. This festered resentment toward them which would often manifest in an emotional blowup. The perceived notion was that Waverley had, over time, turned into this "controlling monster" but no one could see what was really happening to him until it was too late for treatment of his condition. By 1975, the atmosphere around the home had deteriorated. Martha and Cindy emotionally withdrew and had become very secretive. Through bits and pieces of conservation, it had become apparent that his girls may have been considering leaving. They did decide to stick it out until his emotional state reversed itself and the household was once again back together. At this point, the promise he had made to his father-in-law so long ago, returned to haunt him. His health began a downhill spiral as if his father-in-law had been watching over his daughter and was collecting on Waverley's pledge.

This was the year Cindy received her driver's license, which didn't help very much because she didn't have a car to drive. An additional car was really needed in the family since Waverley now worked days and was unable to do a lot of the chores requiring a vehicle. The time had come, and on Saturday afternoon the big day arrived. He drove Cindy downtown to the only car lot around where they found eight beautiful new cars sitting on the lot. He told Cindy to pick one. She glanced over the cars in front of her and inquired into where the other cars were kept. Informed that what she saw was what they had, she really did have a tough time choosing. A 1975 copper colored Dodge Dart was the car she selected. She was now finally able to take the trash to the dump, handle the grocery shopping, and drive her mother shopping or to appointments. This also gave her a more respectable way to attend school, not having to rely on that stupid yellow bus. This was the same way Wave had attended his last three years of high school.

The end of winter was nearing when word came to Waverley and Martha that their son's house had burned down. The children were safe but they had lost everything, including their much loved cat. The family had moved from Early American Attic to all new furnishings and, being underinsured, were now going to have to start all over from scratch. They moved into an apartment near the Navy base and began the daunting task of collecting furniture to outfit their new home. The kitchen table and chairs, along with the beds, were purchased from the thrift shop but mattresses had to be purchased new. Everything else for the home was obtained through another trip to the tobacco barn. This time, however, Waverley was physically unable to participate in moving the furniture but still insisted on towing the trailer of pickings to their new residence. This was also made necessary by the fact that Peg and Wave's new Duster had not come with a towing hitch. The five young Traylor's spent only a short time in their new apartment because the arrival of summer brought Wave and his family a transfer to San Diego for a much overdue shore duty assignment.

With his son now too far away to visit on weekends and help around the house, Waverley became very tough and restrictive to the women in the family. Often the irrational rages would be aimed at the most prized possessions of Martha or Cindy. They learned over time to avoid acknowledgement of a possession being important to them. Those items having real meaning were kept hidden to prevent them from falling into the void of no return. Waverley did, however, maintain an extremely protective attitude for their well being. With Cindy, it was a matter of teaching her whatever skills he thought she would need in life. On a typical afternoon, when she returned home from school, her father was waiting on the steps and as she exited the vehicle he told her to change her tire. As she glared at him perplexingly, he explained that one day she may need this skill and he was going to make sure she was able to perform the task. Since she had watched him perform this job on several occasions, she was sure she knew all of the proper steps. She removed the spare, loosened the lug nuts, jacked up the car, and removed the tire. He then directed her to put the tire back on, which she did without a hitch. This even included tightening the lug nuts in an alternating pattern.

By this point in the life of the family, prediction became the cornerstone by which they survived. All of the children could detect a change in the atmosphere and in the mood as subtle nuances would forecast when an outburst was about to occur. These were the signals to stay clear of dad, for he was about to fly into a rage for no apparent reason. These signals may have included indicators such as a cabinet or door being closed a little too hard, a tool being dropped, or even an eerie silence befalling the area around him. These little signs suggested the vault door was opening and the stress, built up inside, was about to liberate itself. Anyone who was too close at this time would become a casualty of the fallout. Those affected were always the girls. Wave often witnessed the eruptions but could never remember when the irrational outbursts were ever aimed at him.

In this world nothing is certain but death and taxes, and having the shoe drop every time things are looking up. The notice had come in the mail. The owner of the property was going to move back to the farm and per the lease, they had 30 days to vacate the premises. This became a strain on everyone. They had nowhere in which to move and they had horses to deal with. Waverley was tired of renting and not being in control of the situation. He wanted to buy a house but to find one and process the purchase in 30 days would be almost impossible. They found a house located south of town. It was awfully small but it was available and the price was right. They cleared the purchase within the allotted time with two days left to perform the actual move. Using the same trailer he and Allen had built, Waverley and Cindy loaded their possessions and transported them to the new house. The last item to be moved was the horse and Cindy rode her "Smoky" down the road to the new property.

Christmas of 1976 brought a surprise to the Traylors in San Diego. Waverley, Martha, Cindy, plus Wave's aunt and uncle, all came for a visit to the family members displaced by the Navy. It was a wonderful surprise that gave Wave a little hope his father was doing better. This expectation faded when the family spent the day at Sea World. Shortly inside the gate, Waverley had to sit down on an outside bench and there he stayed while everyone else enjoyed the park. He chose to miss out on any entertainment rather than submit to the humiliation of a wheelchair or even a cane. This type of behavior pretty much dominated the remainder of the visit. Martha was convinced that this was Waverley being stubborn and antisocial while in fact, he truly couldn't walk far and the pain he suffered was unimaginable to all but himself. The same problems plagued him on the visit to the San Diego Zoo, but he really toughed it out in order to enjoy some time with his grandchildren.

Their return home brought Cindy into senior-hood at school. She enjoyed her year, although her home life was over restrictive for a healthy and vibrant seventeen-year-old. Highly intelligent, her SAT score showed how much she took after her father. She was also musically talented and a fine artist, all traits of her mother's heritage. She was the child who received all of the great genes.

Over the years, Cindy learned how to get her way from many different angles and nothing in her world acknowledged this better than her procurement of a pet Boa Constrictor. Waverley was not really fearful of snakes in a cage but if they escaped, he knew how to kill them. Martha, on the other hand, was terrified of the creatures and it would never be possible to have her agree on such a pet had it not been for some swift Psychological maneuvering by Cindy. Two girls at her high school were vying for Valedictorian of the class. Both of the young women had straight A's on every subject for the previous four years. The one subject with which Cindy was having trouble was her speech class. Now this was not a required class for her and she only signed up for it because it was the only class that would fit her open time slot. Speech was not a subject you could read or study for, so she was maintaining only a 'B' average.

Early in the year the students were required to give a talk on any subject they so desired. Cindy focused her talk on "How to Tie a Karate Belt." There was a boy in the class who was giving his talk on Hamsters. He arrived in the class carrying a paper sack and telling everyone that he had a baby Boa Constrictor in the bag. Of course when it came time for his talk, he pulled out a Hamster. From that point on, it had become a running joke in the class that anyone who carried a brown paper bag had a baby Boa Constrictor inside.

Cindy realized she must get an 'A' in speech if she had any chance of winning the Valedictorian slot so her brilliant mind started churning. If she were to give a speech on a snake, and actually had a baby Boa Constrictor to show, then she most certainly would get the 'A' she needed. Now came the hard part, convincing Mom and Dad. Approaching her mother first, she explained the circumstances and was very convincing as to how her life would be destroyed if she didn't have this snake. Her mother knew that her father would never ever allow a snake in the house so she told Cindy she could have the pet, but only if her father agreed. She then turned the cart around on the horse and planned her timing to ensure daddy was in a really good mood. She explained the circumstances and how if she didn't have this snake, her entire life would fall into shambles.

Well, being the generous dad which he was, and knowing for an absolute fact that Martha would never, never, never, allow a snake in the house, he told Cindy she could have the snake, but only if her mother agreed. Cindy was a really resourceful young girl; a true Traylor.

Cindy knew of a pet shop in Richmond that sold snakes but her dad told her if she was going to do this, then she had to drive, and her mother had to go with her. They arrived at the pet shop in the mall and bought the snake. The slithery little creature came in a bag, not a box or an aquarium. In a bag! As they headed out of the mall they stopped by the rest room and Cindy asked her mother to hold the bag while she went inside. So there was Martha, standing in the hallway of the mall, holding a bag, with a snake inside. Who'd a thought it. As it turned out, Cindy got her 'A', was selected Valedictorian, and went on to pursue a career with exotic animals.

Wave had completed his shore duty assignment and received transfer orders to another submarine located in Mississippi. They packed up the car and proceeded across country. Wave had taken some leave in order to visit with the Virginia families before settling on the Gulf coast. While visiting the Traylors, they decided to go into the nearest city to catch a movie. The film "The Empire Strikes Back" was playing and the kids were anxious to see this Star Wars sequel. Everyone piled into the grandparent's car. Waverley and Martha in the front seat, Wave, Peg, and Cindy in the back. The grandchildren were placed in the trunk. Needless to say, this was a station wagon that Waverley drove. They reached the theatre where everyone fell out of the vehicle but Waverley decided he was not going in to see the movie. Martha was upset because Waverley was being antisocial again and she knew this would lead to a blowup. The facts, though, were far different from her perception. He stayed in the car because he was in too much pain to walk into the theatre. He was also aware of the theater's policy of keeping the auditorium so cold that his arthritis would flair under the chilly conditions. Martha was correct in her assumption that this would lead to a blowup. When they returned home, she began questioning him about his behavior. He was frustrated enough by not being able to enjoy himself and see the movie, Martha's insistence caused him to boil over the top.

Following two years in Mississippi, Wave left the service. After 13 years, as a Chief Petty Officer, he had not wanted to miss any more of his children's growing up and the family settled back down in Virginia. His father was a bit disappointed with his son's decision and never fully understood the reasoning for this move. In fact, his parents were getting older and not in good health. He wanted to be close to them in their last days.

The Ringling Brothers circus had come to Norfolk that year and Waverley bought tickets for the whole family. They went to see the show on the second of March but Waverley decided he would stay at the house because he wasn't able to handle the stadium seating. Coincidently it had begun snowing that morning. This did not appear to have been a real problem until the show had concluded and it was time to leave for home. It was still snowing very hard and Wave had to install his snow chains on the car. This was fortunate because by the end of the next circus performance, martial law had been declared and the crowd was unable to leave the complex. This also meant the family was unable to leave for home and were stuck in Virginia Beach for the night. Cindy slept in a sleeping bag on the floor while Martha had the living room sofa. Waverley found comfort in the den stretched out in the stuffed lounge chair. In the morning conditions on the roads were still bad but Waverley always had the skill to handle any situation and make it through with flying colors. This he pulled off again and they were home safe in Emporia by mid afternoon. It would be almost another year before Waverley and family visited Wave's home.

The volcano on Mount St. Helens blew its top that spring and Waverley was not too far behind. He had no reason, he didn't need one. The injuries he had suffered during the war would not leave him be. They truly haunted him for the rest of his life. It was also suspected his war buddy, Bobby, would pay him a visit on the anniversary each year of the mortar attack on Okinawa. Christmas the following year they traveled to Virginia Beach to visit with their son's family. Staying only for an afternoon they did enjoy time with their grandchildren. That evening, Waverley treated everyone to dinner out before leaving to return to Emporia. The whole family gathered at an Olive Garden restaurant and were just ordering their drinks when Waverley told his son and daughter-in-law to go ahead and order a drink before dinner if they wanted one. This was the biggest surprise that Wave had ever experienced. While being so strictly against smoking and drinking, he had already allowed Wave and Peg to smoke in his house, and now he was offering to buy them an alcoholic drink. The world must have been coming to an end.

Wave made many more trips to see his mother and dad during those next couple of years. He made it a habit of spending the weekend and doing whatever chores needed doing around the house. The time had come when with each visit Wave found a list of jobs to be done. They needed him to take care of these items because Waverley was no longer able to perform strenuous or very physical deeds. Over this period Wave replaced the rotted bathroom floor. He ripped out the old floor down to the cross beams, put in a new subfloor, and installed new tiles. These were all skills he had learned from his father many years before. He also put up a rail fence around the yard, this time taking only a single afternoon, and made the repairs necessary to the water pump furnishing the fresh well water to the home. These tasks were of great help to the family but things did not often go well. Wave, without being asked, had also cut the grass in the yard. This was the one chore Waverley could still manage on his new lawn tractor and one of a very few things in his life he still enjoyed. By performing this chore, Wave was inadvertently driving his father's depression deeper into the ground.

In July a big Traylor event occurred in the nearby city of Williamsburg. Cindy was getting married to a young man she met while attending graduate school in Fargo, North Dakota. As an alumni, she managed to reserve the Wren Chapel on the

William and Mary campus. She had been really concerned during the week before the wedding because her father had been having a rough go and could barely walk. As a backup, Cindy had asked her brother if he would walk her down the aisle, just in case their father was not able to perform this duty. Waverley took his obligation seriously and just the day before the wedding had visited his doctor requesting a shot in his knees that would help to ease the pain. Fortunately this precaution paid off and the pain abated just long enough for the wedding to proceed on schedule. Wave filled his commitment as best man and the ceremony went off without a hitch.

Cindy's father was determined he would walk his daughter down the aisle.

The wedding reception was held at Wave's house in Virginia Beach and both sides of the family were in attendance. This turned out to be a gala affair itself. There were five large tables, filling two adjoining rooms, for the family style sit down dinner. The meal was prepared by Peg and one of her friends as a "welcome to the family" gesture for Cindy's husband and his family. Waverley had remained in a very good mood throughout the proceedings but he was becoming full of surprises.

Later that year, Wave and his wife were relaxing in their living room watching television when they heard a faint car horn outside. Ignoring the noise, they then heard a second, longer, horn, then a third. Checking to see what was making all of the noise, Wave saw a large white Winnebago parked on the street in front of the house. He went outside to investigate further when his mother appeared at the open door of the vehicle and his father was perched high in the driver's seat. Knowing how much problem his father would have climbing out of the vehicle, Wave called for Peg and they had an impromptu visit right there on the street. This was something Waverley had wanted his whole life and now, through the living will payments he was receiving from his Aunt Marie, he found it possible to purchase such a vehicle.

Waverley and Martha took off for a week and traveled to Cherrystone Campground on the Eastern Shore. Coincidently, their camping space was very near a site occupied by Peg's parents who were camping at Cherrystone that same week. This was indeed fortunate since the Traylors were new to this camping thing and it was good to have a knowledgeable, friendly, family nearby. The Roark's learned a lot about their son-in-law that week and reciprocating, the Traylor's learned much more about their daughter-in-law.

The next year passed with Wave's family visiting Emporia about every other week, always staying overnight to allow him to accomplish more work on his parent's property. During these visits, Wave would perform plumbing work, carpentry, electrical repairs, painting, roofing and auto repair. He would always have his two sons help him with these chores because how else were they going to learn these skills.

The year 1984 arrived with a throb, as Waverley's aches and pains grew to immense proportions and prevented him from going out at all. Cindy was married and living in Minnesota while Linda and family were living in Chesterfield. Wave was still residing in Virginia Beach and was the only child able to *tell* his office when he was taking the day off. Waverley began calling Wave each time his doctor's appointment took him to Richmond. Wave, though, never made an excuse and would simply call in. His boss would cover for him at any meeting requirements and his secretary would reschedule any appointments, conferences, or engagements. The whole firm knew the situation and they all covered for Wave every chance they could get.

Waverley was no longer able to drive more than short distances. Wave was visiting almost every weekend to take the trash to the dump or to make runs to the grocery store. During the week he would take off to drive his father to medical appointments. The doctors had utilized most every treatment they could imagine. The cortisone shots no longer had any impact on his knees. Straps and braces had no positive impact, acupuncture was a joke, and even the lubricating gel shots proved to be useless. This left only one possible treatment for his worn knee, a full knee replacement. In July of 1984, Wave drove his mom and dad to the Chippenham hospital in Richmond where he was to have knee replacement surgery. The procedure went well and he was scheduled for a one week stay. The inpatient recovery time was for working with the physical therapist to get him back on his feet. This was where everything started going bad. In the hospital the nurses took him to therapy twice a day but the severe pain from the surgery kept him from conducting his exercises. Pain was obviously a limiting factor for his workouts and he therefore spent more time in the bed. This was the cause of Waverley contracting pneumonia. Although pneumonia is a very treatable condition, his doctor discharged him from the hospital with this ailment. His health never improved from that point as he laid at home without getting up to walk or performing any of his breathing exercises.

When the time came for his next doctor's appointment, Wave came up to drive him to Richmond. He was unable to walk or even sit up for the car ride. Wave persuaded the local emergency volunteers to come out to the house and help him with getting his father into the car. The only way this could happen was for him to lay down in the back of the station wagon. The trip to Richmond gave the two of them an opportunity to talk confidentially. Wave's dad had admitted that the Marine Corps made it possible for him to own something that could never be taken from him. It was not a gift, and the price was high, but its possession was a lifetime membership in an exclusive fraternity. The requirements to belong have only been met by a few good men and its possession was one he could take with him to his grave. After all, he was a "Devil Dog" by nature, a "Leatherneck" through courage, and a "Marine" through honor. They made the slow trip to the hospital and the Emergency Room staff assisted in getting him up to the doctor's office. Returning home was a little more of a chore since Wave was alone to help his father back into his house.

A return appointment was scheduled for the following month and again Wave was called upon to provide chauffeur services. Upon arrival at his father's home, Wave found his father refusing to attempt the travel to the doctor's office. After nearly an hour of arguing with his dad, something he had never before had the nerve to do, he got him to agree to see the doctor if his son could manage to bring the doctor to him. Wave made the trip to the office of his father's local doctor and found him to be out to lunch. Never having kidnapped a doctor before, Wave was not really sure of the method to use. It turned out that a lot of persuasion was necessary to make the doctor agree to a house call immediately. He diagnosed a prolonged case of pneumonia and congestive heart failure. Waverley found that a trip to the hospital was no longer his own choice as Wave took charge and had the doctor contact the Rescue Squad. That evening Waverley was resting comfortably with around the clock nursing.

Now Wave had always been sensitive about events involving his family and he felt now that this trip to the hospital was one way. His older sister was preparing for a vacation to Aruba and would be leaving in a couple of days. Wave drove to her home near Petersburg and convinced her that it was imperative for her to visit her father before she departed. He also contacted his younger sister in Minnesota requesting she make a visit with her new-born daughter. Both of these visits were very important to Waverley and he managed to see his new granddaughter. This appeared to be the last check on his bucket list because after the visits, his condition worsened.

Wave had left the hospital and joined Peg and the kids that evening at his in-law's home in Colonial Heights. Martha and Cindy were at the hospital that evening when Waverley slid down into the bed. He had been buzzing for a nurse to help him resituate in the bed but there was no response. Cindy offered to help her dad but he wouldn't have it, as he abruptly explained that this was the nurse's job. When there was still no response, Cindy stepped out to get the nurses attention. This action was the trigger to his last blowup in life. This initiated a heart attack that placed him into the Intensive Care Unit. Cindy took her daughter and retreated to her parent's home where she made a phone call to her brother.

Wave had just sat down to dinner when his sister called. He immediately told his wife about the situation and left to return to the hospital. There he found his mother in the waiting room. As he entered she gave him a big hug and explained the situation as best she could remember from the doctor. She then left to spend some time with her husband of 43 years. After a short time, she returned to let Little Waverley visit with his dad. Standing next to his father in the room, he saw him no longer as the man of steel, but as a helpless individual having been dealt a lousy hand in life but lived it as strongly and as proudly as he could. Despite all of his faults and shortcomings, the family had no doubt as to where he would be spending eternity; he really was such a good man. As Wave stood there staring into his foggy eyes, he thought back to how this man had never shown any outward affection. In his own way he shared himself with the family but Wave was not going to let his dad leave that way. He spoke the words to his father that he had never heard spoken in the house before, "I Love You." This was the final gesture of a loving son as he watched his father take his last breath and begin his journey to salvation.

Chapter 17
The Legacy

Shortly after my father's passing, my mother received a certificate from the office of the President of the United States, Ronald Reagan. The purpose of this document was to honor the memory of Waverley L Traylor Jr. for devoted and selfless service to his country. As I thought back on his life I realized I had learned so much from him but I was never aware of how much until after his death. When my father and mother met it had been through the church, their romance was driven by the church, and their life was happy when they shared their commitment to the church. Upon moving away from their friends and their church, their life began a downward spiral. They no longer had a common interest and no longer participated in activities which brought them together. Faith was their prime motivator and I discovered my father also possessed many other attributes which he shared only with me.

These lessons in living made up the Legacy of My Father. Not what to do with your life so much as how to live it. These valuable virtues I learned from his inactions as much as his actions. I had learned these lessons but had not immediately realized the extent of their impact until it had become too late to properly thank him. My life, hereafter, was to be guided by those intangible skills that proved to be the most valuable gifts I ever received.

Love—Never be afraid to openly express love. Even when love is uniquely implied, there is no alternative to the physical expression of any true feelings. Express your strong affection for others through kinship. Work hard to strengthen personal ties to those who share your most intimate thoughts and feelings.

Give in to attraction based on affection and tenderness. Search deeply to acknowledge admiration, benevolence, and common interests. These deep feelings must be allowed to manifest themselves in open expressions of love. Acknowledge your love for a companion, a child, a pet, your country, or your faith. Feel good and be true in your outward expression of your feelings.

Duty—Implies a binding or obligatory force that is morally right. Embrace the moral obligation to show respect to those who are deserving and have earned the homage paid them.

Know yourself and where your allegiance lies. Be true to yourself, your family, your country, and your God. Make decisions based on your principles and never waver from your beliefs. Others may try and influence the way you live but in the end it is your own life and you must live it true to your own feelings.

Honor—Suggests an active regard for the standards of one's profession, calling, or position. Serve with honor. Be honest with everyone you deal with, for dishonesty is a trait which will ruin your life. Honesty implies a refusal to lie, steal, or deceive in any way. First and foremost you must be honest with yourself for without truth, you will fail at all you do. The truth must be held high between you and your family. There is never anyone else who will believe in you more than a family you have served honestly your whole life.

Live your life in such a way as to shine with pride and willingness to share your accomplishments with society. Be proud to stand up for your family, your country, and your God. Never be afraid to sacrifice your life or your body for what you truly believe is right. By embracing a life of honesty, you will forever serve with honor.

Believe in yourself at all times. Never say or even think "I can't." Establish your goals and work diligently to accomplish them. Never give up, never surrender, and never quit. Never be guided by false honor or sacrifice your life needlessly. Honor cannot be served when the cause is unjust or is guided by evil. Resist being tempted by anyone whose purpose is inhumane or immoral. To act and serve honorably, look within yourself for guidance and trust in your faith and your love of God and country.

Courage—Be courageous in all you do. Courage is facing fear and defeating it head on. Develop a state of mind which enables you to face danger, pain, or difficulty without fear. Courage allows you to stand up for your true beliefs and act on your convictions in the face of criticism, intimidation, or threat. Stand up for what you believe to be the righteous path. Never give in to pressure from a peer, a popular figure, or relative if you truly believe that the pressure brought upon you is wrong, illegal, or unethical.

True courage cannot come from an action but must come from within and can only happen when you are alone. It takes a brave man to stand up to his enemies but a courageous man to also stand up to his friends. Have the courage to believe in yourself and follow your heart. If you discover you have erred, have the courage to admit the error and accept the consequences for the path you have chosen. Sometimes it is more courageous to turn and walk away rather than stand and fight. Most importantly, in the face of adversity, have the courage to continue, without fear.

Charity—Look out for others and help when you can. Whether it's a gift, a helping hand, or moral support, always be there when it counts. Charity involves not only giving of a physical possession but embellishes the giving of one's self. Placing the needs of others above your own releases an inner feeling of value and worth. The greatest gift one can receive is to be blessed with the opportunity and ability to give.

Compassion—A virtue which personifies the emotional capacities of empathy and sympathy. It is the result of feelings you have for all living things and acknowledging their God given right to exist and thrive. Being the cornerstone of the interconnection of all life to one another, compassion lends itself to acting for the greater good of others. Compassion too, is a selfless dimension of human existence feeding on the desire to alleviate another's suffering. It is often, though not inevitably, the key component in what manifests in the context of the Golden Rule. *"Do to others what you would have them do to you."* This command can be found in some form in almost every ethnic tradition worldwide and is considered part of common and religious law.

Pride—Be Proud. Proud of your family, your country, and above all, yourself. Always finish what you start but avoid the path of least resistance. Be proud of what you do. Work at what you love and prepare your life by your own desires, not the desires of anyone else. Make your own mark in this world and never rely on others to carry your load. Remember the little things in life for these will be the memories that will guide you through aging.

Hope—Enjoy life knowing that things can always get better with sufficient hard work and forethought. Never give up, for hope is what gives us the courage to face each new day. A hope for the sun to shine, the birds to sing, health to not abandon you, and the love you share with others will not fade. Never face the dawn with fear but with hope for a bigger and brighter tomorrow.

Generosity—Be generous to a fault in giving of your possessions, your time, and your love. Become involved with your family by accompanying your spouse in doing the things they might enjoy. Make time for your parents and call or visit them as often as practical. Most of all though, become involved with your children. The small things you do with them will become the fondest memories for everyone.

Valor—Concerns the strengthening of the mind and spirit, enabling one to confront death face on with firmness, bravery, and an absence of indecision. Valor is to do, without witness, all that can be done before the world; exhibiting bravery, courage, and stability of the soul. Valor is a gift described by Carl Sandburg. "Those having it never know for sure whether they have it till the test comes. And those having it in one test never know for sure if they will have it when the next test comes."

Patience—As you move through life as a turtle, the world will pass so slowly that any bump or ditch can be navigated without consequence. It takes diligence and patience to move a mountain or set the ocean liner into motion. It is passion tamed, and not allowed to run amuck, like finding a wounded animal in the woods and staying with it for its wounds to heal. With patience, traveling through life is akin to the man selected to dig his own grave. Slowly and carefully paying attention to even the slightest detail and stretching the chore knowing he cannot use it until the work is done.

Faith—Have faith in your family and in those you love. Believe they will always be there for you regardless of the circumstances surrounding your own actions and behavior. Never lose your faith in God, for he will guide you through life in both good times and bad. Most importantly though, have faith in yourself. No one will believe in you if you fail to believe in your own self. The world will never like you if you honestly do not like who you are.

Believe in yourself. Follow your dreams and never lose faith that you can do what you want to do and become whoever you truly want to be. Although you will be tested many times in your lifetime, remain true to your beliefs and the pathway to happiness will eventually appear before you. Have the courage and faith to take that path and those who truly love you will follow.

Wisdom—All experiences in life roll together to produce wisdom. Many mistakes will be made but what is learned from these mistakes will make thoughts and opinions more valuable as life brings about age. Great wisdom comes from a deep understanding and realization of people and events which will result in a greater ability to act and inspire others to produce their best. It provides us with the ability to comprehend what is truth, what is right, and what is moral.

Having gained great knowledge does not make wisdom. Claim to know only what is truly known and ensure complete knowledge of whatever is claimed. A wise man has many questions but very few answers. A wise man is very humble while never degrading others. A man who claims great wisdom has none and a man who claims to not have wisdom is very wise indeed.

The Owl has always been considered the wisest of the animals because with each breath, a question is put forth. To be wise is to show an optimism where all of life's problems are solvable and can best be solved by maintaining control while retaining a meditative calm.

Integrity—This philosophic aspect of life addresses the questions about <u>morality</u> and associated behavior. Concepts such as <u>good and evil</u>, right and wrong, and <u>virtue</u> and <u>vice</u>, are constantly at war within everyone. The choices we make will forever impact the way our life evolves. Choosing to live ethically is a difficult decision as we are challenged daily to falter and stray just over the line of the ethical boundary. Venturing over the line may be the easy way, or appear to be too minor for consequence, but in later life, the only true regrets will be those you allowed to slip over the ethical border. Integrity implies trustworthiness and incorruptibility to a degree that one is incapable of being false to a trust, responsibility, or pledge. Remain true and honest with yourself and others. This will allow you to rest and sleep soundly as maturity takes over your very existence.

Respect—Respect is an esteem for, or a sense of worth or excellence of, a person. It involves an indescribable admiration for an individual based on their quality or ability or a manifestation thereof. Respect is a trait which cannot be commanded, but instead must be earned. Authority figures and many groups of people are classified as those who are supposed to be given respect. This is sometimes difficult, if not impossible, to do. Respect can take years to earn or it can almost be earned overnight. It takes the actions of an individual to collectively earn the respect of their superiors, their peers, or their subordinates. It is 10 times easier to lose respect then it is to win. It can be lost in an instant, one word, one decision, or one action can cause a person to quickly lose the respect of another. This in contrast is a trait which everyone wants to have and something that no-one wants to lose.

Fear—Have no fear, but never be afraid to be scared. Fear involves worry of events that have not yet happened resulting in pain, discomfort, or even death. To be scared is to show concern for someone loved. Never let fear stop you from actions. Above all, never have fear of what anyone else will think. It is your life and no one can live it for you. Never panic, because panic breeds fear. Remain calm and approach unexpected circumstances with composure and rational thought. If you can maintain your control while all those around you are losing theirs, than you will be the one who triumphs.

In the context of this book, I pass these thoughts to my children and grandchildren. Hopefully these words can guide their lives and bring happiness in their living the way in which they have nurtured mine. My fondest wish is that my father can realize the respect, the pride, and the love that I feel for having had the privilege of knowing him and calling him my DAD.

SEMPER FI FATHER!

CHAPTER 18
Epitaph

Following my father's passing I took up his quest for the medal that had eluded him for almost 40 years. "PSYCHONEUROSIS HYSTERIA" be damned! This diagnosis was at the time a psychological term denoting "Don't know what's wrong." I am not insinuating a cover up, or any such sinister plot, but giving the dedicated navy doctors the benefit of the doubt since the truth obviously eluded 1945 medicine. My whole life I never understood why he would so often turn his anger inward. Now in researching his life, I have learned the truth and realized it is an all too common occurrence, kept hidden in the dark corners of the minds of thousands of veterans affected by the cruelty of war.

Dad suffered from an Alphabet Soup of problems stemming from his time in service. His immediate affliction resulted from SURVIVOR'S GUILT, or was that too obvious giving the nature of his injury incident. Survivor guilt is often experienced when a person has made it through some kind of traumatic event while others have not. He often would question why he survived. He had been certain his survival was rooted in his Christian life style but then what of his buddy? After all, he was also a very good man. This was why they paired so well. Feeling guilt after the experience of a traumatic event such as this is serious, as it has often been linked to a number of negative consequences. Trauma-related guilt has been found to be associated with depression, shame, social anxiety, and low self-esteem. All of these symptoms manifested themselves in my father. In fact, these conditions were all noted in the medical reports issued by the navy psychologist.

My father additionally suffered from a condition known today as POST TRAUMATIC STRESS DISORDER (PTSD). Unknown prior to the Vietnam Conflict, PTSD manifested itself in flashbacks whereas he would relive his experience over and over in nightmares, including physical symptoms like a racing heart or night sweats. He also suffered from disturbing thoughts based on his time in battle and often would re-experience the events causing upsets in his everyday routine. These may have started from his own thoughts and feelings or from words, objects, or situations that reminded him of the event. He would make it a habit to avoid places, that would remind him of the experience, often feeling emotionally numb, strong guilt, depression, or worry. All interest was lost in activities that were enjoyable to him prior to the war and reminders of these activities, such as Martha's piano playing, would be just enough to momentarily remove him from reality.

Other than in his dreams or keyed by an outside trigger, he had no recollection of his last stand on Okinawa. This was perceived as hating the military because he would never talk about this time. In fact he was very proud of his service and the Marine Corps and would talk of his service with me on several occasions. His primary irritating souvenir from the war was a case of JUNGLE ROT which he picked up on the island as they marched, slept, and fought continuously for over three weeks in mud and water, often knee deep. I learned early on not to approach my father too quietly. He was easily startled and although this never resulted in violent actions, the results were scary. On more than one occasion I thought I had given him a heart attack. He always seemed to be on edge and very tense. Relaxation for him was rare and when it came, we were all very careful not to disturb his rest. With his difficulty having restful sleep, it was important for him to have every moment possible.

PTSD also had a terrifying symptom that manifested in my dad. This being his propensity for having angry outbursts, often for no apparent rhyme or reason.

Also unknown during World War II, and with no diagnostic tool to detect, was a condition now referred to as TRAUMATIC BRAIN INJURY (TBI). Although unable to confirm without a close physical examination, it would be inconceivable to imagine that the incident, such as he had on Okinawa, would not have resulted in this condition. A severe trauma of the brain may not necessarily be the result of external injury. It may also be caused by a direct impact or by acceleration. In addition to the serious damage caused at the moment of injury, brain trauma may also cause a secondary injury which may take place in the minutes or even days following the event. These follow-on injuries affect <u>cerebral blood flow</u> and increase <u>pressure within the skull</u> which in turn may contribute substantially to the damage from the initial internal injury. This condition usually leads to a host of physical, cognitive, social, emotional, and behavioral effects, which often leads to permanent disability.

TBI manifest with emotional instability that can be very quick to appear with great intensity but easily conclude with little or no lasting effect. Often it is no specific event that may trigger a sudden emotional response but a slow buildup leading to the emotional explosion. This may be confusing to family members who may think they may have done something to upset the injured individual. Also disturbing was the fact that the hospital in Dublin, Georgia, had used ELECTROSHOCK THERPY in the treatment of RESTLESS LEG SYNDROM.

It would have been truly outlandish to have even considered a mortar shell exploding within mere feet, would have produced any hearing loss. Of course none of the wide array of test administered on him never once considered that possibility. It seemed like the post engagement hospitals assumed all Marines couldn't hear.

Based on the effects of these conditions and the resulting symptoms constantly presenting themselves in my father's life, it was apparent that only divine intervention allowed him to survive and lead his life as well as he did. After 25 years of demonstrating my theories and arguments I was finally able to obtain the medal my father so wanted and deserved. On Veterans day of the year 2010, I was proud to place a special marker on his grave reminding all of his sacrifice for his country. It was a very simple wooden cross with the words "Honor," "Courage," and "Faith." On the reverse, directly above the phrase "Semper Fi", was attached his long in coming ***Purple Heart***, a tribute to a very special man.

To the veterans that have served honorably in all of our wars who have returned home suffering the consequences, not of giving their lives, but of sacrificing their living;

You Are Not Alone

Epilogue

Waverley Traylor Jr. was honored in a memorial service at Alvin Small Funeral Home, Alvin being an old friend of the family. Among his wife, daughters, son, and brother, not a dry eye was apparent. He was interred at the Blandford Cemetery in the family plot.

Martha moved from Emporia to her sister's house in Petersburg, which she had inherited. Having missed any travel for the past couple of years, she accompanied Cindy on a cruise to Alaska and Linda on an island vacation in Hawaii. She cruised for two weeks in the Caribbean with her son and fell fondly in love with something called a "Pina Colada." After a short time in Petersburg, she became uncomfortable with what the area had become and moved to Minnesota next door to Cindy. She passed gently in her sleep in 1995 and was interred on the Ellis plot in Blandford Cemetery.

Linda remains living in the house her mother and father built in Matoaca. She has three grown children, seven grandchildren, and one great-grandchild.

Cindy moved to the city of Northfield, Minnesota in a home she is seldom in. She has two daughters but no longer any pets. Not very long ago she earned her Doctorate in Conservation Biology and travels throughout the world in her role working for the Captive Breeding Specialist Group. She easily spends more time each year outside the country than she does at home.

Waverley's brother Allen continued his education and finally procured that college degree he worked so hard for. Presently he lives in Ohio and retired several years back from his career with Dupont. His time is spent these days helping his daughter on her farm.

Little Waverley left the Navy after 13 years as a Chief Petty Officer serving on board Nuclear Fast Attack Submarines. His final assignment had him serving as the Weapons Officer aboard USS Sunfish. He went to work for Tracor Applied Sciences, an international engineering firm, and within his 14 year stint, rose to the position of Submarine Systems Program Manager. He turned his efforts to Wildlife Photography and his work appeared in numerous local, national, and international publications. Next on his agenda was a six year job as an Animal Crime Scene Investigator and Dog Fight Investigator. He retired in 2008 on disability from being injured in the line of duty. Physically unable to accomplish any strenuous work, he has turned to writing; this being his seventh published.

Glossary

Abatis—a combat field fortification laid on a trail or roadway, usually made from sharpened sticks or bamboo. Generally the poles were held together with wire and had been known to have been smeared with human excrement.

Amphitrite—a sea-goddess and wife of Poseidon in ancient Greek mythology. Under the influence of the Olympian pantheon, she became merely the consort of Poseidon, and was further diminished by poets to a symbolic representation of the sea.

Antsy—restless, fidgety, impatient, or eager

Asa Kawa—the Asa River lay just north of Naha and was an obstacle to the forces entering southern Okinawa from the north.

Automat—a cafeteria in which food is obtained from a vending machine wall.

Aviation Ordinance—the munitions used to outfit an airplane for battle.

Bailey Bridge—a type of portable, pre-fabricated, truss bridge developed by the British during World War II for military use and saw extensive use by the Marines in the Pacific theatre.

Bailiwick—a special domain encompassing an individual's special field of interest, authority, or skill.

Banika—an island in the Russell Island chain in the South Pacific. Used as a staging point for later battles in World War II.

Banzai—literally means ten thousand years of life. It is a Japanese cheer that can be translates as "Long life!" and is repeated three times to express enthusiasm. During World War II, "Banzai" was used as a war cry. The Japanese soldiers shouted "Tennouheika Banzai" (Long live the Emperor) when they initiated an all-out desperate attack.

BAR—the Browning Automatic Rifle. It was designed to be carried by advancing infantrymen, slung over the shoulder and fired from the hip. The weapon was most often used as a light machine gun and fired from an attached bipod.

Beamer—term used to describe the operator of a Beaming & Winding machine in a textile plant.

Beaming & Winding Machine—After being spun and plied, the cotton thread is taken to a warping room where the winding machine takes the required length of yarn and winds it onto warpers bobbins. Racks of bobbins are then set up to hold the thread while it is rolled onto the warp bar of a loom. Because the thread is fine, often three of these would be combined to get the desired thread count.

Black Gold—crude oil as a naturally occurring, <u>flammable liquid</u>, pumped directly from the ground to be refined into usable energy products.

Boondocks—rough country, outside the realm of civilization, filled with trees, dense brush, or desert. No man's land; a good place for practicing war.

Brannock Device—The Brannock Device is a <u>measuring instrument</u> for accurately measuring a person's <u>shoe size</u>.

Cavalier Beach Club—located in Virginia Beach, Virginia at the Cavalier Hotel and offered outdoor dancing during the Big Band era.

China Road—The main North/South roadway linking southern Okinawa to the northern island.

Cowpox—a mild eruptive disease of the cow, caused by a poxvirus and when communicated to humans protects against smallpox

Defervescence—the subsidence of a fever.

Delineated—to describe with accuracy or in detail.

Depression—a <u>mental disorder</u> characterized by an all-encompassing <u>low mood</u> accompanied by low <u>self-esteem</u>, and by <u>loss of interest or pleasure</u> in normally enjoyable activities.

Devil Dogs—the term has its origins at Belleau Wood during World War I. It was in a dispatch from the German front lines to their higher headquarters explaining the current battle conditions describing the fighting abilities of the new, fresh Americans as fighting like "Teufel Hunden"

or "Hounds from Hell." Thereafter the Marines have been known as "Devil Dogs."

Devil Pups—refers to Marines just out of Boot Camp and fresh on the lines. They are not yet combat initiated.

DI—Drill Instructor. A senior enlisted member of the armed services who instructs new recruits in becoming an accepted member of their branch of the service.

Drill Suckers—the vampire-like unofficial drill instructors indigenous to Paris Island and a most efficient extractor of blood for individual consumption. a.k.a. Mosquitoes.

Easter Fools Day—On the first of April, 1945, Easter fell on April Fool's Day and was the day chosen for the invasion of Okinawa during World War II.

EOD—the Explosive Ordinance Disposal teams are known for defusing bombs and other unexploded ordinance.

Field Day—a military social gathering by direct order, for the purpose of cleaning and polishing, usually in preparation for a command inspection.

Fireside Chats—The "Fireside Chats" were a series of thirty evening radio addresses given by United States President Franklin D. Roosevelt between 1933 and 1944.

Flame Thrower—a mechanical device designed to project a long controllable stream of fire.

Globe & Anchor—the symbol of becoming a Marine. When graduated from Boot Training, the Marine is ceremonially awarded his Globe & Anchor indicating that he has become one of the elite. These devices are worn on the collars of a Marine's dress uniform.

Grasshopper—the name applied to the Piper Cub aircraft used in the Pacific during World War II as spotter planes and for evacuation of casualties.

Great Southern Rebellion—also known as the Civil War or War Between the States. Term primarily used in reference to the southern states response to the unfair treatment by the Federal Government.

Green Monster—a World War II vintage army green weapons carrier, open cab, ten cylinder engine, six wheel drive vehicle.

Gunny—Gunnery Sergeant (E7) backbone of the Marine Corps. Usually the man, short of the Generals, with the most combat experience and the one most likely to keep you alive.

Habu—a Japanese name used to refer to a certain venomous snake found primarily on the island of Okinawa. They grow to a length 7.5 feet and is the largest member of its genus. Slender with a large head, the tail, however, is not prehensile.

Hagushi Bay—located on Okinawa, this site hosted the invasion of the American forces during World War II.

Hand Vertical-Feet Horizontal—delineating the proper method of ascending or descending a cargo net.

Hanza—the village of Hanza was located near the Yontan airfield near the landing site for the Okinawa invasion force.

Industrial History—experience in working within an industrial based business.

Iron Mike—a monument to the graduates of Parris Island who died in World War I.

Japs—Japanese citizens used often in reference to combat soldiers.

Jungle Rot—a tropical ulcer, also known as "Tropical phagedena" is a lesion caused by a variety of microorganisms and is common in tropical climates. Ulcers occur on exposed parts of the body, primarily on the lower limbs and may erode muscles, tendons, and the bones.

Kamikaze—meaning "divine wind"—represents the Japanese people as indestructible and undefeatable. Willing to sacrifice all for the emporia, who was Japan.

Khan Invasion—in 1274 Kublai Khan sent a force to invade Japan. The fleet was crushed by a Typhoon and the Japanese, from that point, felt invincible due to the "divine wind" or "Kamikaze."

Kufau—native to the island of Okinawa the Kufau is considered one of the world's most deadly snakes.

LCA—the Landing Craft Assault vehicles carried the infantry from the troop ships to the beachhead during an amphibious assault.

LCT—the Landing Craft, Tank (or Tank Landing Craft) was an amphibious assault ship for landing tanks on beachheads.

Lead Barter—refers to the heavy exchange of lead used in bullets and associated ammunition.

Liver—a meat served up by the cooks in all military outfits which may be disguised as chicken fried steak, veal cutlet, pork chop, veal parmesan, breakfast steaks, or mashed potatoes.

Love-Day—the designation for the scheduled day troops landed on the island of Okinawa during World War II.

LVT—the Landing Vehicle Tracked was an amphibious vehicles introduced by the Marine Corps during World War II as an assault troop and fire support vehicle. It was often humorously referred to as a "Quack Track."

Machinato Airfield—located on the west coast of Okinawa just north of the city of Naha.

Melanesians—relating to the people, language, or culture of Melanesia; the islands located in the Pacific, northeast of Australia and south of Micronesia including the Bismarck Archipelago, the Solomon islands and the Fijis.

Mogmog—an island in the Ulithia Atoll used in World War II as a recreation site near the end of the war and as a staging area for the troops gathering for the invasion of Okinawa.

Motobu Peninsula—land mass at the northwestern portion of Okinawa on which the heaviest fighting occurred on the island's northern half.

Muleskinner—someone who drives and/or cares for the mules.

Mystery Meat—a delicacy served by all branches of the Armed Services made from a single, or combination of, an unknown meat and/or meat byproducts. Usually made palatable with the addition of a generous helping of gravy, steak sauce, or ketchup.

Nago—the second largest city on Okinawa located on the edge of the Motobu Peninsula.

Naha—the largest city on the island of Okinawa located on the shore of the southwest corner of the island. Location of the headquarters for the Japanese defenses on the island.

Naha Airfield—noted as the last objective in the Battle of Okinawa, it was located on the Oroku Peninsula just south of the city of Naha.

Neptune—the Roman god of water and the sea.

Neurological—referring to the nervous system.

Nips—Nipponese, refers to the citizens of Nippon, Japan. Used in broader terms as another inference to the Japanese people.

Operation Iceberg—The Assault on Okinawa—The Last Battle of World War II.

Paroxysm—a fit, attack, or sudden increase or recurrence of symptoms.

Pollywog—the uninitiated crew members on a ship about to cross the equator. Upon crossing, a Pollywog becomes a full-blooded Shellback.

Precipitous—a very steep, perpendicular, or overhanging rise in the terrain.

Psychoneurosis Hysteria—an emotional conflict in which an impulse that has been blocked seeks expression in a disguised response marked by emotional excitability.

PT—Physical Training conducted to strengthen the body and the mind. Helping the body cope with being subjected to extreme physical stress without succumbing to injury.

PTSD—Post-traumatic Stress Disorder—once referred to as shell shock or battle fatigue. A serious condition that develops after a person has experienced or witnessed a traumatic or terrifying event in which serious physical harm occurred or was threatened. PTSD is a lasting consequence of traumatic ordeals causing intense fear, helplessness, or horror.

Pugil Stick—a heavily padded pole-like training weapon used for close combat training for the military. The stick is marked to distinguish which end represents the bayonet and which end represents the butt of the rifle.

Quagmire—a low lying wetland of deep, soft soil or mud that sinks underfoot.

Rabies—an acute virus disease of the nervous system transmitted through the bite of a rabid animal and characterized by eventual paralysis and death.

Ration Books—during the war, civilians at home were given books containing "ration coupons" allowing him or her to purchase a certain amount of a product each month. Rationing included <u>food</u> and other necessities for which there was a shortage, including materials needed for the war effort such as <u>rubber tires</u>, <u>leather shoes</u>, <u>clothing</u> and <u>gasoline</u>.

Replenishment Draft—men who were drafted into the armed services as replacement troops for those killed or wounded in battle.

Rifle Creed—a set of fundamental beliefs and a guiding principle surrounding the close relationship between a Marine and his rifle.

RLS—Restless Leg Syndrome, tingling in the legs presenting a creepy-crawly sensation. The source of the condition in Neurological in nature.

Romantic Movement—the Romantic Era began in the late 18th century and continued through the late 19th century. Literature of this period was characterized by its emphasis on emotion, passion, and the natural world.

Sand Flea—a flea or chigger found in sandy areas such as ocean beaches and leaping like a flea.

Scuttlebutt—a naval term for the cask aboard sailing ships containing fresh water. On more modern ships it referred to a drinking fountain and finally, rumor or gossip which often was spread as the sailors stood around for a drink of fresh water.

Shellback—those initiated seamen who have crossed the equator and lived to tell their tales.

Shuri Castle—a 15th century Ryukyuan castle located in Shuri, Okinawa. It was the palace of the Ryūkyū Kingdom and in 1945, during the Battle of Okinawa, it was almost completely destroyed.

Slum City—informal reference to the tent cities set up to house troops being assembled for training or preparations for battle.

Social anxiety—is apprehension or worry about social situations, interactions with others, and being evaluated or scrutinized by other people.

Stocking Type Anesthesia—a loss of sensation in the feet.

SToS—The Ship to Shore company handled the stores being unloaded from the transport ships. Success was measured in gross tonnage of supplies moved from ship to shore.

Strafing—to rake (as ground troops) with fire at close range and especially with machine gun fire from low-flying aircraft

Survivor's Guilt—a deep feeling of guilt experienced by those who have survived a catastrophe which took the lives of someone close; derives from a feeling of being unworthy relative to the one who died. Not delineated until after WWII.

Takamotoji Village—A small village located just east of the city of Naha, on the island of Okinawa.

TBI—Traumatic Brain Injury occurs when an external force traumatically causes injury to the brain. Brain trauma may be the result of a direct impact or by acceleration. Causes a host of physical, cognitive, social, emotional, and behavioral effects leading to permanent disability or death.

Tepidness—lacking in passion and marked by an absence of enthusiasm or conviction.

Tetanus—an infectious disease characterized by spasms of voluntary muscles especially of the jaw which is usually introduced through a wound. a.k.a. Lockjaw.

Todd-AO—a large movie film format presentation system incorporating a wide, curved screen with multi-channel sound.

Tracks—combat vehicles that rode on tracks versus wheels. Half track trucks carried supplies and troops, tanks brought forth the mobile artillery, and bulldozers cleared the way.

Troop Train—utilized during wartime to transport troops across or around the country. They provided mass movement of troops, equipment, and supplies.

Trusty—a previously initiated "Shellback." Part of King Neptune's staff who assist in the initiation of the undeserving Pollywogs.

Tun Tavern—located in Philadelphia and served as a founding or early meeting place for a number of groups. It is traditionally regarded as the site where the United States Marine Corps was born on November 10, 1775.

Typhoid—a severe human disease transmitted by body lice and marked by high fever, delirium, intense headaches, and a dark red rash.

Ulithia Atoll—an atoll in the Caroline Islands of the western Pacific Ocean, consisting of 40 islets surrounding a lagoon which is one of the largest in the world.

Varicocele—a varicose enlargement of the veins of the spermatic cord usually resulting in one testicle being larger than the other.

War Dogs—canines trained and used by the military in combat.

"Watch This"—a term used by young boys and rednecks to warn that what follows is a dumb stunt followed by immediate bodily injury.

Wimpy's Hamburger Stand—set up alongside the runway on the island of Banika. Aircraft landing on the island would often hit and kill cattle roaming free on the island. Not to waste fresh beef, the cattle were taken to Wimpy's and prepared by the Marine cooks for troop consumption.

Yellow Fever—an infectious disease of warm regions marked by sudden onset, fever, and headaches transmitted by mosquitoes.

Yontan Airfield—located on the central island coast of Okinawa. This was the sight of the initial landing of the invasion force in World War II.

About the Author

Waverley Traylor attended Virginia Polytechnic Institute and is a decorated veteran who served thirteen years on board nuclear submarines. Among other vocations, he has been a wildlife photographer and is the founder of a wildlife rehabilitation center who is focused on several community projects. Now retired, Waverley lives in rural Virginia with his wife, along with their five dogs and seven cats.